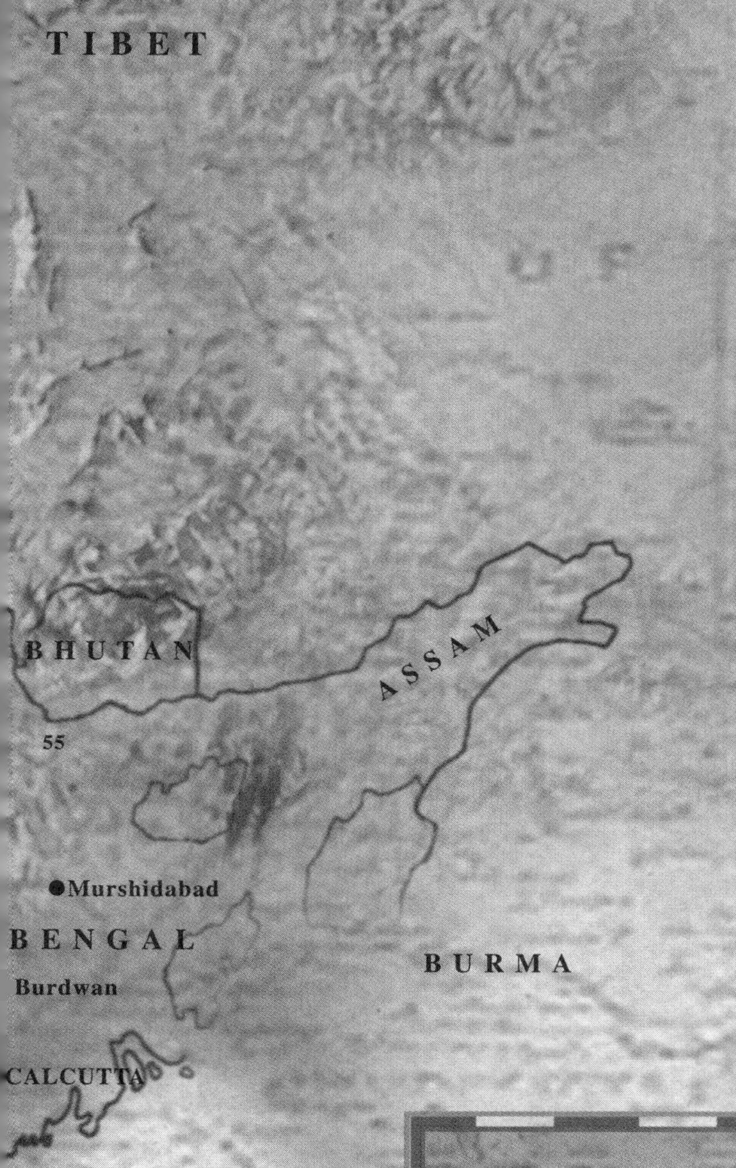

SALUTE STATES MENTION[ED]

RAJPUTANA AGENCY

1. Udaipur (Mewar)
2. Jaipur
3. Jodhpur (Marwar)
4. Bundi
5. Bikaner
6. Kotah
7. Kishengarh
8. Bharatpur
9. Jaisalmer
10. Alwar
11. Tonk
12. Dholpur
13. Dungarpur
14. Pratapgarh

WESTERN INDIA STATES AGENCY

15. Kutch
16. Junagadh
17. Bhavnagar
18. Porbander
19. Dharangdhara
20. Palanpur
21. Gondal
22. Wankaner
23. Palitana
24. Limbdi

WESTERN INDIA STATES AGENCY

25. Indore
26. Bhopal
27. Rewa
28. Dewas Senior
29. Dewas Junior

BALUCHISTAN AGENCY

30. Kalat

34. Kap[urthala]
35. Mandi
36. Faridkot
37. Suket

MADRAS STATES AGENCY

38. Travancore
39. Cochin
40. Banganapalle

STATES IN RELATIONS WITH THE GOVERNMENT OF BOMBAY

41. Kolhapur
42. Idar
43. Janjira
44. Cambay
45. Baria
46. Lunawada
47. Sawantwadi
48. Sangli
49. Bhor
50. Anudh
51. Akalkot
52. Phaltan

STATES IN RELATIONS WITH THE GOVERNMENT OF THE UNITED PROVINCES

53. Rampur
54. Benaras

STATES IN RELATIONS WITH THE GOVERNMENT OF BENGAL

55. Cooch Behar

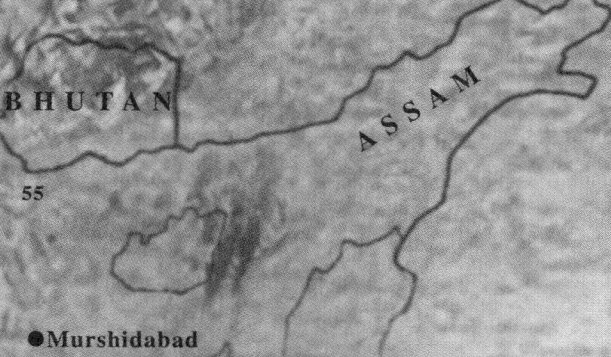

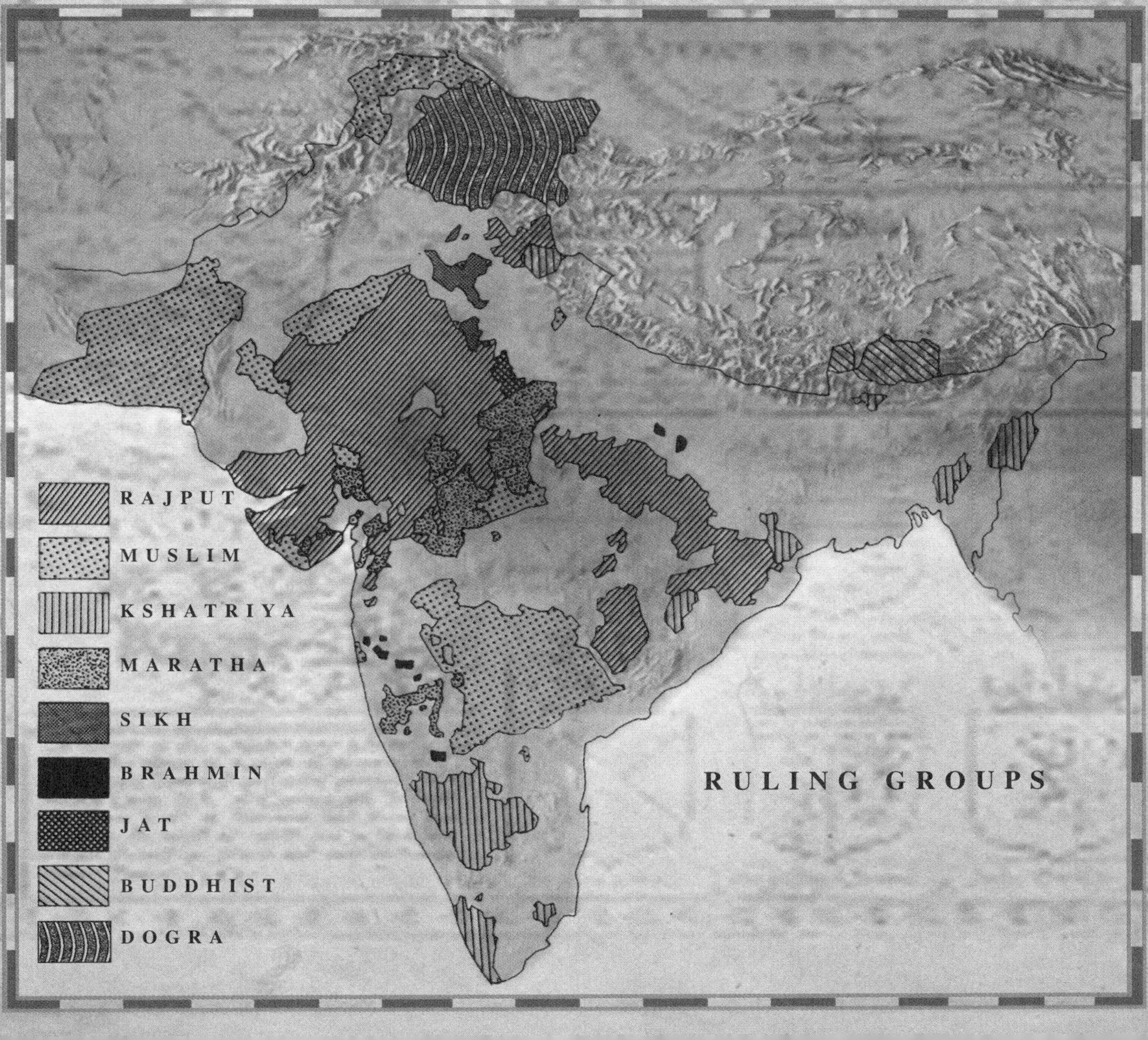

RULING GROUPS

- RAJPUT
- MUSLIM
- KSHATRIYA
- MARATHA
- SIKH
- BRAHMIN
- JAT
- BUDDHIST
- DOGRA

Maharajas

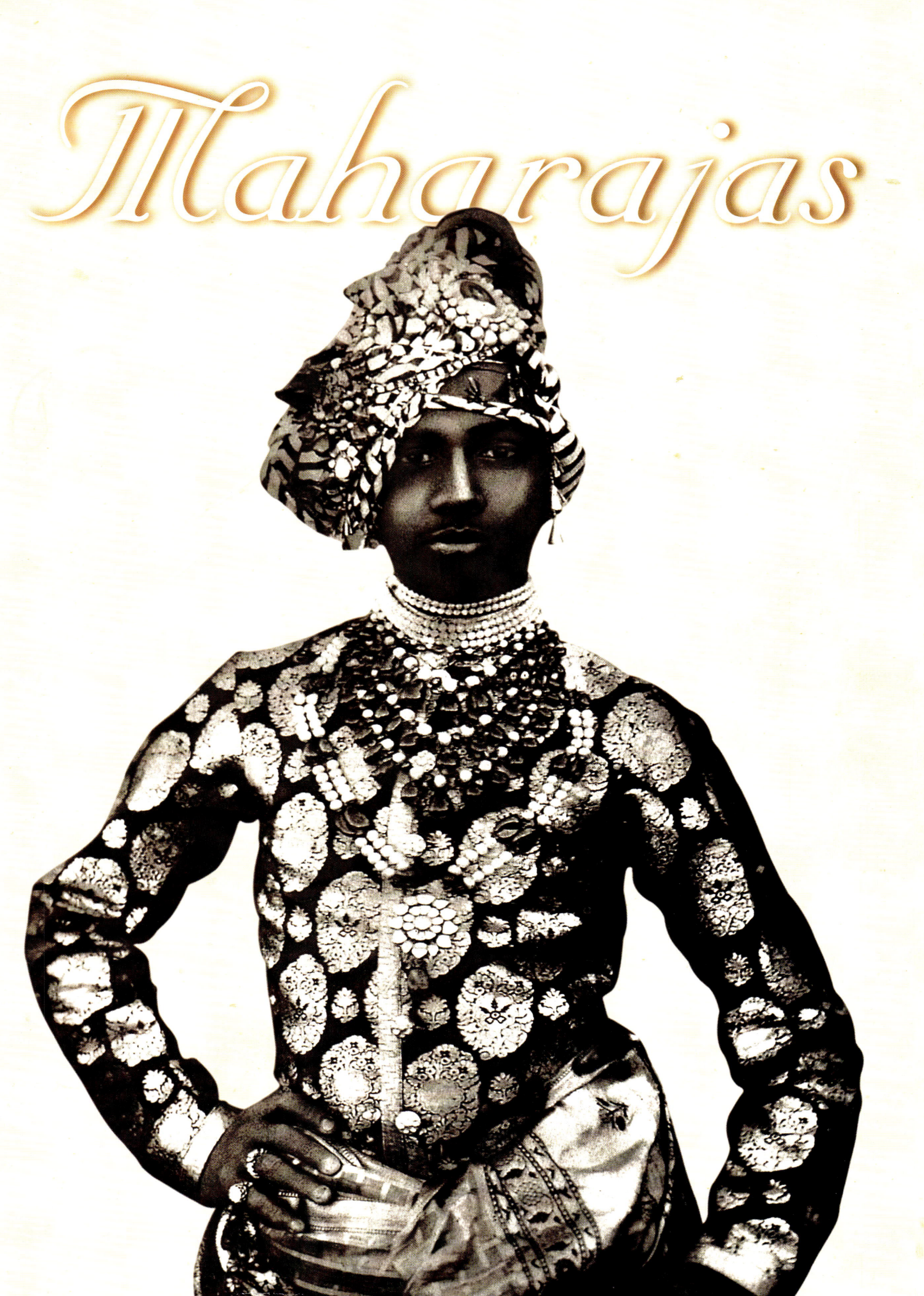

Maha

RESONAN

THE

rajas

A Voice From The Past

Text: Charles Allen
Foreword: Maharaja Ranjitsinh Gaekwad
Photographs: Aditya Patankar

MERCURY BOOKS
LONDON

Published in 2005 by Mercury Books
20 Bloomsbury Street
London WC1B 3JH

Published by Brijbasi Art Press Ltd

Text: Charles Allen

© Photographs: Aditya Patankar
and individual photographers

Project Editor: Veena Baswani

Design: Yogesh Suraksha Design Studio.
www.ysdesignstudio.com

Research: Sundeep Bali

Map of British India and the Indian States
Created by Nilanjan Das

© 2005 Brijbasi Art Press Ltd

All rights reserved.
No part of this publication may be reproduced
or transferred in any form or by any means,
electronic or mechanical, including photograph,
recording of any other information,
storage and retrieval system
without prior permission in writing from the copyright owner

Title: Maharajas: Resonance from the Past
ISBN: 1-904668-674

Printed and bound in Singapore

Contents

10
Foreword

14
Kings and Kingdoms

76
The British Raj
and Princely States

106
Lives of Great Men
All Remind Us ...

140
Artistic Patronage
and Regal Splendour

Fore

There is an immense appetite among people today for that most fascinating phenomenon of the Indian maharaja; an ancient and unique form of kingship, the like of which can never be recreated. That phenomenon continues to be the subject of films, television and the print media.

Even in the days of the Mughal and British Empires, the head of every Princely State, the Maharaja, Raja or Nawab, wielded extraordinary powers. Many states minted their own currencies, had their own armies and, in later years, ran their own railways. It almost goes without saying that many of these rulers built magnificent forts and palaces, which were great works of art and architecture. The Laxmi Vilas Palace in Baroda, with its Indo-Saracenic architecture, is one such example. Post-Independence heirs inherited these memorable structures seeped in history, along with vast fortunes.

The popular image of the Indian princes is often blurred, with the negative becoming magnified and positive contributions being glossed over. It would not be inappropriate of me to mention my great grandfather, Sir Sayaji Rao Gaekwad, who even today can be regarded as one of the most far-sighted statesmen India can ever boast of. His acumen in matters of law, administration, legislation and education were unprecedented. Sir Sayaji's interest in art and architecture was matched by his compassion for the uplift of his people, especially the deprived sections of society.

page 1: THE YOUNG MAHARAJA OF JODHPUR, SARDAR SINGH, IN 1902. HIS FATHER PRATAP SINGH WAS A COURAGEOUS AND CHIVALROUS MAN WHO WAS VERY POPULAR WITH THE BRITISH AND WAS KNOWN AS THE 'BAYARD OF INDIA'.

pages 2-3: A *KHANJAR*, CURVED DAGGER, FROM NORTH INDIA. THE DAGGER IS BEAUTIFULLY SET WITH DIAMONDS, RUBIES, EMERALDS AND PEARLS.

pages 4-5: PRINCE FATEHSINGHRAO, ELDEST SON OF MAHARAJA SAYAJI RAO OF BARODA, WAS HEIR TO THE SECOND RICHEST KINGDOM IN INDIA. AS A CHILD HE RECALLS THAT HIS PALACE, LAXMI VILAS, WAS SO HUGE THAT IT TOOK HIM NEARLY TWO YEARS TO FIND HIS WAY AROUND. HIS FATHER WAS ONE OF THE FIRST TO BRING IN SOCIAL REFORMS FOR THE UNTOUCHABLES AND FOR THE FIRST TIME, MADE PRIMARY EDUCATION FREE AND COMPULSORY IN HIS STATE.

word

He was the first to introduce free and compulsory education for the girl child in India, realising how important it was if women were to be empowered at all. His patronage extended to worthy names such as Maharishi Aurobindo, the revolutionary thinker; Dr B. R. Ambedkar, the architect of the Indian Constitution; Raja Ravi Varma, the renowned artist; and classical musicians like Pandit Bhatkhande and the legendary Ustad Faiyaz Khan. He also envisioned a unique university, which took shape as the Maharaja Sayaji Rao University of Baroda.

The fact is that the maharajas, by and large, were and are patriots, and their love for the country is today second to none. The sacrifice they and their fathers made in voluntarily surrendering their absolute power at the time of Independence, is a forgotten story. So are the contributions made by many illustrious ex-princes in strengthening the democratic process. In the contemporary post-Independence period, many have served as Members of Parliament, the undersigned included, or as members of State Legislative Assemblies. Others have distinguished themselves as Central and State Cabinet Ministers. This is no small measure of their popularity among the people, and their intimate knowledge of the people's aspirations. Moreover, their patronage, especially of cricket, polo and the arts, deserves to be acknowledged by historians and contemporary political or sports commentators. There are illustrious names like Maharaja Karni Singh of Bikaner who won

AN EARLY 20TH CENTURY CHILD'S *TOPI*, CAP, FROM GWALIOR, MADE IN VELVET WITH *KARCHOBE* WORK. **pages 6-7:** PRINCESS YASEEN ALI KHAN OF RAMPUR DRESSED IN TRADITIONAL FINERY DURING HER *NIKAH*, WEDDING CEREMONY. HER BRIDAL COSTUME IS MADE OF PURE *ZARI* BY TRADITIONAL WEAVERS AND WEIGHS MORE THAN TEN KILOGRAMS.
pages 8-9: l to r: MAHARAJ KUMAR BRIJRAJ SINGHJI OF KOTAH, NAWABZADA BAKHTIAR ALI KHAN PATAUDI, MAHARAJA HIMMAT SINGHJI OF JODHPUR AND RAJA HARI SEN OF SUKET POSE FOR A PHOTOGRAPH IN THE DURBAR HALL OF JAIVILAS PALACE, GWALIOR. THEY WERE ROYAL GUESTS AT THE WEDDING OF PRINCESS CHITRANGADARAJE OF GWALIOR. ON THE CEILING HANGS ONE OF THE WORLD'S LARGEST CHANDELIERS. TO TEST THE WEIGHT-BEARING CAPABILITY OF THE CEILING ELEPHANTS WERE MADE TO STAND ON THE ROOF OF THE PALACE.

medals for shooting at the Olympics; Jam Saheb Ranjisinh and Duleepsinhrao of Jamnagar, for cricket and tennis, respectively; my own father and brother, Maharaja Pratapsinhrao and Fatesinhrao, for tennis and cricket, respectively. The great father and son duo of the late Nawab Saheb of Pataudi and the present Nawab Mansoor Ali Khan (Tiger Pataudi), brought laurels to our country in cricket. Maharaja Man Singh of Jaipur and many others patronised and kept alive the interest in polo. There are undoubtedly others too who are worthy of mention.

However, the most significant and perhaps the most ignored contribution of the Princely Order is its ardent involvement in the preservation of the vast and varied cultural heritage of India, including the flora and fauna of the country. On them lies the absolute onus of maintaining and restoring the magnificent and ancient buildings — testimony of unique workmanship and architecture. Housed in most of these buildings are priceless artifacts, paintings, crystal, sculpture, stained glass and much more. Beyond just the material wealth these old buildings are custodians of our country's history and are therefore irreplaceable. Our country's tourism industry is a good example of how erstwhile feudal families have successfully turned crumbling fortresses and palaces of the past into hotels and hospitality houses of international standards, generating employment for thousands of local people — to say nothing of tax revenue. In the words of my own son, Yuvraj Samarjitsinh: 'It is time we turn what we once called white elephants into thoroughbred racehorses'.

Few people today show the inclination or take the time to consider the personal lives and challenges that the erstwhile Indian royalty has had to confront. In a young democracy, they have survived overwhelming personal upheavals in their rights, status and privileges, and yet have continued to assume leadership and contribute significantly to society. Traditions and festivals once celebrated are kept alive by being observed privately — in a continuing effort of a proud people to transmit their culture and values to their progeny.

top left: A SCENE FROM THE AFGHAN WAR, 1878-79. THE PICTURE SHOWS A BRIDGE MADE OF BOATS, WITH FORT ATTOCK IN THE BACKGROUND.
top right: SIR SAWAI MADHO SINGHJI, MAHARAJA OF JAIPUR (1880-1922). HIS ENORMOUS GIRTH HAD ONLOOKERS ASKANCE, AND HIS CLOTHES ARE STILL DISPLAYED AT THE CITY PALACE MUSEUM IN JAIPUR. THE MAHARAJA HAD FIVE MAHARANIS BUT DID NOT LEAVE A MALE ISSUE, AND AS A RESULT HIS ADOPTED SON MAN SINGH II BECAME HIS LEGAL HEIR. SAWAI MADHO SINGH WAS HIMSELF ADOPTED BY SAWAI RAM SINGH II. AT THE TIME HE WAS A SEPOY IN THE TONK CAVALRY. ON HIS TRIP TO ATTEND THE GOLDEN JUBILEE CELEBRATIONS OF QUEEN VICTORIA HE CARRIED TWO LARGE SILVER URNS WITH A SIX-MONTH SUPPLY OF WATER FROM THE GANGES. THE URNS ARE LISTED AS THE LARGEST SILVER OBJECTS IN THE GUINNESS BOOK OF RECORDS, WEIGHING OVER 1.75 TONNES.

I feel privileged to have been born into the royal house of the Gaekwads of Baroda. My childhood was filled with the most amazing sights and experiences. When I look back at those days, it almost feels like a fairy tale . . . Living in this beautiful palace surrounded by acres of greenery that included a riding track, a full-fledged cricket ground adjacent to which was the private Princes' School . . . My father Maharaja Pratapsinhrao Gaekwad, brought us a toy train with a steam engine, which was a made-to-scale model of the Flying Scotsman. Chugging through the palace estate, this little train took us to school. Today we have converted the school building into a private museum, namely, the Maharaja Fatehsinh Museum, which houses among many other artifacts, some of the most reputed paintings of Raja Ravi Varma.

In whatever ways and means available to them, erstwhile royal families all over India today are actively involved in maintaining and restoring these fabulous possessions to the best of their capacities.

This book, *Maharajas: Resonance from the Past* is a crisp and interesting read by the well-known writer on the British Raj and the Indian Princes – Charles Allen. Aditya Patankar of Gwalior, the acclaimed photographer, has travelled extensively in India and known several members of erstwhile royal families intimately over the years. Consequently he has had the opportunity to capture moods and moments unavailable to other professional photographers. In this book he has effectively showcased what I call Lifestyle in Pictures – a lifestyle that is intricately woven with contrasting threads reminiscent of an era of grandeur, abundant wealth and status, as also the harmonious merging into a democratic social republic.

I have great pleasure in introducing the readers to this beautiful book, which vividly brings to life the beauty and aesthetics of a bygone period, which historically speaking, is a treasure house of Indian heritage, nurtured and developed by some of the great princes of India. I hope readers will enjoy this pictorial volume, which is in a sense, heritage preserved for posterity.

A METAL SHIELD, CIRCULAR IN DESIGN, WITH AN UPTURNED RIM, PROBABLY BELONGING TO THE STATE OF AVADH DATES BACK TO THE 18TH-19TH CENTURIES. THE PLAIN ROUNDED KNOBS STAND OUT AMIDST AN INTRICATE SILVER INLAY OF FISH, FLORAL PATTERNS AND CREEPERS.

top left: THE STATE BAND OF PALANPUR ASSEMBLES TO RECEIVE THE NAWAB IN 1937. THE NAWAB IS RETURNING FROM A VISIT TO EUROPE AFTER ATTENDING THE CORONATION OF KING GEORGE VI.
top right: DRUMMERS AND TRUMPETERS IN FRONT OF THE LAXMI VILAS PALACE AT BARODA ADD TO ITS GLORY. THE PALACE, CREATED BY CHARLES MANT, A MAJOR IN THE ROYAL ENGINEERS, WAS A BLEND OF SCIENTIFIC EUROPEAN DESIGN ALTERED TO SUIT THE TASTE OF THE NATIVE STYLE. MAJOR MANT, OBSESSED WITH THE FEAR THAT THE BUILDING WOULD COLLAPSE, BECAME INSANE AND KILLED HIMSELF.

Kings and

Kingdoms...

EARLY IN JUNE 1947, as British India's last Viceroy began the countdown leading to independence for India, officials of the Political Department in New Delhi set fire to a huge pile of documents. All of them were related to the so-called Indian Princes and rulers of Native States: the maharajas, *maharanas, maharawals, maharaos,* rajas, *ranas, rawals, raos, thakurs,* nizams, nawabs, *mirs,* khans, *taluqdars* and other local rulers with whom the British Crown had entered into political relations. Intended to prevent these same documents falling into the hands of the new government, this bonfire was also highly symbolic: it marked an end to the protection which India's Princes had long enjoyed under the British – and the beginning of the end for the Princes themselves.

But who were these Princes and rulers of Native States? Were they, as many alleged at that time, an artificial and alien institution foisted on India by the British rulers, or were they, as they and their admirers claimed, India's true kings – rajas and maharajas – with roots going back to the dawn of history?

Roots

The institution of kingship in India is a very ancient one, based on the authority of the raja – one who rules. It can be traced back to the arrival of the Vedic Aryan tribes on the plains of northern India in about 1500 BCE, and it began with the selection of warlords from among the Kshatriyas, a warrior caste whose duty it was to protect the tribe from its enemies. These first rajas ruled only with the support of a council of their peers. Very soon, however, the hereditary principle was established, with the raja gaining his authority not by selection but through his anointing by a *purohita* or head priest from the Brahmin priestly caste. A raja without a *rajpurohita* was likened to an elephant without a mahout, elephant driver, and his kingdom could never flourish. From this time onwards rulers and priesthood were bound up in a symbiotic partnership in which the one depended upon the other to maintain their joint authority as leaders of Indian society.

These early Indian kingdoms were known as *janapadas,* footholds of the tribe, and it was the duty of every raja to extend his *janapada* by conquest into a *mahajanapada,* greater foothold, to which lesser kingdoms should pay tribute. So from an early age the idea of the maharaja and the raja, the great king who ruled over lesser kings, became established. Its apotheosis was the maharaja-*adhiraja,* the king of kings, an emperor to whom all viceroys and vassal kings, great and small, had to pay tribute.

As well as enlarging his kingdom, the raja also had a duty to preserve social order and ensure the material well-being of his people. In return, his subjects were expected to give him their obedience as well as a sixth part of their produce, livestock and gold – and the fairest of their daughters. In the great Vedic epics such as the Mahabharata, much is made of the state of *arajaka,* anarchy, that exists without the leadership of a raja, when little fish are devoured by bigger fish. The first such raja was the mythical King Prithu who formed an ideal government under which the whole earth prospered. Since he gave his people happiness they offered him the royal title of raja, while the god Vishnu entered his body to infuse him with a spark of divinity. In the *Code of Manu,* the ancient manual of laws proposed by the sage Manu, the raja is seen as the incarnation of the eight guardian deities of the Hindu world – Surya, the sun;

WITH A STAR OF INDIA ON HIS CLOAK, MAHARAJA SIR PRATAP SINGH OF BUNDELKHAND POSES FOR NORZ COWELL, A PHOTOGRAPHER, C. 1900. THE BRITISH DURING THEIR RULE IN INDIA BESTOWED VARIOUS TITLES AND HONOURS ON INDIAN PRINCES IN ORDER TO FLATTER AND APPEASE THEM.

facing page: MAHARAJA RUDRA PRATAP SINGH OF PANNA WEARS AN ELABORATE *SARPECH*, TURBAN, LARGE *TIKKA* ON HIS FOREHEAD AND JEWELLED ARMBANDS, AMIDST OTHER REGULAR ROYAL ADORNMENTS.

pages 14-15: A JEWEL-ENCRUSTED SWORD HILT FROM KASHMIR, WHICH WAS THE BIGGEST OF INDIAN STATES.

Chandra, the moon; Agni fire; Vayu, the wind; Indra, rain; Kubera, wealth; Varuna, demons; and Yama, death – taking on all their qualities in his kingship. From this time onwards it became accepted, firstly, that the raja came from a royal family divinely appointed to rule, and secondly, that once the raja had undergone the anointing ceremony of the *rajasuya* performed by his Brahmin *rajpurohita*, he became infused with divinity, making him godlike. But this divinity still came with strings: however much of a god he might be, the raja still had a sacred duty to treat his subjects as a father to his children, to observe the sacred laws and to respect his Brahmin priests.

Ancient Indian kingship was thus a complex two-way compact between ruler and ruled, with strict obligations on both sides. And what made this ancient raja-*praja* (king-people) compact unique was its staying power. The first documented period of Indian kingship begins in about 268 BCE with the king-emperor Ashoka. Although a convert to Buddhism, his ideas on kingship remained essentially Brahminical. 'All men are my children,' reads one of Ashoka's famous rock and pillar edicts. 'On behalf of my own children, I desire that they may be provided by me with complete welfare and happiness in this world and in the other world.' Two thousand years later, the same code of kingship was still being applied within the scores of Rajput principalities which had managed to cling on to various degrees of self-government within the crumbling Mughal empire. The concept of the ruler as the father and mother of his people can still be found in many of the former princely states of Rajasthan to this day, where even after being divested of every scrap of legal authority or title, the current clan chief is still widely addressed as *ma-baap*, father-mother, or as *annadata*, giver of bread.

Some historians claim that the torch of Aryan tradition was handed down from ruler to ruler, dynasty to dynasty, throughout the centuries without a break. They argue that today's maharajas are the descendants of the ancient Aryan Kshatriyas of northern India who, after the old ruling dynasties fell apart in the sixth century CE, re-emerged a century later to pick up and re-ignite the torch dropped by their forefathers. This theory ignores the disruptive impact of successive invasions of *mleccha*, a disparaging term meaning

THE ORDER OF MERIT, EARLY 19TH CENTURY AWARD. EMERALDS ARE INLAID IN ENAMELLED GOLD.
top: PRATAPSINH GAEKWAD, THE LAST RULING MAHARAJA OF BARODA, POSES FOR A FAMILY PICTURE IN 1939. SEEN STANDING ON HIS MOTHER'S RIGHT IS LT. COL. FATEHSINGHRAO GAEKWAD, THE LATE MAHARAJA, AND SEATED BETWEEN HIS PARENTS, THE CURRENT MAHARAJA RANJITSINH GAEKWAD.
facing page: SIR SADIQ MOHAMMAD KHAN, NAWAB OF BAHAWALPUR, WHICH IS NOW IN PAKISTAN. THIS PHOTOGRAPH TAKEN IN THE LATE 19TH CENTURY SHOWS THE NAWAB IN THE ATTIRE TYPICAL OF THE RULERS OF HIS STATE. THE NAWAB'S GRANDFATHER WAS A PINDARI ROBBER CHIEFTAIN IN CENTRAL INDIA. WHEN BROKEN UP BY THE BRITISH FORCES ONE GROUP ESCAPED WESTWARDS BEYOND THE DESERT LANDS OF BIKANER AND LAID CLAIM TO A VAST LAND, EAST OF THE RIVER INDUS.

barbarians, used to describe the waves of nomadic tribes of central Asian origin who, from the second century BCE onwards, descended on northern India through mountain passes from Afghanistan to the plains of the Indus. These invasions wore down the long-established royal dynasties of the region and the social system that supported them.

The impact on northern and western India of the Huna or White Huns, in particular, from about 460 CE onwards was particularly cataclysmic, because they and the tribes who followed in their footsteps eradicated all urban culture in northern India, severing all family and clan links with the past. Numismatic evidence shows that the Hun leader Toramana held sway over much of upper India as far south as Malwa. In about 515 CE he was succeeded by his son, who took the Indian name of Mihiragula, sunflower. Some fifteen years later he was defeated by a local ruler in Malwa, and withdrew northwards to the region of Kashmir. But damaging as these invasions were, they fail to explain the 'dark age' that followed. One possible explanation is that some sort of natural catastrophe occurred in about 536 CE, producing a disastrous drop in temperatures throughout the globe for about a

A GROUP OF RAJPUT PRINCES POSES FOR A FORMAL PHOTOGRAPH.

pages 20-21: AN 18TH CENTURY MARWAR PAINTING OF THAKUR PADAM SINGH (R.1720-42) OF GHANERAO IN A DURBAR SCENE. THE PAINTING SHOWS HIM SEATED ON A TERRACE, SURROUNDED BY TWO CHILDREN, NOBLES AND ATTENDANTS. GHANERAO IS A SMALL *THIKANA*, PROVINCE, ON THE BORDERS OF MEWAR AND MARWAR.

decade — a climate change so severe as to cause a breakdown in civil government in many parts of the world. What is beyond dispute is that a 'dark age' lasted in northern India for about three-quarters of a century, from which there emerged an almost entirely new order of kings.

Each of the earlier invaders from the north-west had dislodged and pushed his predecessors deeper into the subcontinent so that when, in the first quarter of the seventh century CE, Raja Harsha Vardhana briefly succeeded in imposing himself as King of Kings over the Gangetic plain, many of his vassal kings and tributaries were of foreign origin. After fighting a ferocious campaign that won him a swathe of territory right across central India from the Bay of Bengal to the Arabian Sea, Raja Harsha set about transforming the ancient town of Kanauj on the southern bank of the upper Ganges into a magnificent capital. But with his death in 647 CE the region was fractured into a number of small kingdoms ruled by a new order of kings, who soon claimed for themselves an absolute right to rule as members of a loose confederacy of tribes who later named themselves the *chatis raj-kula*, the thirty-six royal families.

YOUNG COUSINS OF MAHARAJA GAJ SINGHJI OF JODHPUR DRESSED FORMALLY ON THE OCCASION OF A ROYAL FAMILY WEDDING. IN RAJPUT WEDDINGS ONLY MEN GO IN THE *BARAAT*, WEDDING PARTY, WHILE THE WOMEN STAY AT HOME. ALTHOUGH THE OCCASIONS IN BOTH PICTURES (THE ONE ON THE FACING PAGE AND ABOVE) ARE FORMAL, THEY ARE SEPARATED BY ALMOST A CENTURY AND SHOW A MARKED CONTRAST NOT ONLY IN THE DRESS OF THE PRINCES BUT ALSO IN THEIR PHYSICAL APPEARANCE.

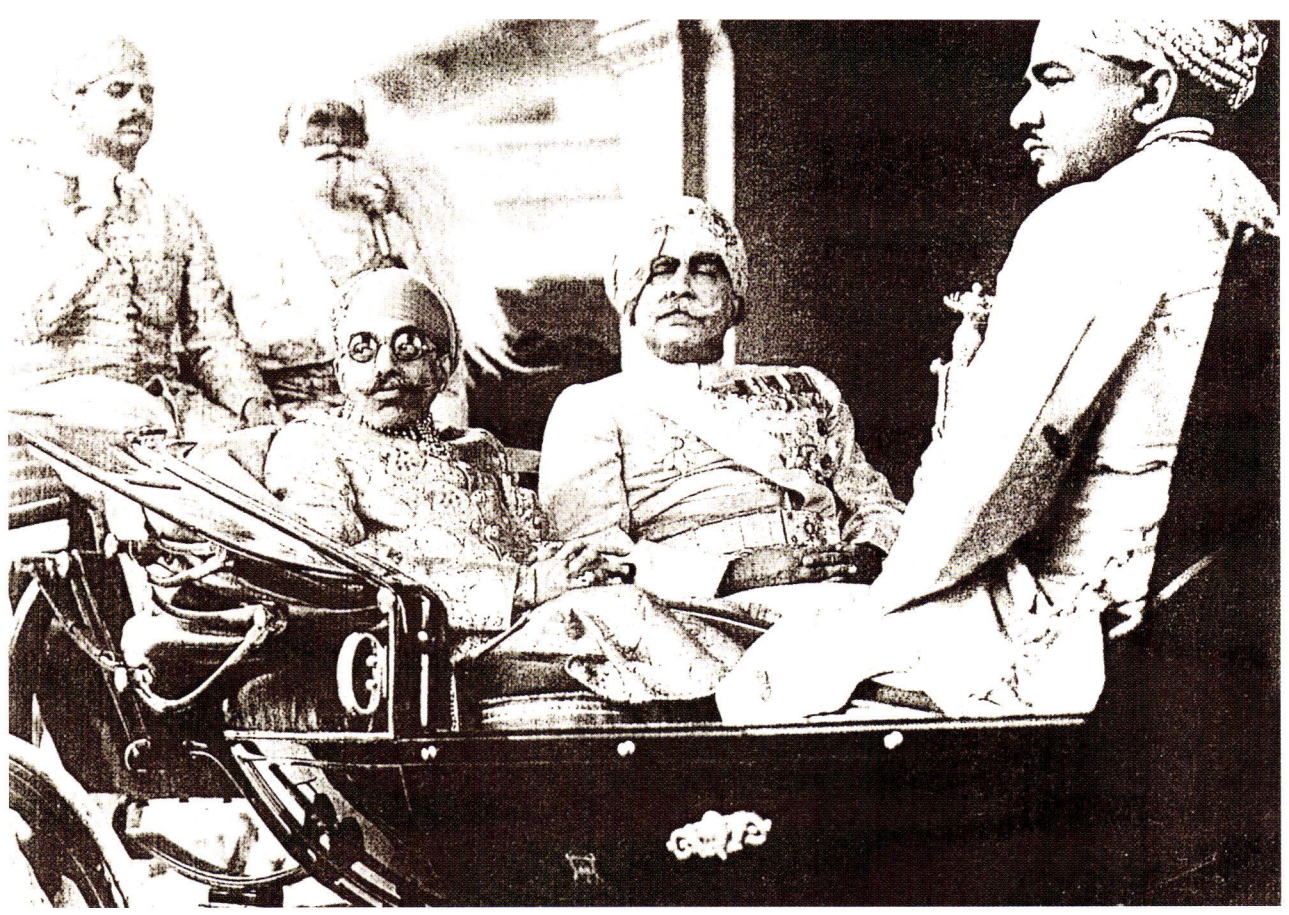

Maharaja Ganga Singh of Bikaner and Maharana Bhupal Singh of Udaipur in a Bikaner state carriage. The Maharaja of Bikaner celebrated his Golden Jubilee as a ruler of the state in 1937. Under his rule Bikaner was transformed from a state lost amidst the sands of the Thar Desert to the granary of Rajasthan, prosperous and healthy in its appearance. By influencing the King and the Viceroy he gained access to the river Sutlej and built the Ganga Canal in 1927, which irrigated a thousand square miles. Maharana Bhupal Singh was crippled after an operation that affected his spine and could not walk. The Maharana succeeded his father to the throne of Mewar in 1933.

pages 26-27: Birthday celebrations of the Maharaja of Benares, Vibhuti Narain Singh. His daughters and son smile in the background while his grandson, in his lap, seems oblivious to the goings-on. The Viceroy gave Vibhuti Narain Singh the powers of a Maharaja on 11 July 1947 but his powers lasted only for five weeks, after which the princely states were merged into one unified India.

The Rise of the Rajputs

To belong to this new and exclusive club of rulers it was necessary to be a Rajput. The Sanskrit word *Rajaputera*, son of a ruler, predates the appearance of the Rajputs by at least a thousand years. It implies royal ancestry and common lineage, which is precisely what the Rajputs claimed for themselves. The majority of the Rajput *chatis raj-kula* refer to themselves as *Suryavansha*, children of the sun, and claim descent from Rama and the sun; while the remainder are *Chandravansha*, children of the moon, and trace their lineage back to Krishna and the moon. All claim direct and unbroken links with the ancient Kshatriya caste found in the great epics of the Mahabharata and Ramayana. The ancient Sisodia ruling dynasty of Mewar (known today as Udaipur) is *Suryavanshi* and its symbol is a golden sun. The Sisodias have always proclaimed themselves to be the legitimate heirs of the throne of Rama by direct descent from his elder son Kush, Rama himself being the fifty-seventh king since Vaivasvata Manu, the Vedic Noah. Every other surviving Rajput clan has a similar genealogical family tree that details its claim to be authentic descendants of the earliest kings of India.

But to this day a huge question mark hangs over the true origins of the Rajput tribes. The general consensus among historians is that most, if not all, of the Rajput clans were drawn from one or other of those same central Asian tribes who entered India from the second century BCE onwards, fanning out as far west as Kathiawar and Kutch and as far east as Orissa. In their search for new homelands, these invaders took on the local indigenous tribes of the forests, mountains and deserts, conquered and subjugated them and then set themselves up as local chieftains. The chronicles of the illustrious Sisodia clan, also known as the Guhilotes

facing page: This photograph is from the album given to the Maharaja of Dharangdhara by the Maharaja of Ratlam in 1880. At a time three or four centuries ago, when the house of Jodhpur was expanding, the family members separated and founded the states of Bikaner, Ratlam and many others. Dharangdhara, a senior house of the Jhala clan, was one of the 8 richest states out of the 282 odd states present in the Kathiawar peninsula in Western India in the 1930s. In 1527, one of their ancestors Ajoji was the commander of the combined forces of the Rajputs that fought the forces of the Mughal invader, Babur, at Khanua.

(Gehlote), cave-born, state that they came from the north but were driven westwards to the Kathiawar seaboard before finally making their way into the Aravalli hills of Rajasthan, where in the second half of the sixth century CE, their common ancestor Guhil, the cave-born, formed an alliance with local Bhil aboriginals and became their chieftain. According to the annals of Mewar, Guhil was a refugee brought up by a Brahmin priest in ignorance of his royal parentage, who preferred to hunt in the jungles with the forest-dwelling Bhils rather than study. One day the other boys elected Guhil as their leader and to indicate his selection, one of them cut his thumb with an arrowhead and marked Guhil's forehead with a bloody thumb print. When the elders heard of this they held a council and decided that Guhil should be declared the chief of their tribe, their *rawal*. All the lands they hunted over then became his, over which he and his descendents, the Guhilotes, offspring of Guhil, ruled. On Guhil's death his son was appointed chief of the Bhils and the *tikka*, mark of blood, was smeared on his forehead by the son of the Bhil who had performed that same office on his father. This tradition of blood-anointing continued through the centuries right up to the present day. When the ceremony was last performed, at the anointing of the seventy-sixth Maharana of Mewar in 1986, the man who cut his thumb and applied it to Maharana Mahendra Singh's brow was a descendant of that same Bhil who had made the first cut some fourteen centuries earlier. The *Raj-tilak*, anointing ceremony, of many other Rajput clans in and around Rajasthan also involved the participation of Bhil tribal chiefs as a symbol of this ancient alliance between rulers and ruled.

The dispute over Rajput origins is unlikely to be resolved. What is certain is that in the seventh and eighth centuries CE an extraordinary number of proto-Rajput ruling dynasties began to emerge all over northern India who later claimed membership of the *chatis raj-kula*. By the middle of the tenth century about a dozen of these dynasties stood head and shoulders above the rest. They included: the Tomara in the Jamuna region, where they built the first of the many cities of Delhi; the Pratihara further downstream in the

top left: The last ruling Maharaja of Bikaner, Sadul Singhji, sits astride his pony at the age of four. The Rajput and his horse were inseparable, and almost as soon as he could walk, a Rajput boy was put on a horse. Sadul Singh succeeded his father in 1942. He was also an excellent shooter as described by his son, Karni Singh.
facing page: Raja of Bansda.
pages 28-29: *Ghodi Pujan*, worship of the bridegroom's horse. Princess Rita Kumari of the Rathore clan of Jodhpur feeds a caparisoned mare before her brother rides away to get married. In Rajput weddings the groom traditionally rides to the ceremony on a mare rather than a stallion.

Tuladan ceremony of Maharaja Ganga Singh of Bikaner at *Yagya Shola* in Lallgarh Palace. Being weighed in gold, which was then distributed among the subjects, was a common practice. The Maharaja reigned from 1898 till his death in 1943 and after he saw the fate of hundreds of his subjects who died in the Chapna Kaal famine at the end of the 19th century he was obsessed with the thought of getting water and of greening his desert state. He also wanted to get the railways to his state so that fcod could be transported quickly. He had a remarkable personality, a voice like a tiger, and was a hard taskmaster.

upper Gangetic plain, with their capital at Kanauj; the Chandella to their south and east; the Paramara in the Malwa country west of the Chandella kingdom; the Solanki and Sisodia in the Gujarat area; the Chauhan and Bhatti in the western desert; the Jhala in Saurashtra; and the Jadeja in Sind and Kutch. From these last two families are descended no less than ten of the princely salute states and a large number of lesser chieftainships that formed part of the Western India States Agency until 1947: Dharangdhara, Wankaner, Wadhwan and Limbdi – all Jhala; Nawanagar, Morvi, Dhrol, Rajkot, Gondal and Kotda Sangani – all Jadeja.

To the Fire Born

How these interlopers first established the loose confederacy that became the *chatis raj-kula* and were absorbed so completely into the Hindu caste system is another great mystery. However, the evidence suggests that to legitimise themselves as rulers and to win popular support, the first proto-Rajput chiefs underwent purification. An important clue to this transformation process can be found in the legends relating to the origins of the Rajputs who call themselves *agnikula*, fire-born families. Four of the most important of the thirty-six royal families, the Pratiharas (Parihars), Paramaras (Pawars), Chaulukyas (Solankis), and the Chauhans (Chahamanas), are said to have emerged from a fire-pit situated near the summit of the rocky plateau in western Rajasthan known today as Mount Abu. The story of their fire-birth is told in the epic poem *Prithviraj Rasa*, which runs into a hundred thousand stanzas and might well be termed the Ramayana of the Rajputs. It relates how the original Kshatriya warriors were destroyed, leaving the Brahmins unprotected and causing great disorder: 'Ignorance and infidelity spread across the land, the sacred books were trampled upon and mankind had no defence against the monstrous brood of the *daitya* and *mleccha* [demons and barbarians].' So all the sages gathered on Mount Abu and prayed to the gods to regenerate the warrior caste. The first god to respond was Indra, who created a warrior that emerged from the fire-pit shouting, 'Kill! Kill!' and was therefore called Paramara, slayer of the enemy. The next god, Brahma, created a warrior named Chaulukya. The god Rudra created the third warrior, who slipped as he went forth to fight the demons and was therefore demoted to the role of gatekeeper and named Pratihara, gatekeeper. The fourth warrior, created by Vishnu, was the most powerful, and being given four arms to fight with, was named Chauhan, four-armed. The Chauhan warrior overcame the demons and the four *agnikula* apportioned lands to rule over.

The fire-pit legend shows the process by which the four tribes involved were elevated from non-Hindu barbarians to high-caste Hindus by an act of purification involving fire – a ritual in which the Brahmins played a major role. This gave them the necessary status to become true rajas who would be acceptable to those they ruled over. The Brahmins also gained in this transaction, because with the decline of the original Kshatriya caste they had lost their traditional allies and protectors. Now with the upsurge of a new warrior class they saw the perfect opportunity to rebuild the old Brahmin-Kshatriya alliance – by upgrading and making the new rulers respectable by performing ritual purification.

As might be expected, these four fire-born tribes of the Rajputs were among the earliest to make their

THE YOUNG PRINCESS INDIRARAJE GAEKWAD OF BARODA, DAUGHTER OF MAHARAJA SAYAJI RAO GAEKWAD. SHE IS DRESSED IN A TRADITIONAL *ANGARAKHA*, BODICE AND *KARCHOBE* WORK *TOPI*, CAP. INDIRARAJE WAS VERY HEADSTRONG AND IN 1910, AT EIGHTEEN YEARS OF AGE, SHE WENT AGAINST HER PARENTS' WISHES AND REFUSED TO MARRY THE FORTY-TWO-YEAR-OLD MAHARAJA MADHAV RAO SCINDIA OF GWALIOR. IN 1911 AT THE DELHI DURBAR SHE FELL IN LOVE WITH THE HANDSOME PRINCE OF COOCH BEHAR AND EVENTUALLY HAD HER WAY BY MARRYING HIM.

facing page: THE YOUNG SON OF THE MAHARAJA OF BANSDA RIDES AN ELEPHANT. THE *CHATTRA*, UMBRELLA, A SYMBOL OF ROYALTY, PROTECTS HIM ABOVE. ELEPHANTS WERE USED NOT ONLY CEREMONIALLY BUT ALSO IN BATTLE AND DURING SHIKAR. EACH MAHARAJA'S *HATHIKHANA*, ELEPHANT STABLE, SPECIALISED IN ELABORATE DECORATION AND PAINTING OF THESE ROYAL BEASTS.

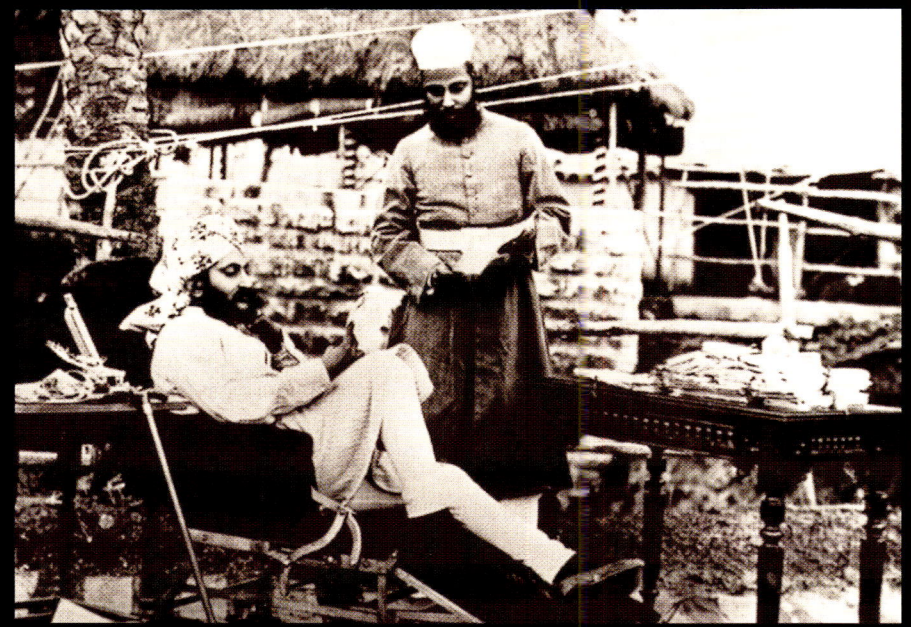

above: Dull, brown walls surrounded the King Kothi Palace in the heart of Hyderabad. The ostentation of the interior, however, spoke of the immense wealth of the Nizams.

top left: Mahboob Ali Khan, the sixth Nizam, working in an informal relaxed atmosphere. **pages 34-35, top centre:** This late 19th century Hyderabadi shield comprising two sheets is inlaid in gold. Four leaf-shaped windows and steel knobs surround a seven-petal flower in the centre.

right: Gold, rubies, diamonds and emeralds decorate this 19th century pair of *paizebs*, anklets, from Nizam Asaf Jah's collection in Hyderabad. **facing page, top right:** A rare necklace of table-cut diamonds interspersed with smaller ones, toning down in size at the back, and ending in a suspended triangular diamond, surrounded by small ones. Set in gold, this is a 19th century piece.

facing page, right: Lost in thought, this young prince stands with the swagger akin to that of his peers.

Hyderabad and Berar

1654
Khwaja Abid was one of Aurangzeb's most trusted generals. After his death his son Mir Kamruddin Khan was appointed Nizam-ul-Mulk, Regulator of the State, of the southern Deccan. Thus began the Asaf Jah dynasty.

The Asaf Jah family claimed a line of descent on the male side from the Khalipha, the Prophet Mohammed's successor, and on the female side from the Prophet himself. This Muslim dynasty ruled over a largely Hindu population in the southern Deccan.

Second half of the 18th century
Problems over succession occurred after Mir Kamruddin's death. Amidst murders and intrigues, Hyderabad lost a lot of territory to the British, French, Marathas and Mysore.

1779
Treaty signed with the East India Company, making Hyderabad its most important ally.

19th century
Salar Jung, a capable administrator, pulled the state out of impending bankruptcy.

20th century
Loyalty to the British earned the Nizam the title of His Exalted Highness. Mir Osman Ali, the tenth and last Nizam, tried unsuccessfully to exert his independence in 1926.

1940s
When the Princely States were invited to merge with either India or Pakistan, Osman Ali declared Hyderabad an independent state. The Indian government sent in troops and finally Hyderabad merged with India.

mark. The first to claim the holy mountain of Mount Abu were the Paramaras, of whom it was said in the eleventh century that 'the world is the Paramaras'. Two centuries later, the Paramara ruler was overthrown by his rivals, the Chauhans, and the survivors fell back on their last stronghold at Mount Abu. It is said that the Chauhans then proposed that twelve Paramara princesses should marry twelve Chauhan princes, to end the quarrel between their tribes. But as the princesses and their escorts descended from the mountain they were set upon by Chauhan warriors hidden in ambush. All the men were killed, the princesses were taken as captives and the Paramaras disappeared from history. Their descendants, known today as the Lok, can still be found in Mount Abu. They still hark back to this ancient betrayal by refusing to marry their daughters to any Rajput plainsmen.

The first *agnikula* family to make an impact on Indian history was the Pratihara, usually referred to by modern historians as the Gurjara-Pratihara. A rock inscription dated to 959 CE links the family to the area of central Rajasthan known as *Gurjararatra-bhumi*, the homeland of the Gurjara. The modern state of Gujarat in western India derives its name from these same Gurjara or Gujars, a tribe of nomadic pastoralists descended from the Khazar of the south Russian steppes, who are thought to have entered India in the wake of the more warlike Huna. References to Juzr in the writings of Arab historians from the ninth century, declared there to be 'no greater foe of the [Islamic] Faith' than these people, the finest cavalrymen in India. This could explain how these low caste Gujars gained the name of Pratihara. A ninth-century stone pillar recovered from a lake in Gwalior names the ancestor of the Pratihara kings as Lakshman, younger brother of the hero-king Rama, and calls him *pratihara* in recognition of his defence of the land against Rama's enemies. The Gwalior pillar also names the clan's first ruler as Raja Nagabhatta of Jalor, who fought against the first Arab invaders from Sind at the start of the eighth century, which suggests that it was this that earned him and his clan the title of gatekeepers – as the first line of Hindu India's defence against Muslim invasion from the west.

The Pratihara clan soon emerged as the dominant power in the Malwa area, going on to rule a broad swathe of northern India from Gujarat to the Gangetic plains. In about the year 816 CE Raja Nagabhatta II captured Kanauj, which remained the seat of the Pratihara clan for the next two centuries. His successors conquered more territory, including in about 846 CE an enormous rock bluff that dominates the plains country between the Chambal and Narmada rivers and serves as the key to the control of central India. This was the ancient hill fort of Gwalior.

Another *agnikula* family, the Solanki, may also be of Gujar extraction. In its years of glory it ruled what is now south Rajasthan, but for centuries its power-base was much of present Gujarat. Gujar pastoralists make up a large part of the agricultural population of eastern Rajasthan, being outnumbered only by Jat cultivators, who are believed to be descendants of Shaka invaders who broke into India some two millennia ago. In the sixth or seventh century these people took up swords and spears, and moved up the Hindu hierarchical ladder to become Kshatriyas and Rajputs.

The decline of the Pratiharas coincided with the rise of the fourth of the *agnikula*, the Chauhans. It is said that they were originally Brahmins, but probably this distinction was conferred on them after their coming to power to give the name greater lustre. They too have early links with the Gujarat region, but the name of the clan founder, Chahamana, has phonetic ties with Toramana and other leaders of the Huna. An early text known as the *Prabandha Kosh* mentions 551 CE as the date of Chahamana's accession as clan warlord – about a quarter century after the Huna had suffered a severe defeat that forced them to withdraw to Kashmir.

According to their annals, the Chauhans' first seat was established at Nagaur near the Sambhor lake, a hundred and sixty kilometres west of Jaipur. They were ejected from there by the Pratiharas in the mid-seventh century. Under the command of Ajaipal the survivors made their way south along the Aravalli range in search of a new home. They settled in Ajmer and within five generations, recovered their fortunes sufficiently, challenged the Paramaras and the Pratiharas, and became the new power in the land.

The Kshatriya Warrior-kings

Whatever today's Rajputs claim about their racial purity as Kshatriyas, we can be sure that their Rajputisation began with alliances between the conquering *mlecchas* and the conquered indigenous Indian women, often the local aboriginals known today as Adivasis, first people. In their search for new homelands, the proto-Rajputs took on these indigenous tribes of the forests, mountains and deserts, conquered them, made themselves their rulers and married their daughters.

Once they had transformed themselves into legitimate Kshatriya rulers, the Rajputs then underwent a second and equally dramatic transformation. Within generations they had reshaped themselves to become paragons of all the Kshatriya virtues, abandoning almost every trace of their nomadic, central Asian heritage in favour of the religion, language and customs of their adopted land. As befits a warrior people, they chiefly became devotees of Shiva and his female counterpart, worshipping the former in the form of the *lingam* or phallus, and the latter either in the martial form of Durga or as the black goddess Kali, protector and destroyer of evil. So complete was this assimilation that the word Rajput soon became virtually synonymous with Kshatriya. This assimilation was also accompanied by a remarkable crystallising of Rajput culture.

It must have become apparent to these Rajput rulers at an early stage that if they were to claim

Vahan pujan being performed in the Sharbata Courtyard of the City Palace, Jaipur, by Maharaja Bhawani Singhji during Dussehra. In this puja, the Kshatriya worships the various modes of transport he uses, such as the elephant, the horse and the ox-cart. These animals played a very important role in the lives of the Indian princes, as they were instrumental in moving armies and entourages from place to place.

strengthened through carefully planned matches between sons and daughters. In this way strong political alliances were often maintained for centuries between ruling families, to the advantage of both houses, although not always to the personal happiness of those directly involved as marriage partners. However, these marriage alliances also led to a constant cross-fertilisation of ideas right across the regions where Rajput rule held sway and resulted in the rise of a vibrant Rajput culture throughout northern and central India — one that lasted for over a thousand years and which still remains a dominant force in regions such as Rajasthan.

Arab Invasions

The Rajputs' fixation on military valour and loyalty to the head of the clan may have been their defining characteristic, but it also proved their undoing. It led to constant rivalry and warfare among rulers, and often left them incapable of uniting against a common enemy. Ultimately, it proved fatal, for the rise to power of the Rajput dynasties coincided with the first raids by Arabs and their Muslim successors. Two new and opposing elements, militant Islam and the no less militant Rajputs, appeared on the Indian scene at the same time, and Hindu-Muslim conflict became inevitable.

But the Muslim armies, highly motivated by their religious beliefs, taught to regard unbelievers as fair game and given both religious and material incentives to wage war, proved to be well-nigh invincible. In the year 711 a viceroy of the eastern provinces of the Khalifa of Damascus embarked on a campaign designed to extend the Islamic empire eastwards. Under the command of his seventeen-year-old cousin, Muhammad ibn Qasim, an invading force of twelve thousand Syrian cavalrymen and camel-riders was sent into Sind. His campaign began with an assault on a seaport defended by four

exclusiveness for themselves as a ruling caste, then they had to marry only amongst themselves. The result was an absolute taboo placed on marriage outside the thirty-six royal families, which in turn led to marriage becoming a key political weapon. However, because of their warrior ethic the Rajputs were as often at war with their neighbours as they were at peace with them. The survival of a ruling family often depended on the strength of its political alliances and these alliances were

The Maharaja of Jodhpur, H. H. Sir Jaswant Singh Bahadur of the Rathore clan from Marwar in the 1880s. The Maharaja is wearing a necklace with several Columbian emeralds. Two centuries ago one of his ancestors by the same name was one of the greatest heroes of Marwar. He valiantly held back Aurangzeb and in 1659 led 30,000 brave Rajput soldiers in battle against him. A huge number died in the battlefield and when he returned to his fort with the remaining soldiers, his Rani closed the gates of the fort on them and told them to either vanquish or die.

facing page, top left: The young Nawab of Bahawalpur, Sadiq Muhammad Khan, and his Council of Regents.

thousand Rajputs together with three thousand Brahmins who served the temple. When the walls had been breached they were invited to embrace Islam and on refusal, all were put to the sword. Their wives and children were enslaved, with seventy-five of the fairest being transported to Damascus to join Al-Hajjaj's harem, together with a fifth of the spoils – the rest being divided amongst the troops. This ferocity encouraged other towns inland to open their gates to the invaders and it was not until Muhammad ibn Qasim crossed the Indus that he found himself opposed by a Rajput force under the king of Sind. Arab historians described this king, Rao Dahir, as a Brahmin but he was married to a Rajput woman, and she and her daughters behaved with characteristic Rajput courage after Rao Dahir had been killed in battle. As so often happened in these engagements, the death of their leader was the signal for a general retreat. 'The idolaters fled', writes the historian Al-Biladuri, 'and the Mussulmans [Muslims] glutted themselves with massacre'.

The survivors retired to the fortress of Rawar, where Rao Dahir's widow, Rani Bai, took charge of the defence. When resistance was no longer possible she assembled all the womenfolk in the fort and ordered them to preserve their honour by performing the Rajput rite of *jauhar* (derived from the Sanskrit word for warrior, *yodhri*), an act of mass suicide. This rite, together with sati, the burning of a widow on her husband's funeral pyre, were to become the cornerstones of Rajput custom. At Rawar, however, no mass suicide took place, for the fort was assaulted while Rani Bai and her womenfolk were still preparing themselves for mass immolation. Muhammad ibn Qasim made the queen his wife and moved on to the city of Alor, 'the greatest city of all Sind', which gave in after a month.

WORN IN THE FRONT CENTRE OF A TURBAN, THIS *KALGI*, DIADEM, OF THE 18TH CENTURY IS MADE OF GOLD AND SET WITH RUBIES, EMERALDS, BERYLS AND DIAMONDS ON THE FRONT AND THE BACK.

below: COLUMBIAN EMERALDS, CAREFULLY MATCHED FOR COLOUR, LUSTRE AND PURITY, ARE SET IN GOLD AND COMPLEMENTED WITH DIAMONDS IN THIS *SARPECH* BELONGING TO THE NIZAM OF HYDERABAD.

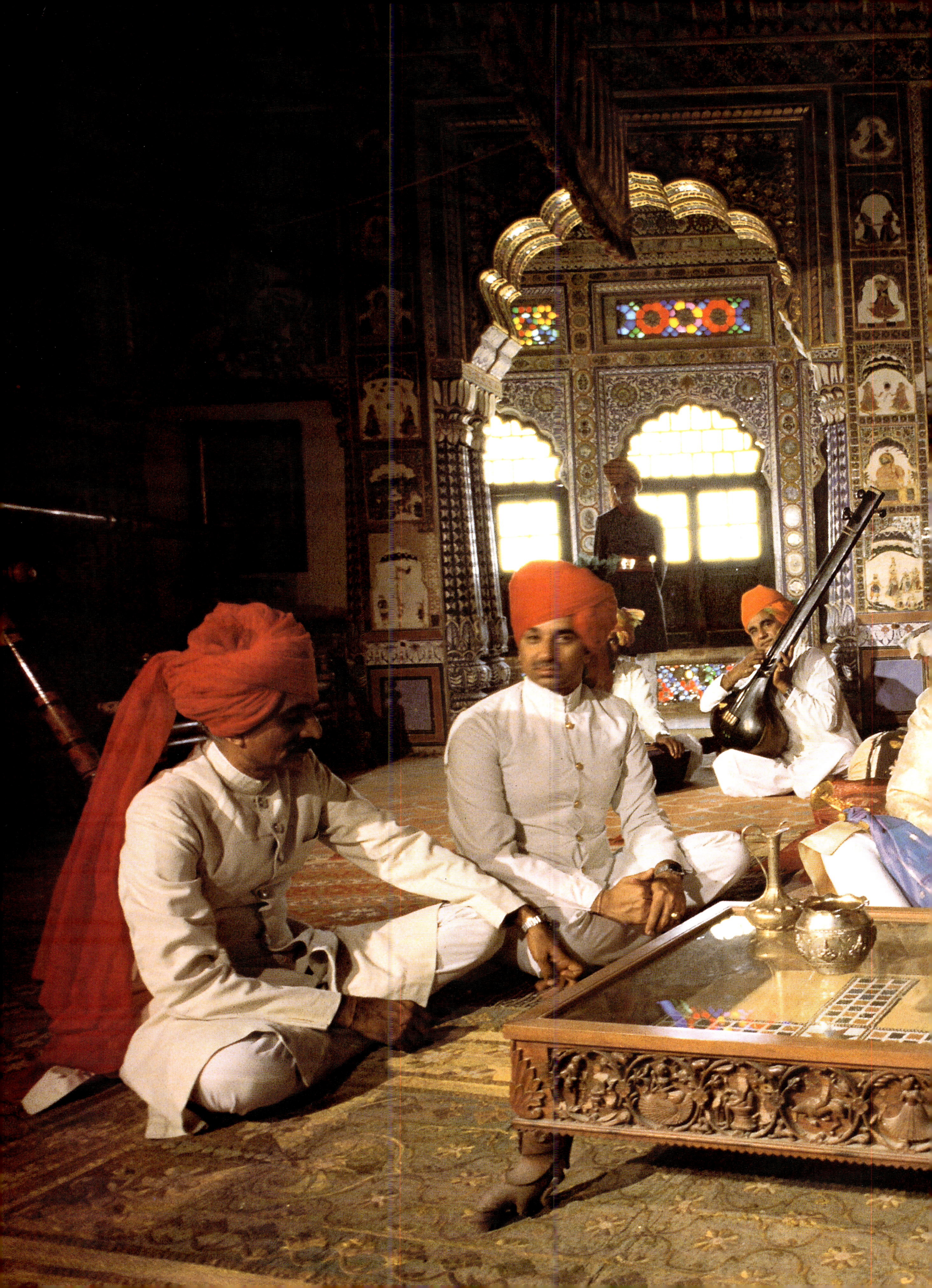

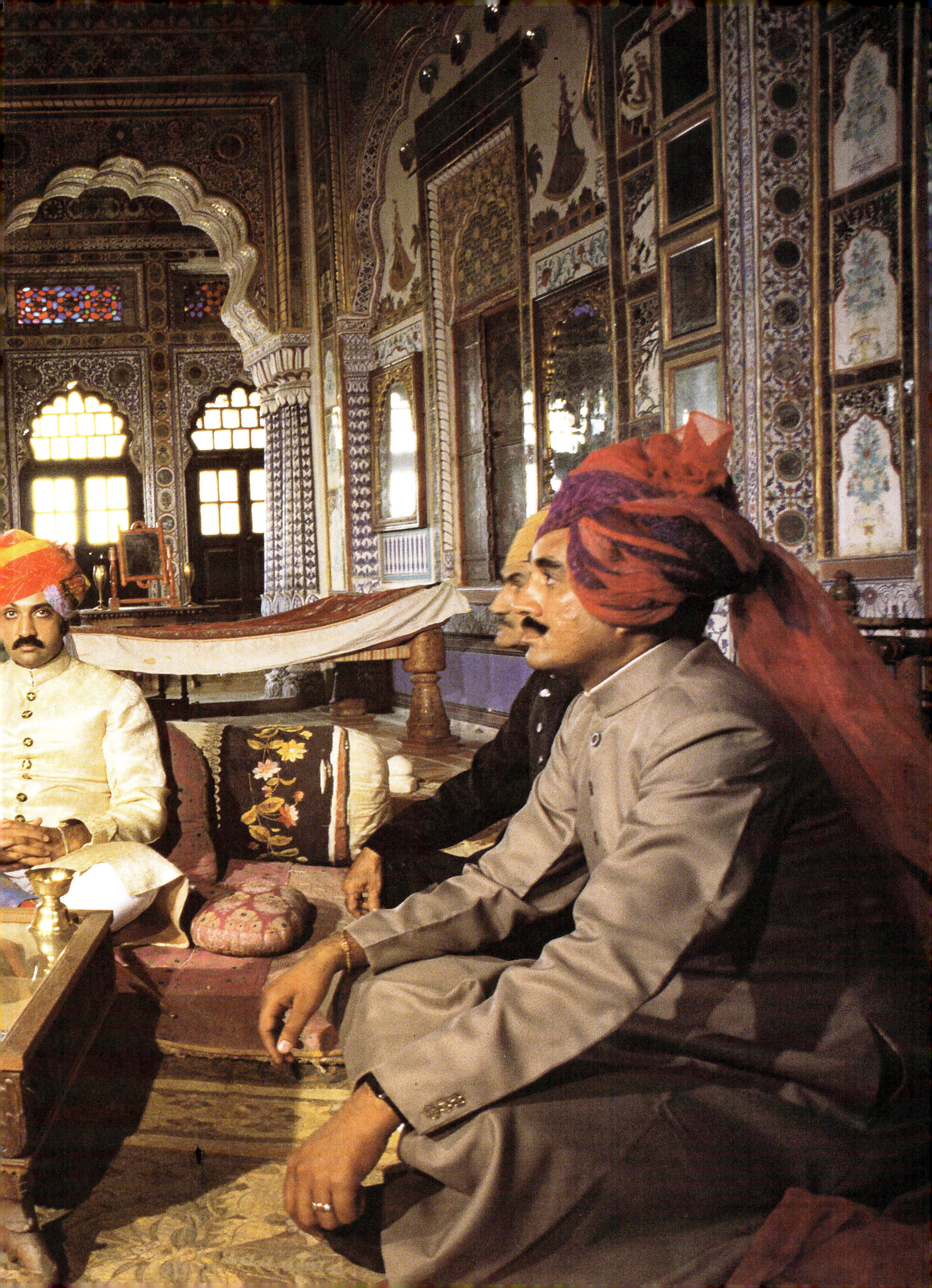

Soon after this a Muslim missionary made his way from Sind across the Great Indian Desert to Ajmer, in the heart of Rajput country. This was the capital of the Chauhans. Here the Muslim visitor was unwise enough to dip his thumb into a bowl of yogurt intended for the clan chief. The offending digit was immediately cut off and its owner bundled out of the town. According to Arab accounts, the disjointed member was taken to Mecca, where it was recognised as belonging to the saint — from which we may assume that the offended missionary returned to Sind demanding retribution. A punitive expedition was at once assembled and despatched in the guise of a caravan of horse-traders. It evidently caught the garrison of the fort above Ajmer off guard because the first casualty was Lot, the son of the ruling chief, who was playing on the battlements when he was struck by an arrow. Both boy and father were killed and the Chauhan capital fell to the Arabs. Thirteen hundred years later this first fatal encounter with Islam is still remembered by the Chauhans.

The boy Lot was deified and became one of the prime household gods of the Chauhans, and to this day his death anniversary is marked with prayers. The silver anklet that Lot was wearing when he died is still preserved in the Chauhan fort at Kota, and no Chauhan child has worn such an anklet from that day to the present.

So Ajmer briefly became a Muslim enclave in the heart of Hindu Rajasthan and is today recognised as one of the holiest places of Islam outside Arabia, because it contains the tomb of a *pir*, Muslim saint, popularly known as Khwaja Gharib Nawaz, Protector of the Poor, who brought the mystical form of Islam known as Sufism to India. Preaching love and understanding, he helped to convert many non-Muslims to Islam.

Ajmer's star fortress was recaptured by the Chauhan's new clan-chief Manika Rai, whose numerous sons set out to establish their own chieftainships as the family

A LATE 19TH CENTURY *KATAR*, DAGGER, FROM JAIPUR. EXTREMELY POPULAR DURING THE MUGHAL ERA, THESE WERE TUCKED INTO THE WAISTBANDS OF THE EMPEROR AND HIS COURTIERS. ELABORATELY ENAMELLED AND SET WITH PRECIOUS STONES, EACH PIECE WAS TREASURED BY ITS OWNER.

TOP RIGHT: IN THE 1860S, THE MAHARAJA OF JAIPUR KEPT PET CHEETAHS. THEY ARE SEEN HERE WITH THEIR KEEPERS. THESE CHEETAHS WERE SPECIALLY TRAINED TO HUNT DEER.

PAGES 42-43, CENTRE: A 17TH CENTURY MUGHAL DAGGER. ITS WATERED STEEL BLADE IS TOPPED WITH A LIGHT GREEN NEPHRITE HILT. INLAYS OF GOLD AND JEWELS ON THE HILT DO NOT BELIE ITS STURDINESS.

grew in strength. Many of these petty principalities were in the western desert, where they formed the front line against the Arab and Muslim advance. The Arab historian Ferishta records that in the year 765 Muslims launched fresh raids into India and 'the Raja of Lahore, who was of the family of the Raja of Ajmer, sent his brothers against these Afghans'. Seventy engagements were fought within five months. 'Sometimes the infidel carried the war to the mountains and drove the Mussulmans before him; sometimes the Mussulmans, obtaining reinforcements, drove the infidels by flights of arrows to their own borders, to which they always retired when the torrents filled the Nilab', blue water, the Arab name for the River Indus.

Further Arab assaults took place during the Caliphate of Al-Mamun, son of the celebrated Harun-al-Rashid of Baghdad. In 813 CE Al-Mamun launched a military expedition that took his army as far west as the celebrated rock fortress of Chittor, which had now become the family seat of the Sisodias. Arab historians have made little of this campaign, which has led others to ignore it – but the reason for this silence is because it was one of those rare instances when the invaders met with severe reverses. It was also one of those rare occasions when the Rajputs set aside their quarrels to eject the invader. According to the *Khomain Rasa*, the oldest of the sagas of Mewar, thirty-nine Rajput princes came to defend Chittor, each at the head of his own contingent of mounted vassal-knights, foot soldiers and bowmen. The list of the gathered clans and tribes, as quoted by James Tod in his *Annals and Antiquities of Rajasthan*, provides a valuable roll-call of Rajput power as it stood at the start of the ninth century:

A 17TH CENTURY MUGHAL HELMET. A BAYONET-SHAPED SPIKE TOPS THE STEEL BODY, INLAID WITH GOLD FLORAL AND BIRD ENGRAVINGS.

pages 40-41: MAHARAJA GAJ SINGHJI OF JODHPUR AND HIS COURTIERS ENJOY LISTENING TO HINDUSTANI CLASSICAL MUSIC IN MEHERANGARH FORT, JODHPUR.

THE ROOM IS RICHLY DECORATED WITH GOLD LEAF, MIRROR INLAY, MIRRORS AND WALL PAINTINGS IN TRADITIONAL RAJPUT STYLE. HINDUSTANI CLASSICAL MUSIC OWES A GREAT DEAL TO THE PATRONAGE GIVEN TO IT BY INDIAN PRINCELY FAMILIES. AS A RESULT, EVEN TO THIS DAY INDIA HAS SOME VERY IMPORTANT

GHARANAS, SCHOOLS OF MUSIC, LIKE THE JAIPUR, GWALIOR, RAMPUR AND BENARES GHARANAS.

43

'From Gajuni came the Gehlote; the Tak from Aser; from Nadolaye the Chauhan; the Chalook from Rahirgurh; from Mangrole the Macwahana; from Jeitgurh the Joria; from Taragurh the Rewur; the Cutchwaha from Nirwur; from Sanchore the Kalum; from Joengurh the Dussanoh; from Ajmer the Gor; from Lohadurgurh the Chundano; from Kasoondi the Dor; from Delhi the Tuar; from Patun the Chawura, preserver of royalty; from Jalore the Sonigurra; from Sirohi the Deora; from Gagrown the Keechie; the Jadoo from Junagurh; the Jhala from Patri; from Kanouj the Rahtore; from Chotiala the Balla; from Perungurh the Gohil; from Jesulgurh the Bhatti; the Boosa from Lahore; the Sankla from Roneja; the Sehut from Kherligurh; from Mandelgurh the Nacoompa; the Birgoojur from Rajore; from Kurrungurh the Chundail; from Sikur the Sikurwal; from Omergurh the Jaitwa; from Palli the Birgota; from Khunturgurh the Jareja; from Jirgah the Kherwur; from Cashmer the Purihara.'

This army marched under the leadership of the Gehlote warden of Chittor, Rawal Khuman II, who engaged the invaders in no less than twenty-four encounters, first defeating the Arabs on the Chittor plain and taking their general captive, and then harrying them as they retreated westwards. Khuman's reward was to have his name preserved in Mewari memory. Tod records, 'If you make a false step, or even sneeze, you hear the ejaculation of "Khuman aid you!"'

As early as the end of the ninth century CE the Rajputs had come to see themselves as the champions and protectors of Hindu religion against Islam, a role which they continued to maintain in the public mind for the next nine hundred years.

Perishing under Afghan Might

Rawal Khuman II's victory over the Arabs at Chittor in 813 is as significant as Charles Martel's outside Poitiers in 752, for these two confrontations marked the eastern and western limits of Arab expansion, the

Maharaja Colonel Sawai Bhawani Singhji of Jaipur with his sardars and ADCs dressed in traditional white *achakans*, long coats, and red turbans on the occasion of Dussehra. The Maharaja served as a paratrooper officer in the Indian Army and has been awarded the 'Mahaveer Chakra' for his very distinguished military services.

facing page: *Tilak*, engagement ceremony, of Bhanwar Ijyaraj Singhji of Kotah in the Durbar hall of Umaid Bhawan Palace. Behind him stand liveried attendants carrying yak hair flywhisks, swords and shields – all symbols of Indian royalty. The ceremony is being conducted by the royal priests of Kotah and is witnessed by family members and select guests.

turning points after which these empires began to fall apart. One after another the eastern provinces threw off their allegiance to Baghdad, with local governors setting themselves up as independent sultans. One of these was the ex-slave Sultan Subuktagin, Amir of Ghazni, who in 978 began 'girding his loins for a war of religion', and set out to ravage eastern Afghanistan and northern Punjab where a Hindu dynasty known as the Shahi had come to power early in the ninth century. Although not listed as one of the thirty-six royal families, there is evidence linking them to the Bhattis, whose annals speak of ancestors ruling large tracts of Afghanistan before being driven eastwards. The Shahi ruler, Raja Jaipal, was unable to stand up to Subuktagin's raiders and appealed to the Rajput chiefs of northern India to come to his aid. This brought together for the second time a confederacy of Rajputs said to number a hundred thousand, giving them overwhelming superiority. The opposing forces met in the Karram Valley, south-west of Peshawar, where a pattern of battle was established that would be repeated time and again. The Rajput army consisted of a score of individual corps, each flying the banners of their own commanders and owing allegiance only to them. Although composed of cavalry, infantry and archers, they relied heavily on a front line of war-elephants to push the enemy before them. By contrast, their opponents were united under the green banners of Islam and the soldiers were, by the standards of the day, highly disciplined. However their greatest strength lay in their light cavalry brigades mounted on the best horseflesh in central Asia, which came at the close-packed Rajput forces from all sides and wore them down. Finally, in clouds of choking dust so thick that 'swords could not be distinguished from spears, nor men from elephants, nor heroes from cowards', they closed in for the kill. The Rajput army was utterly devastated and destroyed; no prisoners were taken and a permanent foothold on the northern Indian plains was secured.

page 46: MAHARAO RAGHUBIR SINGH BAHADUR OF BUNDI. THIS 19TH CENTURY RULER WAS ONE OF THE FEW INDIAN RULERS WHO MANAGED TO SUSTAIN UNDER BRITISH RULE, THE SAME STANDARDS AS HIS ANCESTORS DID BEFORE THE BRITISH RAJ. HE IS SEEN HERE IN AN *ANGARAKHA* AND A *PAGRI* WITH A *TILAK* ON HIS FOREHEAD. THE STATE OF BUNDI, SITUATED IN SOUTH-EASTERN RAJASTHAN, IS FAMOUS FOR THE SCHOOLS OF ART THAT, ENCOURAGED BY THEIR KINGS, CREATED GREAT FRESCOES AND MINIATURE PAINTINGS.
page 47: MAHARAJA SIR BHANWAR PAL OF KARAULI.

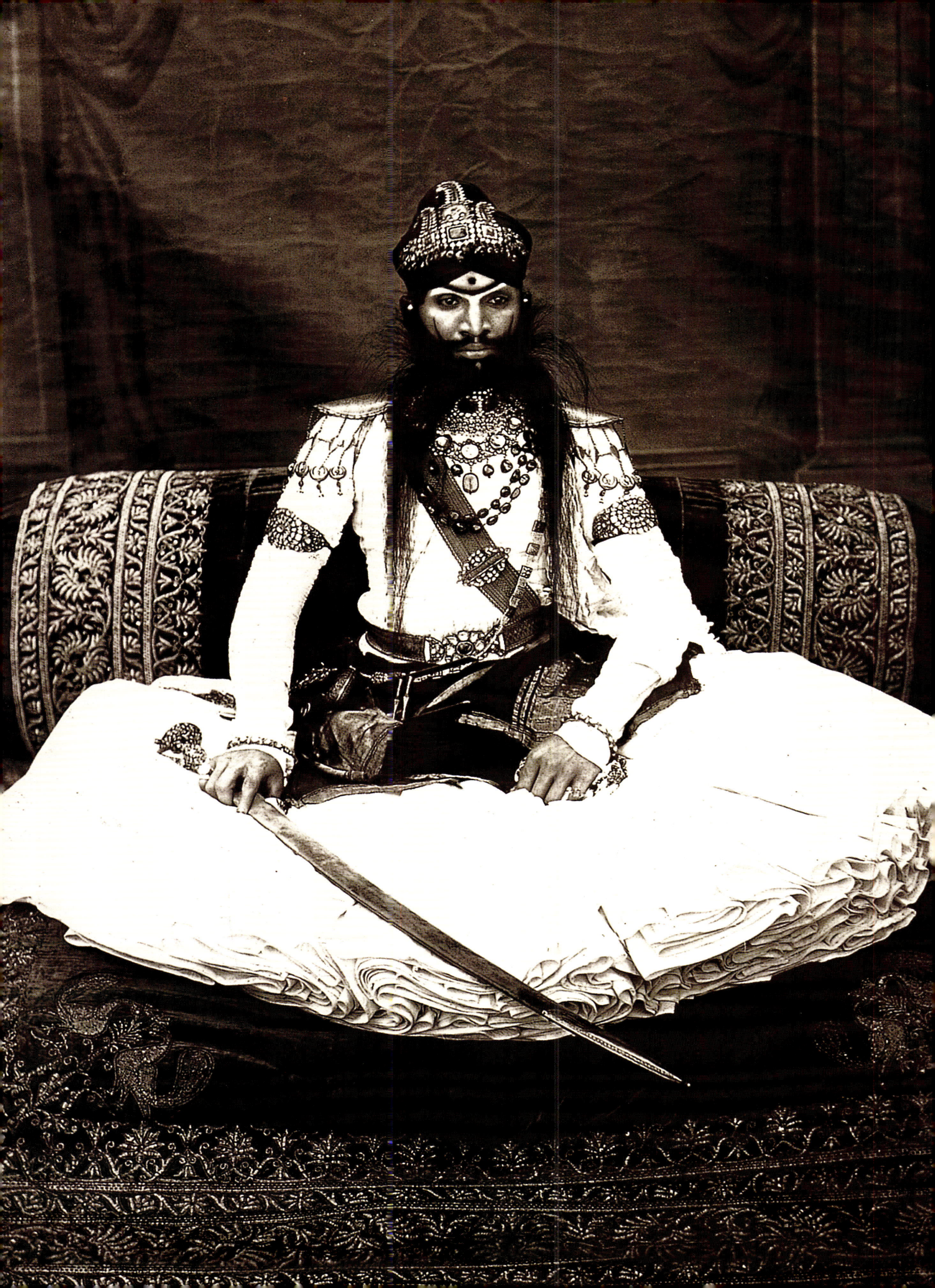

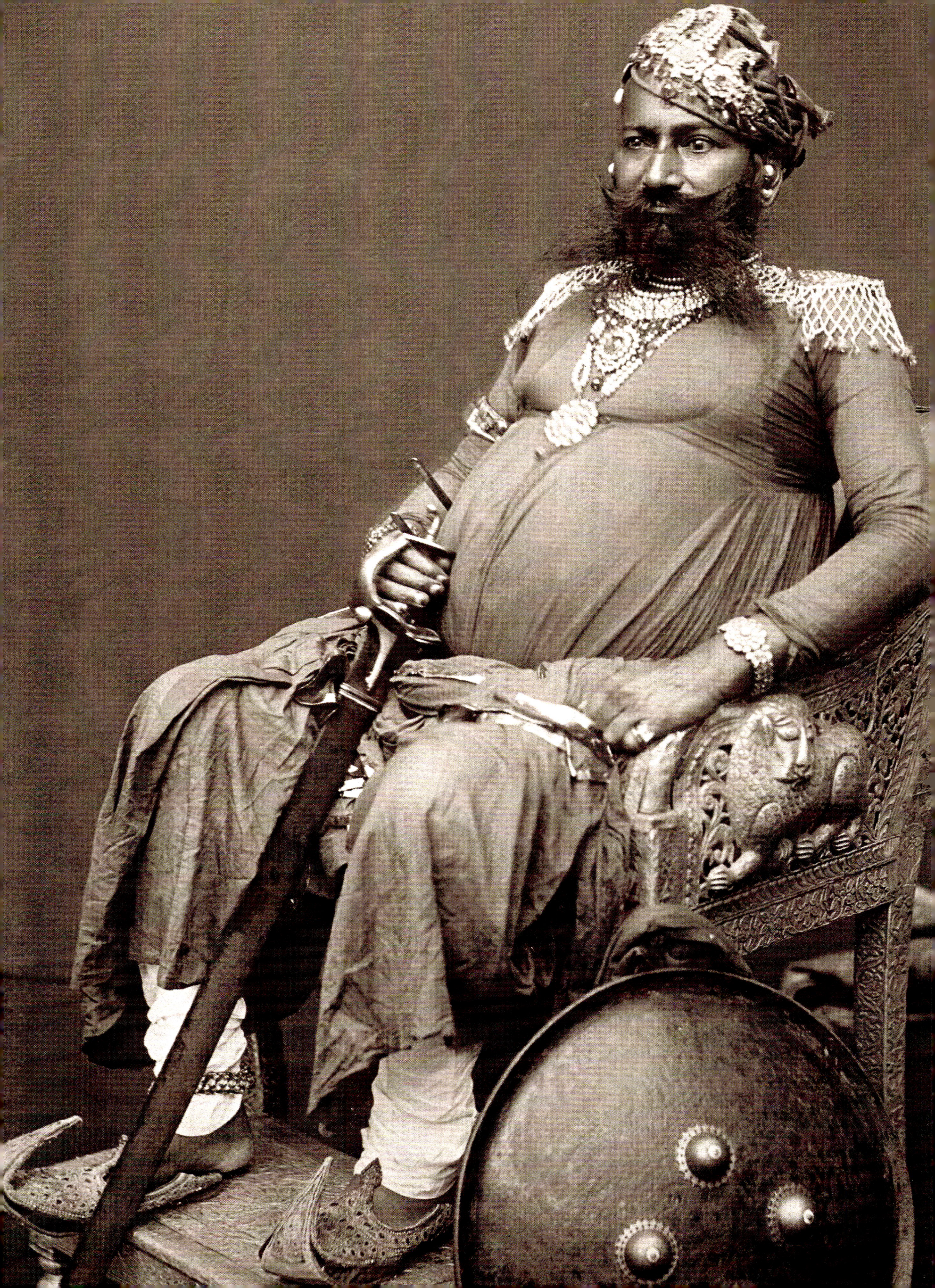

In 997 Sultan Subuktagin was succeeded by a son whose generalship bordered on genius: Sultan Mahmud of Ghazni, who over the next three decades struck no less than seventeen mighty blows against the heathen, earning himself such accolades as Sword of Islam and Idol-breaker. To many Hindus, Jains and Buddhists he came to be regarded as a devil incarnate who brought devastation to northern India. Almost every autumn from the year 1001 onwards Mahmud of Ghazni rode down through the Khyber Pass to strike at one or more cities in the Punjab, killing every infidel who offered resistance, destroying all traces of idolatry and returning to Ghazni with as much booty and as many slaves as his army could handle. Ghazni soon became the slave capital of the world, to which merchants flocked from distant cities.

In 1004 the main target was Bhatia on the River Jhelum, the stronghold of the Bhatti prince Bijai Rai. As the Muslims were about to breach his city's defences, Bijai Rai gave the order for the Rajput male's equivalent of the *jauhar* – the *saka* – in which every Rajput male above the age of twelve dons saffron robes, signifying sacrifice, and then charges forth, sword in hand, to meet his death in battle. According to the Rajput code, the head of the family or his heir had to be kept alive at all costs, so it was arranged that Bijai Rai should slip away to safety while his men diverted the enemy's attention by making their last desperate charge. In the event, their sacrifice was in vain, because Bijai Rai was hunted down and killed himself with his dagger rather than surrender.

In 1005 Sultan Mahmud's attack on the grand city of Multan brought together another great Rajput army under the command of Visaladeva, leader of the Chauhans of Ajmer. There was another pitched battle, which turned against the Rajputs when the elephant carrying their leader was struck by a flaming arrow, causing it to panic and bolt. This was construed by those around him as flight and they followed suit. Soon the entire Rajput army was in retreat, hotly pursued by the Muslim cavalry. The chase continued for two days and two nights and left twenty thousand Rajputs dead on the field. Returning to Ghazni, Mahmud put some of his booty on display for the ambassadors attending his court. 'He ordered the courtyard of his palace to be covered with a carpet, on which he displayed jewels and unbored pearls and rubies, shining like sparks, or like wine congealed with ice, and emeralds like fresh sprigs of myrtle, and diamonds in size and weight like pomegranates.'

Further raids into the Punjab and Kashmir led to the collapse of the house of Shahi, allowing Mahmud to push beyond the Sutlej river. In 1018 he launched his boldest venture, leading his army of one hundred thousand Turkoman cavalry and twenty thousand Afghan infantry on a series of forced marches that took him to the very outskirts of Kanauj, the capital city of the Pratihara. The unexpected appearance of this vast array at his gates so unnerved the Pratihara ruler, Rao Rajyapala, that he abandoned both his capital and its seven surrounding forts, which all fell to the enemy in a single day in January 1019. Mahmud pushed on to the temple-city of Mathura, where its scores of temples were looted and then 'burned with naptha and fire and levelled to the ground'. Included in the booty were two hundred solid silver idols and five of red gold, each 4.6 metres high. One had eyes of rubies 'of such value that, if any one were to sell such as are like them, he would obtain fifty thousand dinars'; another had a sapphire 'purer than water and more sparkling than crystal; the weight was 459 *miskals*' (nearly 2.7 kilograms).

There is evidence to suggest that at this low point both Rajyapala and Visaladeva, the Chauhan general, gave up the struggle and converted to Islam, as many

left: A STRAIGHT-BLADED DAGGER BELONGING TO THE MUGHAL PERIOD. THE ENGRAVED GOLD HILT IS ENCRUSTED WITH RUBIES, EMERALDS AND GREEN GLASS.
extreme left: *ANKUSH*, ELEPHANT GOAD. THE FLAUNT TIP OF THE GOAD IS USED BY THE MAHOUT TO PROD THE ELEPHANT'S SKULL WHILE RIDING. THE CURVED PRONG IS USED BEHIND THE ELEPHANT'S EAR. THIS PARTICULAR PIECE IS RICHLY DECORATED WITH FLAT DIAMONDS AND GREEN ENAMEL WORK ON GOLD.
facing page: A MOST UNUSUAL USE OF THE ELEPHANT IN INDIA. THESE LOYAL-TO-MAN PACHYDERMS WERE USED EVEN TWO THOUSAND YEARS AGO BY THE MIGHTY ARMIES OF EMPERORS LIKE ASHOKA. HUNDREDS OF ELEPHANTS ARE KNOWN TO HAVE LOST THEIR LIVES DURING THE BATTLE OF KALINGA. THE PICTURE SHOWS MUGHAL-STYLE PUNITIVE ACTION THAT INCLUDED BEING TRAMPLED UPON AND EXECUTED BY ELEPHANTS.

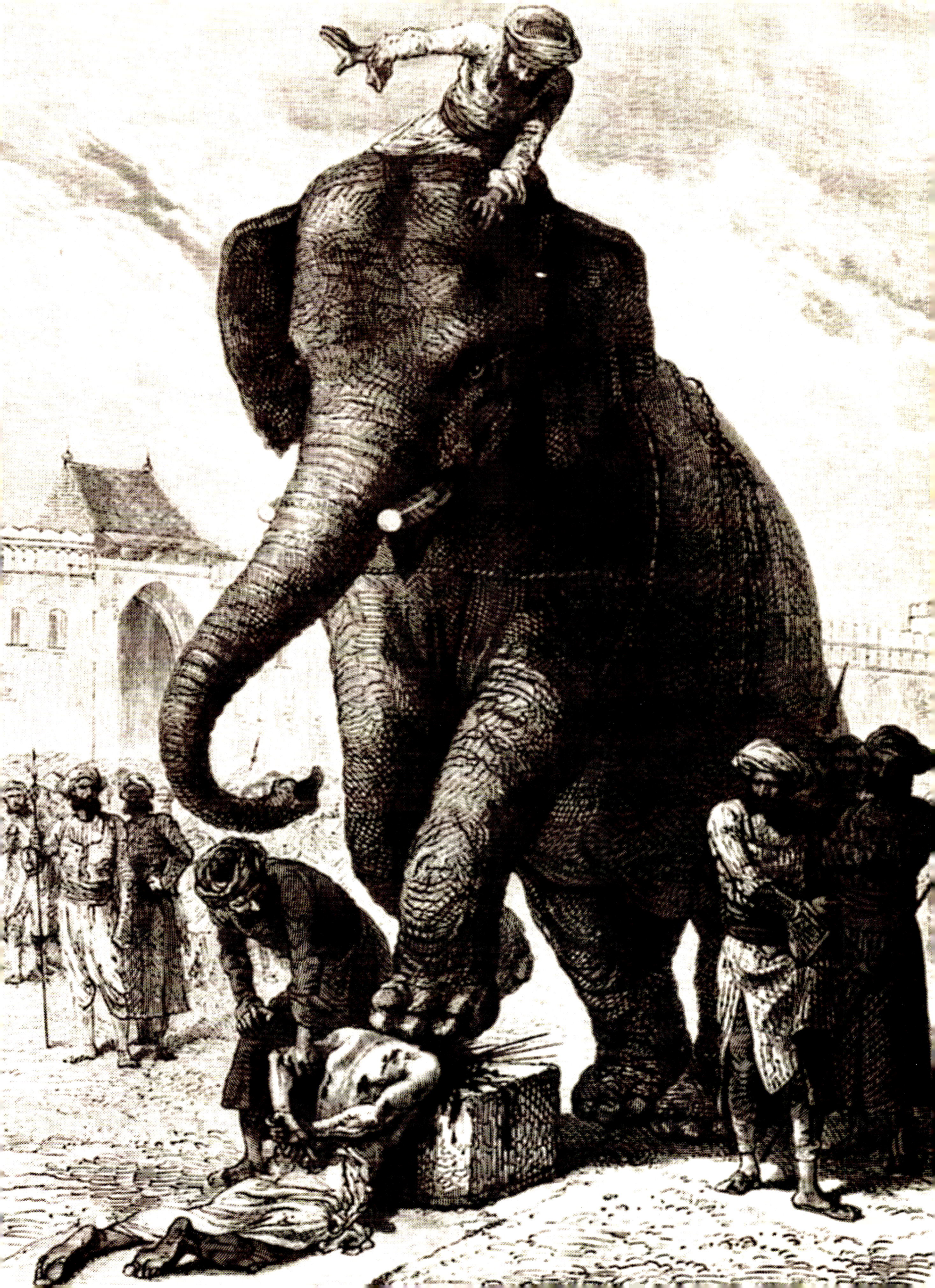

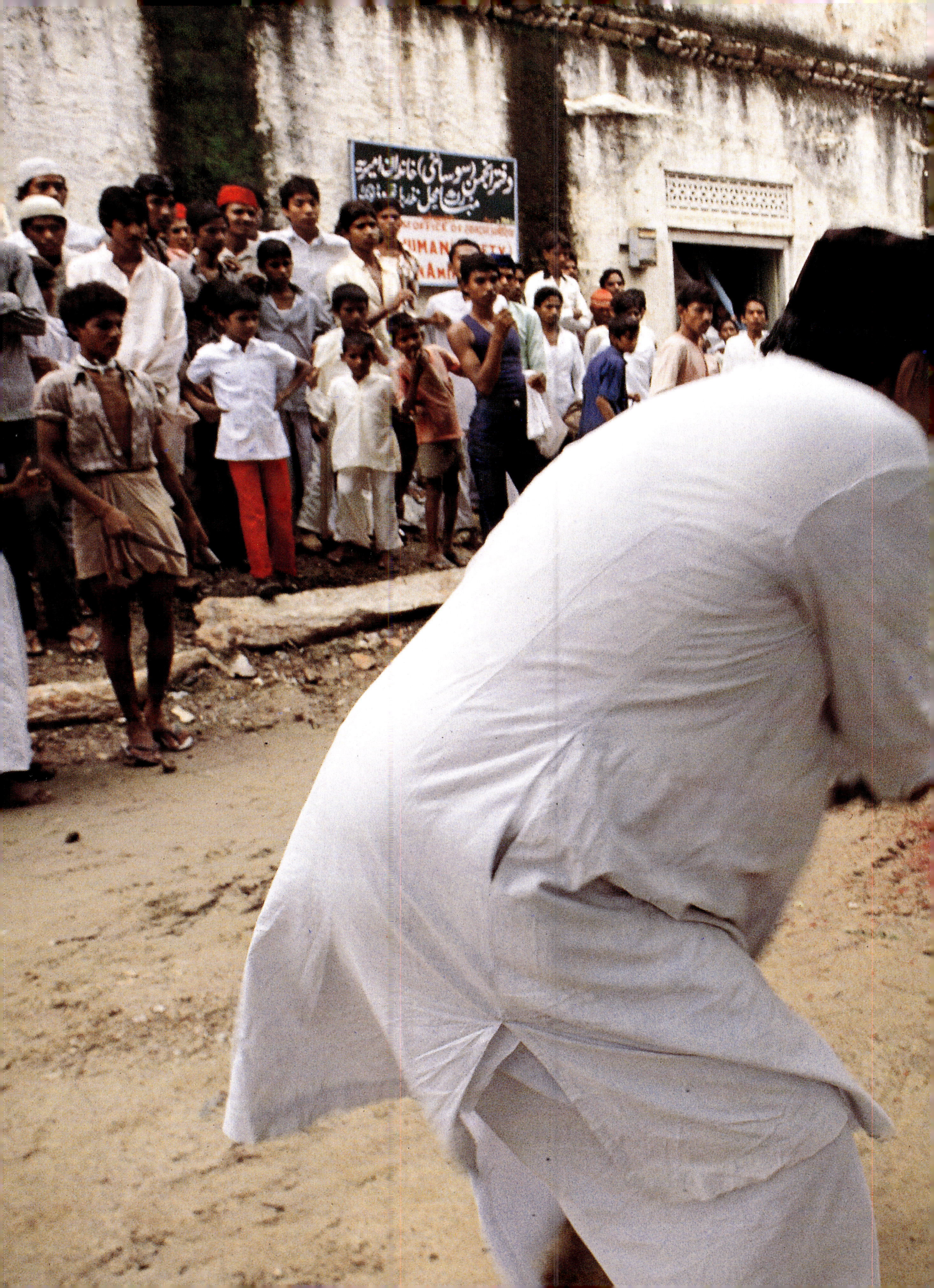

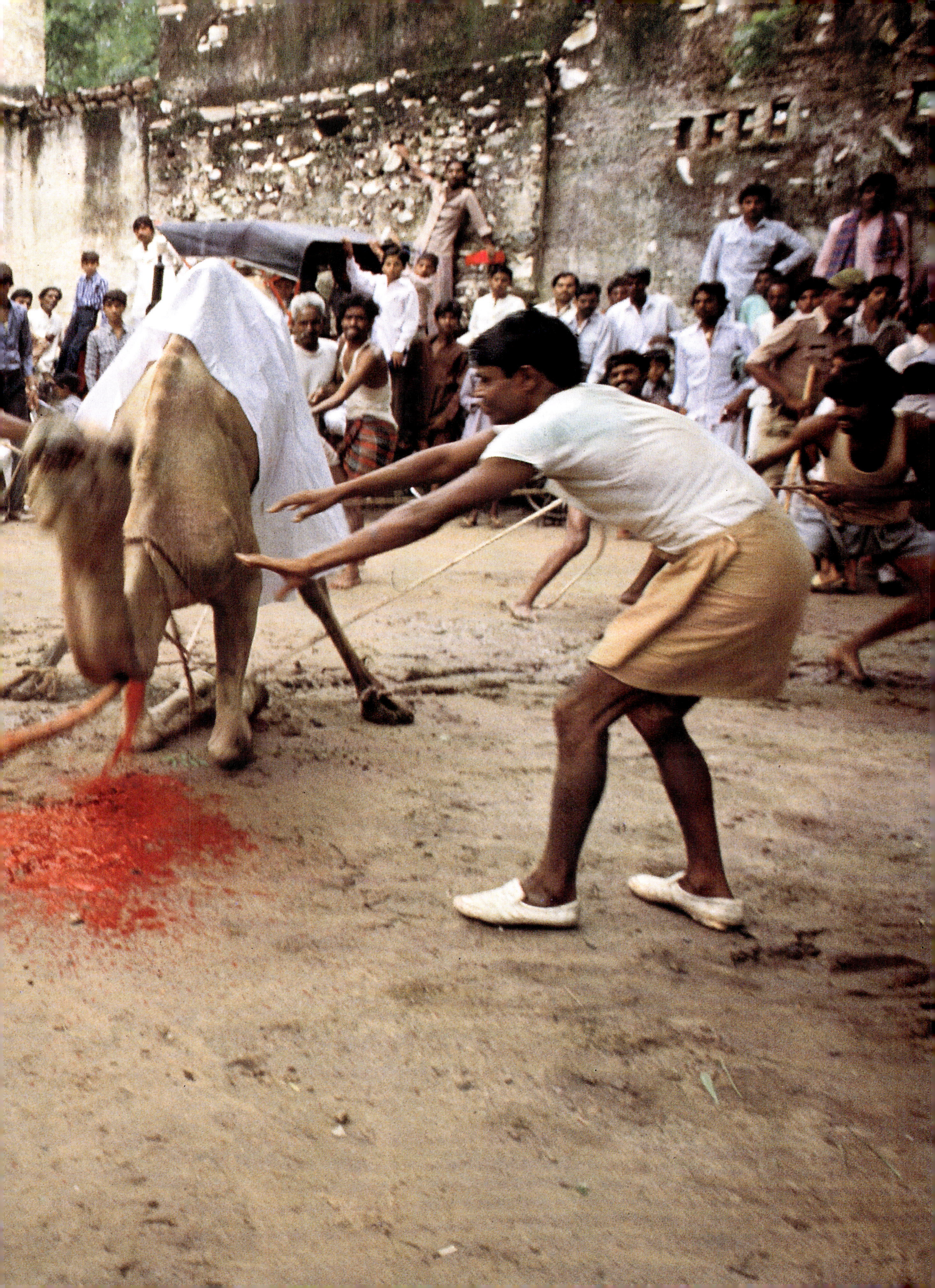

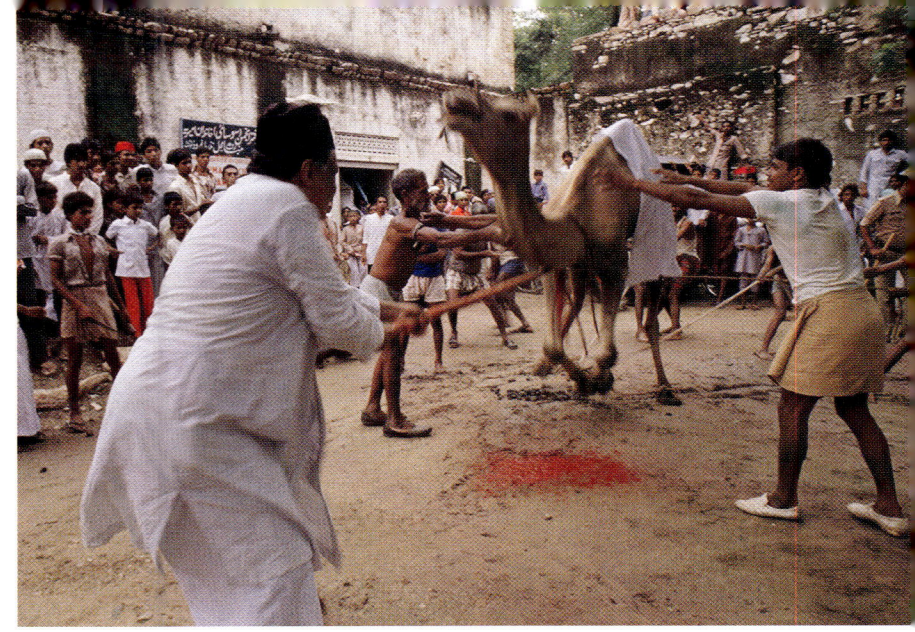

pages 50-51:

QURBANI, CAMEL SACRIFICE, PERFORMED ON THE OCCASION OF BAKR ID IN THE DESERT STATE OF TONK IN RAJASTHAN.
THE UNDERLYING FORCE BEHIND A SACRIFICE WAS TO GIVE UP A POSSESSION OF VALUE, HENCE, THE CAMEL — THE SHIP OF THE DESERT — IS PROFFERED.

Hindus and Buddhists in the Punjab had already been forced to do. The eastern Rajputs, under the leadership of the Chandellas, responded by turning on Rajyapala and killing him. As for Raja Visaladeva, he appears to have recanted and atoned for his loss of courage by becoming an ascetic. The task of defending central India from Mahmud now fell to the Chandella Rajputs and their allies. They lost the first round at a cost of five hundred and eighty elephants and were forced to buy off Mahmud when his army returned in 1021, but by holding on to their two great forts at Gwalior and Kalinjar they were able to claim a victory of sorts.

Mahmud next turned his attentions south, by sending in 1024, a fast-moving corps of camels and horses in a thousand-mile dash across the Rajasthan desert to Gujarat and Saurashtra. Here his main target was the famous Shaivite temple-city of Somnath. Abandoned by their ruler, the inhabitants prayed in vain to Lord Shiva to save their city. The historian Ibn Asir writes how 'band after band of the defenders entered the temple of Somnath, and with their hands clasped round their necks, wept and passionately entreated him. Then again they issued forth until they were slain'. In what Ibn Asir himself calls the 'dreadful slaughter' that followed, the death toll exceeded fifty thousand. The giant stone *linga* at the core of the main temple was stripped of its jewels and its outer covering of beaten gold. The inner core of stone was then smashed to pieces, with Sultan Mahmud himself attacking it with his sword. In 1030, as Sultan Mahmud lay dying, he wept at the thought of all the treasures and arms he was leaving behind. Having made no attempt to impose any form of civil order in the territories he overran, he left behind a fragile empire that was soon torn apart by rivalry between his successors. His one lasting legacy among non-Muslims was a hatred of Islam that would linger for centuries.

Of the many Rajput families driven from the Punjab, three branches of the Shahis recovered to re-establish themselves as ruling powers elsewhere: the Jadeja in Kutch, the Jadun in central Rajasthan and the Bhatti in the Thar desert. After wandering over the Thar desert for several decades a handful of Bhatti clansmen under Rawal Jaisal established a settlement on several low hills in the desert that came to be known as Jaisalmer. The foundations of this remarkable desert city were probably laid in about 1186. Thereafter its rulers did their best to keep out of the main political arena, relying for their defence almost entirely on the great wastes of sand and wilderness that surrounded them. Jaisalmer's position as an oasis at the Great Desert's crossroads also served it well, providing its people with a source of revenue from trade, which they supplemented from time to time by raiding caravans.

This last pursuit took the Bhatti twice to the brink of extinction. An old hermit had prophesied to Rawal Jaisal that his new capital would suffer the horror of *jauhar* two and a half times. The first of these took place in 1294 after a son of the ruler ambushed a caravan bearing tribute money from Gujarat to the Sultan of Delhi. For eight years a punitive army tried and failed to breach Jaisalmer's double ring of stone walls but eventually the defenders were starved out and committed the customary double act of *jauhar* and *saka*. According to the annals, 'twenty-four thousand females, from infancy to old age, surrendered their lives, some by the sword, others in the volcano of fire. Blood flowed in torrents, while the smoke of the pyre ascended to the heavens: not one feared to die, every valuable was consumed with them, not the worth of a straw was preserved for the foe'. The next day, after securing a promise from the Muslim general that the lives of the rulers' two young sons would be spared, the men followed their womenfolk to their deaths.

At this nadir in the clan's fortunes the head of one of its lesser branches was called upon by Sultan Ghiyas-ud-din Tughlaq Shah (1321-1325), one of the sultans of the so-called Slave Dynasty in Delhi, to give his daughter in marriage to the sultan's brother. This was a shocking idea to any Rajput and the Bhatti ruler refused, whereupon his little kingdom was invested by the sultan's troops. After suffering much hardship, the young woman in question, Princess Naila, went to her father and told him that it was in his people's interests to hand her over, and that henceforward he was to look upon her as dead. The marriage took place and in due course the Rajput princess gave her husband a son who later came to the throne of Delhi as Sultan Feroze Shah.

Jaisalmer's second *jauhar* and *saka* took place during Feroze Shah's rule. Over the intervening years one of the two Bhatti princes who survived the first *saka* had been allowed to reclaim the royal throne of Jaisalmer and to repopulate the city. However, its trading links were now broken, so the Bhattis had to rely increasingly on banditry, and soon became a menace to their neighbours. A raid on Sultan Feroze Shah's stud of matchless Arabian horses from his camp beside the Anasagar Lake near Ajmer brought about the Bhattis' second downfall. An army again laid siege to Jaisalmer and again the ghastly suicides and massacres were performed. This time sixteen thousand women and children perished and seventeen hundred males.

Rise of the Delhi Sultanate

Damaging as these early Muslim invasions were, it was not until the appearance of the Afghan Mohammad of Ghori on the Indian scene that they became conquests. Hoping to take advantage of the rivalry between the leading Rajput kingdoms, he marched on Delhi in 1191, calling on Rao Prithviraj III of Ajmer to join forces with him against his main rivals, Raja Jayachandra of Kanauj and Rana Somarsi of Chittor. The Rajputs, however, briefly laid aside their quarrels to unite against him.

The two armies met at Tarain, on an expanse of open plains, a six days' march north of Delhi that has served as a battlefield from the days of the Mahabharata through to the so-called Indian Mutiny of 1857. This first battle went well for the Rajputs, but a year later Sultan Mohammad was back with a stronger army of one hundred and twenty thousand armoured and forty thousand unarmoured horsemen. This force of heavy and light cavalry also deployed two modern innovations hitherto unknown in India: the stirrup, which gave the rider far greater stability in the saddle, and the crossbow. Used together, they proved a winning combination, and the Muslims defeated the largest Rajput army ever assembled, drawn from over a hundred Rajput clans. So confident were the Rajputs of victory, says the Arab historian Ferishta, that they spent the night before the battle 'in riot and

facing page, top left: Late Nawab Masoom Ali Khan of Tonk stands ready with a *ballam*, spear, to perform the *Qurbani*. *pages 52-53, top centre:* The spear is thrust into the camel's jugular vein. As the bleeding camel drops to the ground, onlookers perform *halal*, slow bloodletting, and then dismember the animal. *top right:* An onlooker walks away with an entire leg of the camel, his vest bloodied by the scramble for the animal's flesh. Within half an hour of the camel being speared, not a bit of the animal's flesh is left on the scene as the onlookers loot the sacred sacrificial meat. Sometimes the scramble for the loot can get extremely violent and thus a police force is usually on standby.
The gelatinous footpads of the camel are considered to be a great delicacy.

revelry', waking up next morning to find themselves surrounded on all sides.

By a process of steady attrition – of attack, withdrawal and again renewed attack – the massed Rajput force was worn away, until at sunset Mohammad launched his heavy cavalry in a direct assault. 'He put himself at the head of twelve thousand of his best horses, whose riders were covered in steel armour, and making one desperate charge, carried death and destruction through the Hindu ranks.' The charge broke the Rajput centre and finally, as Ferishta recorded, 'this prodigious army, once shaken, like a great building tottered to its fall'. Not for nothing has this second battle of Tarain been called the most decisive battle in the history of India. Rao Prithviraj III fled the battle but was captured and put to death. In the battle itself died his gallant brother-in-law Rana Somarsi, the Gehlote ruler of Chittor, a score of other lesser chiefs and Rajput retainers estimated to number one hundred thousand or, as the historian Hasan Nizami puts it in his *Taju-l Ma-asir*, 'a hundred thousand grovelling Hindus swiftly departed to the fire of hell'. With them died all hopes of halting the spread of Islamic rule beyond Sind and the Punjab, for Mohammad Ghori now possessed 'the key to the gate of Delhi', which his able slave-general, Qutb-ud-din Aibak soon secured on his behalf. The city was 'freed from idols and idol-worship, and in the sanctuaries of the images of the gods, mosques were raised by the worshippers of one God'.

A year later the victorious Sultan saw to the building of the precursor to Delhi's great mosque, the Jami Masjid, adorned 'with the stones and gold obtained from the temples which had been demolished by elephants'. He then marched on Kanauj, India's premier city, which again fell with little resistance.

Raja Jayachandra of Kanauj was drowned as he attempted to escape across the Ganges but two of his sons survived. One fled deep into the *terai* jungles and foothills of the Himalayas with his retainers, where their many descendants can still be found. The other moved south and then west into the Great Desert, where his son Rao Sheoji settled in the region of Marwar and offered his services to the powerful Solanki Rajputs.

After reducing mighty Kanauj to ruins, Sultan Mohammad marched on Ajmer, the Chauhan capital, which he found to be a city of gardens filled with fountains, trees and brightly-coloured birds. Here he 'destroyed the pillars and foundations of the idol temples and built in their stead mosques and colleges, and the precepts of Islam, and the customs of the Law were divulged and established'.

At this point the annals of Bundi and Kota begin to focus on a lesser branch of the Chauhans, the Hada clan, which had been all but been wiped out in the second battle of Tarain. Rao Govind became its new leader and led the survivors deep into the mountains of Rajputana with Sultan Mohammad Ghori's forces in hot pursuit, 'passing over hill and desert like a wild ass or an antelope'. They made their way to the isolated jungle fortress of Ranthambhor, which they wrested from its occupants, a branch of the Jadun Rajputs, and made their new home.

The last major Rajput house to be brought down by Sultan Mohammad Ghori was that of Raja Govind of Benares. In 1193 the Sultan's general Qutb-ud-din Aibak marched down the Ganges plain, first destroying Kol (renamed Aligarh) and then moving on to Benares, Hinduism's most sacred city. 'When the two armies met there was great carnage', writes the thirteenth century historian Ibn Asir. 'But in the end the infidels fled, and the faithful were victorious. The slaughter of the Hindus was immense; none were spared except women and children, and the carnage of the men went on until the earth was weary. The Hindu king was slain, and no one recognised his corpse but for the fact of his teeth, which were weak at their roots, being fastened with golden wire.'

In 1194 Bihar's chief fortress was taken and the ancient Buddhist university of Nalanda flattened. In

RANI RAMESHWAR SINGH OF SUKET DRESSED IN A TRADITIONAL YELLOW *TILAK*, PERFORMS THE *SASU AARTI*, MOTHER-IN-LAW'S GREETING, TO BHANWAR IJYARAJ SINGHJI OF KOTAH BEFORE HIS MARRIAGE CEREMONY WITH HER DAUGHTER. THE *TILAK* IS A CUSTOM THAT IS ONLY PRACTISED IN CERTAIN HILL STATES OF INDIA.

facing page: AFTER HER MARRIAGE TO YUVRAJ VIKRAMADITYA SINGH OF KASHMIR, THE VEILED PRINCESS CHITRANGADARAJE OF GWALIOR IS ESCORTED FOR THE *GRIHA PRAVESH*, ENTRY INTO HER HUSBAND'S HOME, IN DELHI BY HER SISTER-IN-LAW PRINCESS JYOTI OF KASHMIR. BOTH ARE DRESSED IN THE TRADITIONAL DOGRI KURTAS THAT ARE HEAVILY EMBROIDERED ON THE FRONT YOKE, PANELS, SEAMS, CUFFS AND HEM. RICHLY DECORATED *DUPATTAS*, VEILS, COVER THEIR HEADS. THE ENSEMBLE IS COMPLETE WITH A NAVY BLUE CHURIDAR, TIGHT TROUSERS, AND ANKLETS ON THE FEET.

18th century
Gaekwads, protectors of cows, were a humble family.

1720
Damaji Gaekwad became deputy commander of Maratha army, pushing into Gujarat.

1731
Damaji's successor, Pilaji Gaekwad, pushed Mughal forces out of Gujarat.

1734
Pilaji captured Baroda; his son made it their capital. The Gaekwads consolidated their position, extending into Kathiawar.

End of 18th century
British took control of those areas in Gujarat which the Peshwa had claimed as his. Gaekwad kingdom was still substantial. Malhar Rao, the next ruler, succeeded to the throne after an unsuccessful attempt to poison his brother and the latter's subsequent death.

1881
Sayajirao III, a distant relation, was crowned ruler.

above right: NAUTCH-GIRLS WERE COURTESAN-DANCERS WHO TAUGHT TEENAGED BOYS ETIQUETTE AND URDU, APART FROM PROVIDING THEM WITH ENTERTAINMENT. THESE WERE VERY DIGNIFIED AND CLASSY WOMEN WHO WERE SKILLED AT VARIOUS ARTS. **left:** A TURBAN AND JEWELLERY FROM THE HOUSE OF GAEKWADS. **top:** A GROUP OF CAMELS WAS USED TO PULL AN OPEN CARRIAGE (EARLY 20TH CENTURY). **facing page, top left:** MAHARAJA SAYAJI RAO III, MAHARAJA OF BARODA. **facing page, top right:** APPARENTLY ORDERED FOR THE GAEKWAD OF BARODA IN THE 19TH CENTURY, THIS MAGNIFICENT NECKLACE BOASTS THREE ROWS OF BRILLIANT GOLCONDA DIAMONDS AND COST APPROXIMATELY RUPEES SIX MILLION. **facing page, below:** ROYAL GUESTS IN FRONT OF THE LAXMI VILAS PALACE AT THE WEDDING CEREMONY OF PRINCESS ALAUKIKARAJE GAEKWAD OF BARODA.

Baroda

Cooch Behar

15th century
Muslims overran Bengal but did not settle there. Tussle between warring tribes

16th century
The Koch, a tribe, took control (hence the name Cooch).

1773
British East India Company made a treaty with the ruler to protect its expansion in Bengal.

1780
Under pressure from the East India Company, the ruler signed away half his territory to the British.

1863
Due to dynastic feuds, the British Government in India moved in to administer the state, encouraging the ruler to adopt British ways

top: INDIRA DEVI OF COOCH BEHAR (1892-1968), DRESSED IN A SIMPLE WHITE WIDOW'S GARB, AT A DURBAR HELD TO MARK THE YOUNG MAHARAJA'S BIRTHDAY. HER SONS, MAHARAJA JAGADDIPENDRA NARAYAN AND MAHARAJ KUMAR INDRAJITENDRA NARAYAN, ARE SEATED ON EITHER SIDE. THIS IS A VERY UNUSUAL PHOTOGRAPH OF A MAHARANI IN DURBAR. THE MAHARAJA WAS A GREAT PATRON OF POLO AND WAS THE FIRST ROYAL TO PLAY A PROMINENT ROLE IN CALCUTTA HORSE RACES. bottom: MAHARAJA JITENDRA NARAYAN OF COOCH BEHAR.

1196 Qutb-ud-din Aibak's army marched on Gwalior, 'the pearl of the necklace of the castles of Hind, the summit of which the nimble-footed wind from below cannot reach, and the bastion of which the rapid clouds have never cast their shade'. Here the Kachhawa ruler Rai Pal sued for pardon, and having agreed to 'place the ring of servitude in his ear', was allowed to keep his fort. In the following year it was the turn of Gujarat. The city of Anhilwara was taken and the kingdom of Gujarat came under Muslim dominion. In 1199 Bengal's capital, Nuddeah, was captured and a new centre of administration set up which would ensure that this most fertile of provinces remained under Muslim control for the next five and a half centuries. Four years later the stronghold of the Chandella Rajputs at Kalanjar, with defences 'as strong as the wall of Alexander', surrendered after a long siege, opening the way for the conquest of Bundelkhand.

These were only the major milestones in an extraordinary series of campaigns that within the space of fifteen years, saw every Rajput kingdom in northern and central India destroyed or reduced to the status of a vassal state, forced to acknowledge the suzerainty of Mohammad Ghori and his successors. His assassination in 1206 led to his general, Qutb-ud-din Aibak, being proclaimed the first Sultan of Delhi, initiating the so-called Delhi Sultanate and three centuries of tyrannical misrule in northern India, during which successive Turkic and Afghan dynasties – the Slave Kings, the Khiljis, the Tughlaqs, the Sayyids and the Lodis – fought as much among themselves as they did against the Hindus. A pattern of behaviour now became established in northern and central India that would be followed for the next six centuries: while the Sultans of Delhi were strong and their armies were winning victories, Rajput rulers hastened to court to pay homage and taxes, but the moment their authority was challenged, their vassals would neglect to pay their dues and shun the capital. A new form of local rule began to emerge as provinces ruled by Muslim governors and supported by local Muslim aristocracies broke away to form their own independent Sultanates, mostly notably in the Deccan and in Gujarat. Armed with their own very different canons, these rulers were egalitarian in recognising talent from within all classes in their own ranks but often oppressive in their persecution of non-Muslims. Nevertheless, in some of these Muslim-governed local Sultanates a happy fusion of Hindu and Muslim cultures developed.

THE RATHORES OF MARWAR

Unable to oust the Muslim rulers of Delhi, the Rajput kingdoms in northern and central India turned on each other in an endless succession of campaigns. In the Rajput code of honour, *vair*, revenge, takes second place only to loyalty to the chief, resulting in blood feuds between families that often lasted for generations. The annals of every clan are filled with tales of bloody encounters and massacres, none more bloody than that of the Rathores of Marwar (known today as Jodhpur). Under the dynamic leadership of Rao Chunda, the wandering Rathores found their first real home in the desert at Mandore, whose ruins lie tucked away on the edge of an escarpment that rises dramatically up out of the plain west of the Aravalli range in the desert. One rocky spur sticks out beyond the rest, a hundred and twenty-metre high bluff over which the extended wings of the *cheel* or kite can always be seen turning in the sky. Known as Bhakurcheeria, the mountain of the birds' nest, this was in Rao Chunda's day occupied only by a solitary hermit. But hidden behind this bluff is a narrow gorge overlooked by the ochre sandstone rocks that still provide the city of Jodhpur and the surrounding region with its main building material. Water is always to be found here, even in the worst

above: Wall painting from Kota fort showing one of the rulers riding an elephant in procession. This particular school of painting became very well known as the Kota *kalam* and was patronised by the rulers of Kota.

pages 60-61, top centre: A wall painting from Kota fort depicting a ceremonial occasion inside the fort. The elephant is seen in a salutary position of obeisance, while soldiers and retainers mill around.

bottom: A wooden door in Juna Mahal Palace, Dungarpur. On either side are painted scenes of celebration, including fireworks and dancing girls. On the top right, a retainer is seen walking a domesticated caracal in a harness, rather like a dog! Indian princes were fond of keeping exotic animals as pets.

page 59: Nawab Sher Muhammad Khan Zorawar, Diwan of Palanpur, photographed in 1902. The Nawabs of Palanpur were the descendants of Pathan tribesmen from Afghanistan. The Muslim-ruled state of Palanpur had a predominantly Hindu population with only 15-20 per cent Muslims. The Muslim rulers merged their beliefs in kingship with their Hindu counterparts and also shared the latters' love for jewels and adornment in dress. Palanpur was not renowned for its jungles and the only game available was in the monsoon season when birds migrated from the Deccan jungles and returned in winter. Poaching an animal or cutting bamboo in the tiger preserve was punishable by law.

years of drought – which is why the ancient town of Mandore came into being. In Rao Chunda's time Mandore was being claimed by the Parihara Rajputs. One account says he took it by force; another account maintains that he married a daughter of the ruling house and gained the fortress and city of Mandore as her dowry.

Today its walls, towers and temples are heaps of stone, but when the banner of Rao Chunda fluttered from its battlements, Mandore was in its prime. The Rathores' control of the trade routes that crossed their desert made them wealthy as never before. In 1424 Rao Chunda of Marwar was killed in battle and his son Rainmal was anointed as clan chief. He was a giant of a man, and if the pair of his pantaloons on display in the museum at Meherangarh Fort is anything to go by, of massive girth. When his neighbour, the Rana of Mewar, died leaving a six-year-old son named Prince Mokal by his marriage to his Marwari queen, Rao Rainmal intervened to ensure that this nephew, Prince Mokal, was anointed as the new ruler of Mewar. According to the annals of Marwar, this boy was then murdered by his older half-brother, provoking his uncle Rainmal to hurl his *safa*, turban, to the ground and vow that he would not wear another or sleep in his bed until he had avenged the death of his nephew. The avenging uncle then rode to Chittor, killed the murderer and married his daughter, forcing her to sit on her father's headless body during the marriage ceremony. He was then himself murdered in his bed – a terrible fate for a Rajput for whom death in battle is the only proper end.

The Sisodia version of the story is probably closer to the truth. By this account the little prince was not murdered but his uncle, Rao Rainmal of Marwar, appointed himself regent of Mewar and then began to eliminate all rival claimants to the royal *gaddi* or throne of Mewar, beginning with one of Rana Mokal's two older half-brothers. The other, Prince Chunda of Sisodia, had voluntarily given up his claim to the royal throne and gone into exile. He was now approached by a group of Sisodia loyalists who begged him to rid Mewar of the Rathore tyrant.

The fortress of Chittor, the capital of the Sisodias, was the strongest in Rajputana. Shaped like a long, narrow ship, it rose out of the plain to form a plateau surrounded on all sides by sheer one hundred and fifty-four-metre high cliffs. If ever a piece of high ground was designed by nature to serve as a fortress it is Chittor, its access further limited by seven gates set at intervals along the single road that climbs up the side of the spur on which the citadel stands. Prince Chunda had taken with him into exile two hundred huntsmen, whose families had been left behind in Chittor. On the pretext of visiting their families at Diwali, the autumn festival of lights, these huntsmen returned to Chittor and offered themselves to the gatekeepers as temporary guards during the holiday period. This allowed Prince Chunda and forty horsemen to reach the seventh gate before they were challenged. The guards there were cut to pieces and every Rathore then killed without mercy.

Both annals agree that the giant Rao Rainmal died in his bed. He had become smitten by the charms of one of his sister's maids and had fallen asleep in her arms, drunk on wine and opium. The noise of the tumult outside failed to wake him but it roused the maid who, being a Sisodia, knew where her duty lay and tied Rainmal to his bed with his immensely long Marwari turban. When the Sisodia warriors burst into the bedroom the Rao awoke to find himself helpless and immobile. Nevertheless, he was strong enough to turn the bed over and get to his feet, and then using only a brass water pot as a weapon, struck down two of his assailants before he was overcome and slain. Since then it has been the custom for Rathore men to sleep on short beds – just in case they should find themselves in a similar position to Rao Rainmal and have to fight for their lives tied to a bed!

But not every Rathore was killed. One of Rao Rainmal's twenty-four sons, a teenager named Jodha, was asleep below the walls of Chittor when he was woken by the sound of a *nagara* or kettledrum, used by army commanders to pass messages. A loyal drummer in the citadel above had grasped what was happening

top: A BEAUTIFULLY PRESERVED WALL PAINTING OF MAHARAWAL UDAY SINGHJI II RIDING IN PROCESSION FROM THE JUNA MAHAL PALACE IN DUNGARPUR. THE ELEPHANT IS RICHLY CAPARISONED AND PAINTED WHILE RETAINERS CARRY THE INSIGNIA AND SYMBOLS OF ROYALTY AT THE BACK.

bottom: A MAGNIFICENT WOODEN DOOR IN JUNA MAHAL PALACE, DUNGARPUR. ON EITHER SIDE ARE PAINTED BANANA TREES AND PEACOCKS. AMONG THE HINDUS THE BANANA PLANT IS CONSIDERED VERY AUSPICIOUS AND HAS MANY USES IN RITUALS AND EVERYDAY LIFE. ITS LEAVES ARE USED AS DISPOSABLE PLATES WHICH ARE BIODEGRADABLE.

pages 62-63: JAUHAR SAMOROH: MAHARAJA GAJ SINGHJI OF JODHPUR, MEWAR, PAYS HIS RESPECTS IN FRONT OF A PAINTING DEPICTING *JAUHAR*, MASS IMMOLATION, OF RAJPUT WOMEN AT THE HISTORIC FORT OF CHITTOR. WHEN THEIR MEN WERE DEFEATED IN BATTLE *JAUHAR* WAS PERFORMED BY RAJPUT WOMEN TO AVOID FALLING INTO ALIEN HANDS. RANI PADMINI AND SCORES OF OTHER WOMEN PERFORMED ONE OF THE MOST TRAGIC AND WELL-KNOWN *JAUHARS* WHEN CHITTOR WAS TAKEN OVER BY SULTAN ALLAUDIN KHILJI OF DELHI. EVERY YEAR A COMMEMORATION IS HELD AT CHITTOR TO HONOUR THE WOMEN WHO PERFORMED *JAUHAR*. CHITTOR WAS SACKED THREE TIMES BY MUSLIM ARMIES BUT WHEN THE MEN WERE LOSING, THEIR WOMEN EITHER WENT BRAVELY INTO BATTLE AND SACRIFICED THEMSELVES OR ENTERED THE PYRE AND GAVE UP THEIR LIVES TO AVOID SURRENDERING TO THE INTRUDERS.

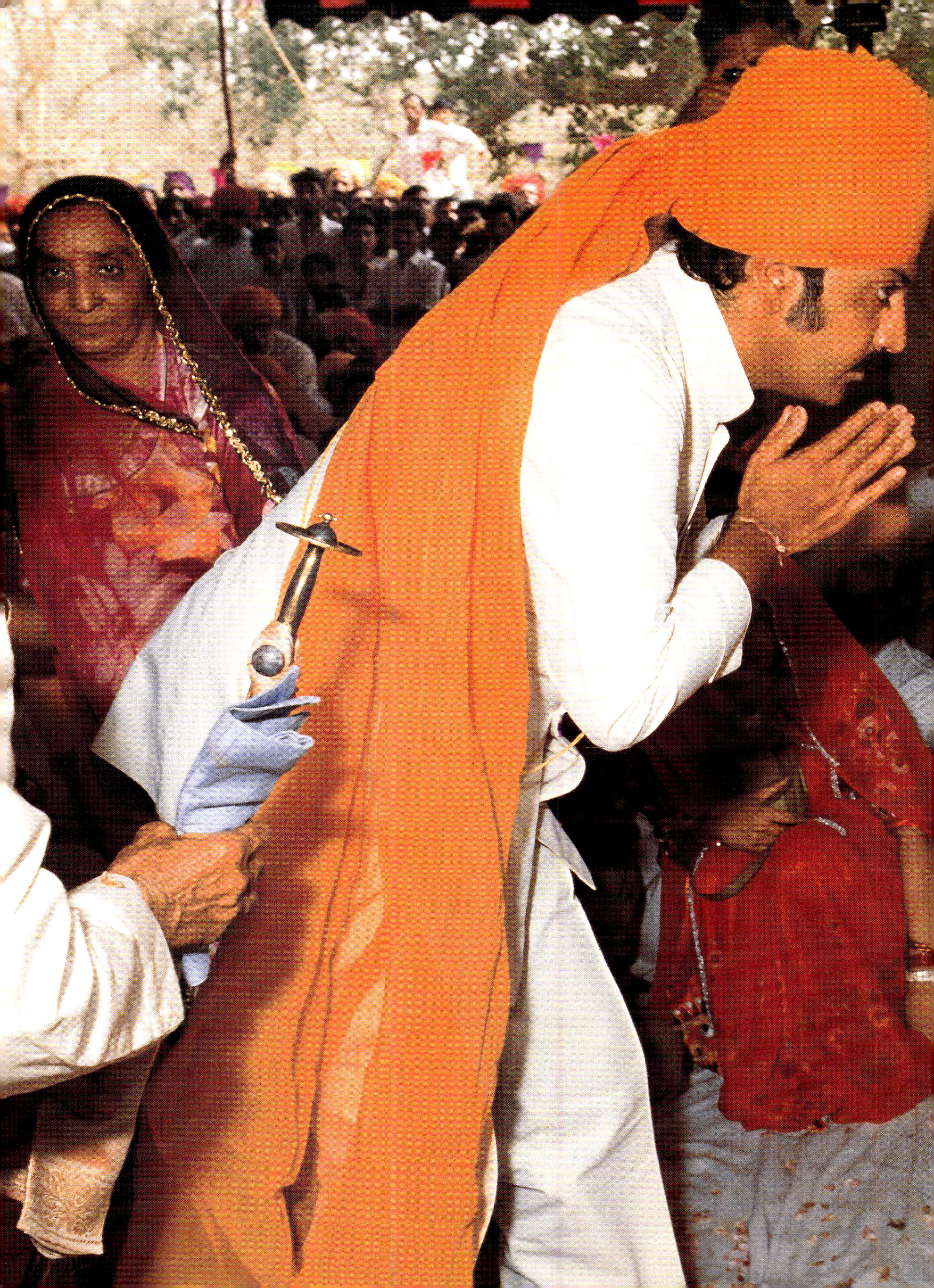

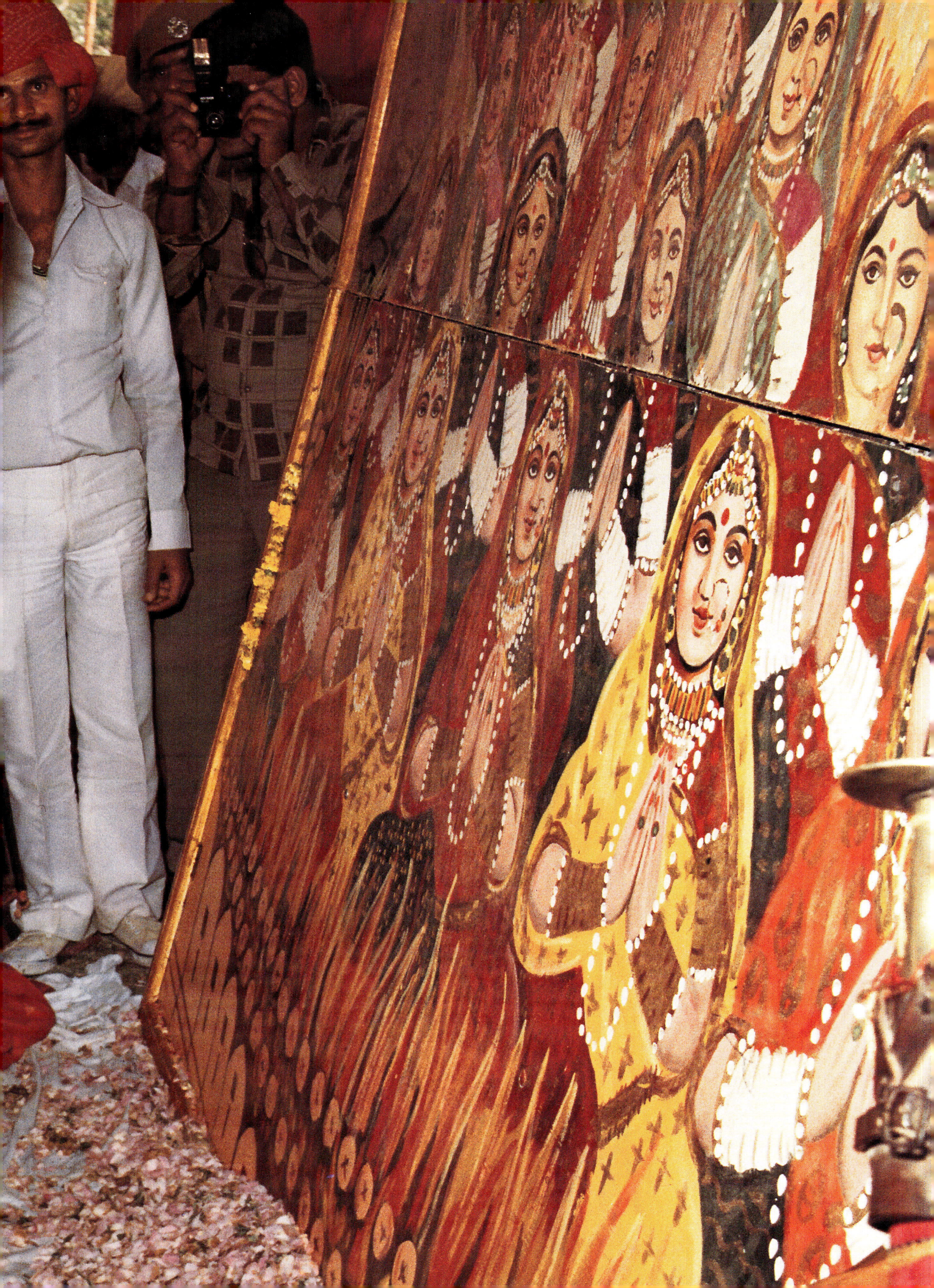

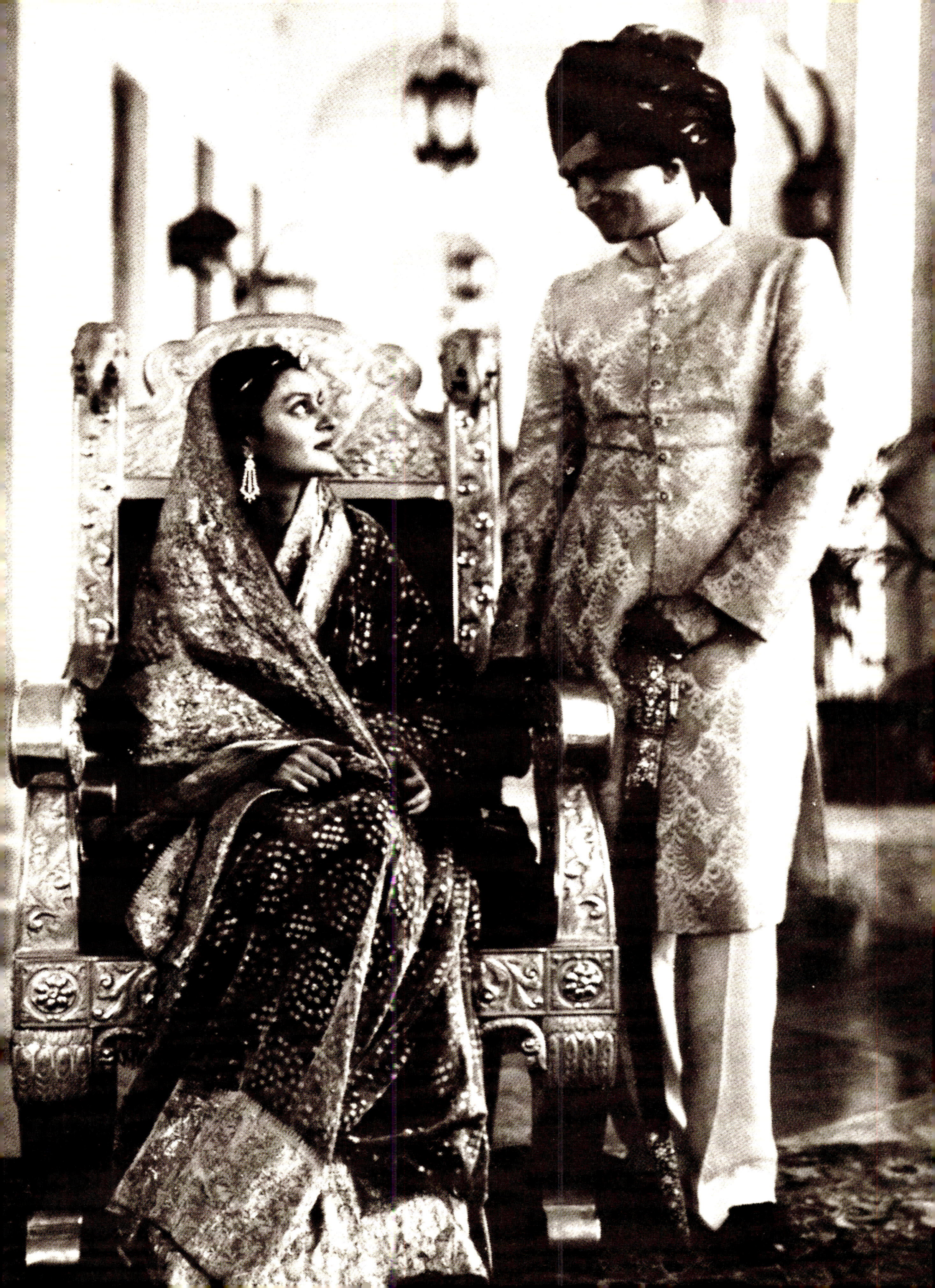

and before he was silenced, tapped out one brief message: 'Chunda has returned, has come back from Mandu. Jodha, Rainmal is dead, run if you can, run'. As a result of this warning Prince Jodha was able to make good his escape, together with one hundred and twenty followers.

Determined to rid Mewar of the Rathore threat once and for all, Prince Chunda Sisodia harried Prince Jodha and his men relentlessly all the way through the Aravalli hills and into the desert, a chase that lasted for a night and a day. Knowing that the young prince had to survive, the Rathores responded with a classic Rajput tactic: every few miles a group of Jodha's men peeled off to make a last stand, knowing that their deaths would buy time for the rest. Their gallantry cost them dear because by the time Chunda called off his chase only Prince Jodha and six of their number remained alive. So swift was this pursuit that Prince Chunda reached Mandore before news of the Chittor massacre had reached the Rathore capital. Mandore had been left only lightly garrisoned and the town fell to the Sisodias almost without a struggle.

Prince Jodha survived but it took him twelve years to reclaim Mandore. After one of many failed attempts he found refuge in the hut of a simple Jat peasant whose wife, unaware of his identity, fed him a bowl of plain millet gruel known as *kheech*. The hungry Jodha took the bowl and reached for a drop of butter that lay melting at the centre, only to burn his fingers — whereupon the woman declared him to be 'almost as stupid as Rao Jodha'! He was mortified to be told that it was because the Rao always attacked Mandore while ignoring the surrounding country — 'just as you reached for the centre of the bowl and ignored the cooler food at the edge'. Only after conquering the lands around Mandore could he win the prize of Mandore itself. Rao Jodha took the Jat woman's advice and in 1453 finally recaptured Mandore.

In recapturing his city Rao Jodha killed two of Prince Chunda's sons, whose deaths had now to be avenged. However, in defiance of the Rajput code, Rao Chunda declared an end to the feud. The two leaders and their armies met at Nadole, roughly midway between Chittor and Mandore, and here, Rao Jodha of Marwar and Rana Chunda of Mewar agreed that the boundary between their two kingdoms should be at Godwar, where Prince Chunda's son Manda had fallen. Here the yellow flowered shrub known as the *aonla*, which grows in abundance in the kinder soil to the south and east, gives way to the far hardier thorn tree known as the *babul* or *baoli*, common to the deserts of Marwar. This gave rise to the popular Rajasthani folk song which declares:

Where the *babul* tree grows,
that is Marwar;
Where the *aonla* grows,
that is Mewar.

Thus peace came to Marwar, and Rao Jodha was anointed as the fourteenth ruler since

A PAIR OF KADAS, THICK BANGLES, FROM 20TH-CENTURY RAJASTHAN. THE SOLID GOLD LION-HEAD TERMINALS WERE POPULAR AND SYMBOLISED BRAVERY AND VALOUR. FLORAL-SHAPED MOTIFS IN CUTWORK GOLD ARE SET WITH DIAMONDS. top: THE ENAMELLED REVERSE OF A HASLI, RIGID NECKLACE THAT SITS ON THE COLLARBONE. MADE IN BIKANER IN THE 19TH CENTURY, THE FRONT SIDE IS A GOLD NECKLACE WITH A BLUE ENAMEL GROUND, ENCRUSTED WITH DIAMONDS. A ROW OF LARGE PEARLS RUNS ALONG THE OUTER EDGE. WOMEN IN RAJASTHAN VERY COMMONLY WEAR THIS ORNAMENT.

facing page: ONE OF THE MOST ROMANTICISED MARRIAGES WAS THAT BETWEEN GAYATRI DEVI OF COOCH BEHAR AND MAHARAJA SAWAI MAN SINGH II OF JAIPUR. GAYATRI DEVI WAS SMITTEN BY THE DASHING AND GLAMOROUS YOUNG MAHARAJA WHO CAME TO STAY AT HER LARGE HOUSE 'WOODLANDS' DURING THE CALCUTTA POLO SEASON. THE MAHARAJA WAS A WORLD-FAMOUS POLO PLAYER AND AT ONE TIME HIS TEAM BECAME THE WORLD CHAMPIONS AT DEAUVILLE, FRANCE. TRAGICALLY, HE ALSO DIED ON A POLO FIELD IN ENGLAND. THE FIRST TIME THAT GAYATRI DEVI MET HIM WAS WHEN SHE WAS FIVE AND HE WAS THIRTEEN YEARS OLD, DURING A VACATION IN THE HILL STATION OF OOTACAMUND. IT WAS HERE THAT SHE EVENTUALLY ALSO WENT FOR HER WESTERN-STYLE HONEYMOON, A RARITY IN THOSE DAYS. THEIR MARRIAGE TOOK PLACE AMIDST MUCH DISAPPROVAL ON BOTH SIDES (SHE WAS TO BECOME HIS THIRD WIFE AND IT WAS A NON-RAJPUT ALLIANCE). HOWEVER, GAYATRI DEVI WENT ON TO DO JAIPUR PROUD, TAKING AN ACTIVE INTEREST IN THE STATE'S WELFARE, IN PARTICULAR, IN WOMEN'S EDUCATION.

Panna Bai's Sacrifice

When the nobles of Chittor placed Bunbir on the throne during the minority of Udai Singh, son of Rana Sangha, the former hatched a plot to remove Udai Singh, who was at the time about six years old. Having gone to sleep after his dinner, Udai's nurse, Panna Bai, heard screams from the womens' section of the palace, whereupon a *bari*, cuisinier, informed her of the plot to assassinate the minor prince. James Tod narrates of how 'the faithful nurse put her charge into a fruit basket and, covering it with leaves, she delivered it to the *bari*, enjoining him to escape with it from the fort'. She then replaced the boy in the cradle with her own son. When Bunbir entered and asked for the prince, she pointed to the cradle and 'beheld the murderous steel buried in the heart of her babe'.

Barely did she have the time to shed tears on her son's demise, when she hurried out to the faithful *bari* who was waiting for her with the child who was fortunately still asleep. After being refused shelter with two rulers, she took him to Kumbalgarh and placed him on the governor's lap, pleading with him to 'guard the life of his sovereign'. The governor was persuaded by his mother to do so and provided Udai Singh with refuge till he became an adult and returned to claim his inheritance. Panna Bai's story has gone down in history as the epitome of ultimate sacrifice and loyalty.

Rao Sheoji. He now began to look around for a site for a new fortress that he could make the strongest in Rajputana. There was an obvious spot just five miles from Mandore on that high bluff known as the birds' nest mountain over which kites were always wheeling – even though it lacked a water supply. It was, however, inhabited by an elderly yogi who called himself Cheerianathji, Lord of the Birds, who had lived there undisturbed for many years. If the yogi could survive up there, Rao Jodha reasoned, so could others. The yogi was politely but firmly ejected and given new quarters below the hill. But he went with a curse: that whoever lived in Jodha's fortress should always suffer from a scarcity of water. The curse has not been forgotten, and to this day the citizens of Jodhpur, the city of Jodh, still attribute the city's water shortages to the wrath of the Lord of the Birds.

Mughal Suzerainty

The building of the great rock citadel of Meherangarh at Jodhpur coincided with a resurgence of Rajput power under the leadership of Rao Kumbha of Mewar, who built a ring of thirty-two fortresses, among them the mighty hill fortress of Kumbha, with its thirteen kilometres of ramparts and its three hundred and sixty-five temples. Under his leadership the Rajputs inflicted the first serious defeat to a Muslim foe in over a century, but it offered only a temporary respite, for in 1526 a new invader appeared at the gates of Delhi after defeating Sultan Ibrahim Lodi on the battlefield of Panipat – a Mongol warlord named Babur.

To establish his Mughal dynasty as the new rulers of India, Babur and his successors had to wage a series of brutal campaigns against the newly invigorated Rajput kingdoms of central India. Leading this opposition was a warrior-king considered by many as the greatest of the many rulers of Mewar, the one-eyed and one-armed Rana Sangram, who in eighteen years, won eighteen battles and, prior to Babur's arrival, had been set to overthrow the weakened Ibrahim Lodi, whose dynasty had ruled over Delhi since 1451. However, it was the Mughals under the leadership of Babur who first took Delhi and then advanced south to confront the Rajputs.

In 1527 the two armies met at Khanna, one hundred kilometres west of Agra. 'The holy warriors of the faith advanced in ranks straight as fir trees', Emperor Babur was to dictate for his autobiography years later. 'The vain Hindus scattered abroad like teased wool and broke like bubbles of wine.' Rana Sangram's body was found with over eighty wounds inflicted by sword or spear. In the following year the Sisodia capital of Chittor fell to the Sultan of Gujarat to the accompaniment of the terrible twin rites of mass suicide by its warriors and their women. But once again the heir to the royal throne of Mewar, the infant Udai Singh, was smuggled away, and after years of hiding in the Aravalli hills, established himself beside a small lake, founding a new capital which was named after him as Udaipur.

The struggle continued under the leadership of the kings of Jodhpur until the arrival of the third and wisest of the line of Mughal emperors – Akbar, the Great Mughal, who won the allegiance of his predominantly Hindu subjects by measures designed to reconcile them to his rule. Those rajas who offered *nazar*, tribute, to the Great Mughal as tokens of their submission were permitted to continue as rulers of semi-independent feudal states, while those who refused were worn down by a combination of

Rana Sangram Singh II of Mewar. This 18th century watercolour on paper is set with pearls and precious stones. The Mewar Rajputs are renowned for their brave deeds on the battlefield. The Rana's ancestor by the same name is said to have lost an arm and an eye, and had eighty-four wounds inflicted on his body at the time of his death. These rulers from the Sisodia clan claimed descent from the sun and called themselves Suryavanshis or 'the race of the sun'. The dynasty is perhaps the oldest known in India and founded Mewar in 800 CE.

facing page, top: *Dosti* London coins of Udaipur.
facing page, bottom: The ethereal-looking Jag Nivas or lake palace Hotel, as it is better known today.

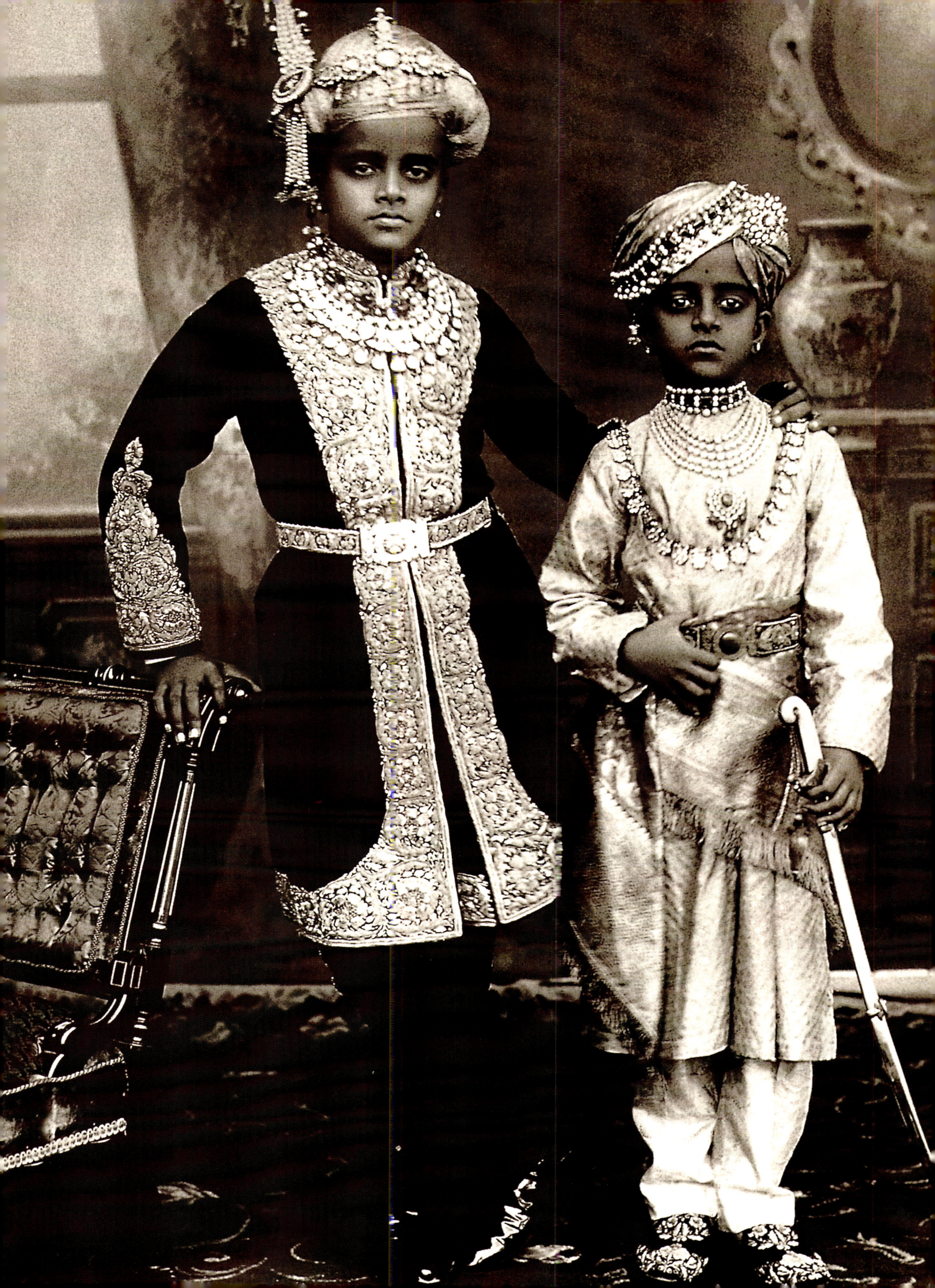

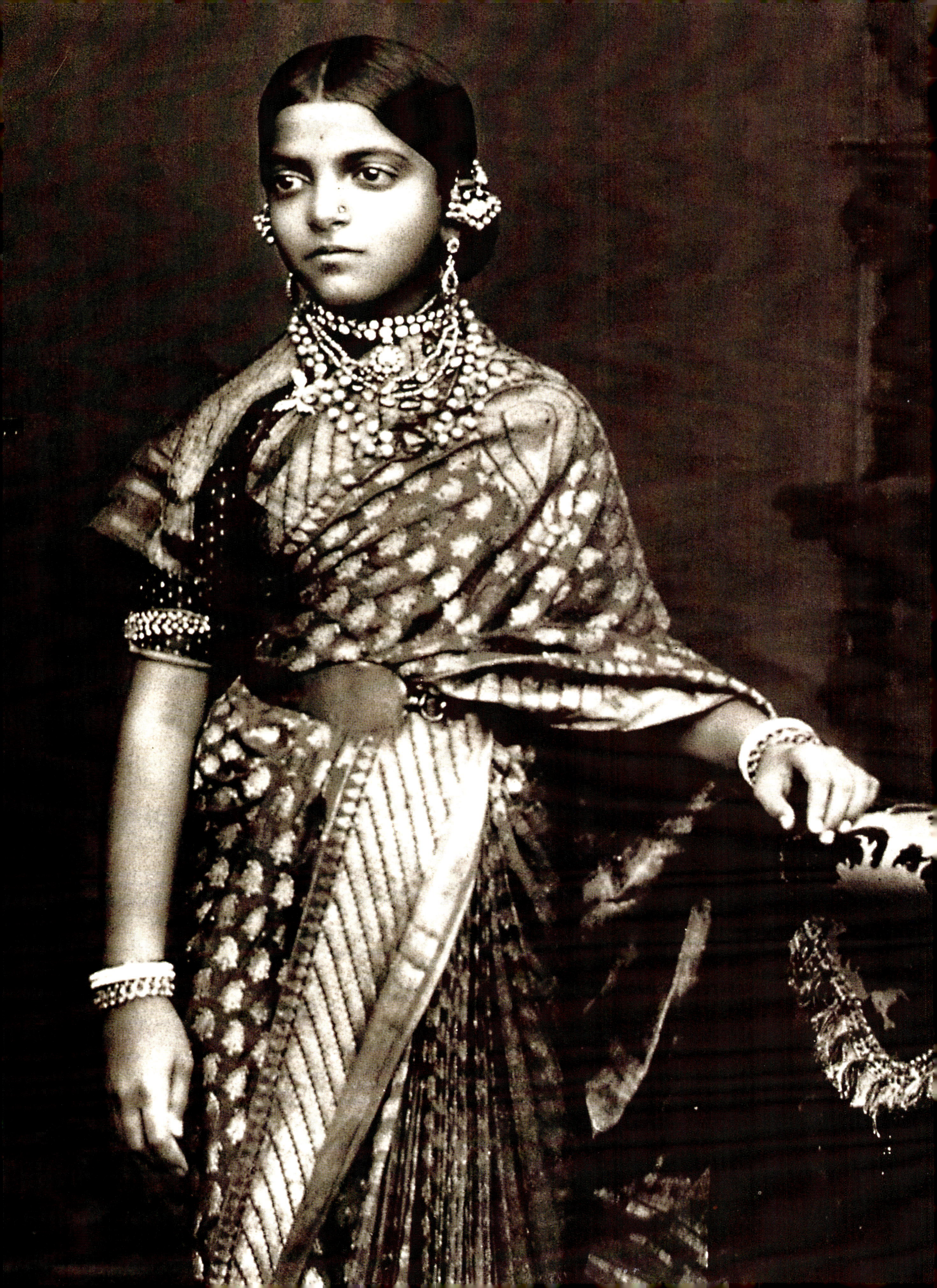

SEATED BETWEEN HER PARENTS, THE MAHARAJA AND MAHARANI OF JAIPUR, PRINCESS DIYA KUMARI IS GREETED BY A RAJPUT LADY ON THE OCCASION OF HER BIRTHDAY. BEING THE ONLY CHILD OF THE MAHARAJA, HER SON HAS NOW BEEN ADOPTED BY HER PARENTS AND WILL BE THE NEXT MAHARAJA OF JAIPUR.

pages 70-71, top centre:
COLOURFULLY DRESSED RAJPUT LADIES ASSEMBLED IN THE ZENANA *DEODI*, LADIES' WING, OF THE CITY PALACE IN JAIPUR ON PRINCESS DIYA KUMARI'S BIRTHDAY.

ruthlessness in the battlefield and carefully calculated acts of friendship. The two powerful Rajput kingdoms of Amber (known today as Jaipur) and Jodhpur presented the greatest threat to Akbar because of their proximity to Delhi and Agra, so it was here that he concentrated his diplomatic offensive. The first to 'bend the knee' was the Kachhawa ruler of Amber, Raja Bhagwandas, who, as James Tod puts it, 'sullied Rajpoot purity' by giving his daughter in marriage to Akbar's son Prince Salim – who later ruled as Emperor Jehangir. In acknowledging Akbar and his successors as the paramount power in India, Raja Bhagwandas not only ensured the survival of his kingdom but also brought great wealth to himself and his successors. His son, Maharaja Man Singh, became one of Akbar's most brilliant generals and his example was followed by other Rajputs from Amber, many of whom took up arms against their fellow Rajputs. From this period onwards rulers such as Man Singh who showed proper loyalty to the Mughal emperors, were rewarded with grand titles, honours and land, many earning the title of maharaja or its local equivalent.

By contrast, Rajput rulers who spurned Akbar's offers of friendship were given no quarter. The old Sisodia stronghold of Chittor once again became the Rajputs' main rallying point until in 1567 it finally fell to the Mughals. Tod records that in this third and last fatal sally eight thousand Rajput warriors died, while

FORMALLY DRESSED COURTIERS, WOMEN WITH GARLANDS AND THE LOCAL PEOPLE OF JAIPUR GATHER IN THE CHANDRA MAHAL TO GREET MAHARAJA SAWAI BHAWANI SINGHJI ON HIS BIRTHDAY. A MAN PAYS RESPECT TO THE MAHARAJA BY TOUCHING HIS FEET. THE WALLS OF THE PALACE ARE BEAUTIFULLY DECORATED WITH PAINTINGS OF FORMER MAHARAJAS AND ON THE CEILINGS HANG CRYSTAL CHANDELIERS. THE CELEBRATION OF ROYAL BIRTHDAYS IS CUSTOMARILY PERFORMED IN MOST ROYAL HOUSEHOLDS AND INVOLVES SPECIAL PUJAS FOR THE LONGEVITY OF THE FAMILY MEMBERS. HERE THE MAHARAJA HAS JUST RETURNED FROM A VISIT TO THE TEMPLE OF THE FAMILY DEITY, GOVIND DEVJI.

'nine queens, five princesses, two infant sons and the families of all the chieftains perished in the flames'. For good measure, Akbar also put to the sword thirty thousand of Chittor's less illustrious inhabitants. However, one group survived: Chittor's armourers and smiths, who then made a vow that they would never return to Chittor until their land had been freed of invaders. Their descendants are known today as *gadhia lohars*, blacksmiths of the carts, and can often be seen camping by the roadside in Rajasthan with their decorated carts, still plying their trade as tinkers and metalworkers. Shortly after India became independent in 1947, its first prime minister, Jawaharlal Nehru, led the leaders of the *gadhias* back into Chittor and offered them land there – but they had become accustomed to the nomadic way of life and refused to settle.

After this third sack of their capital the Sisodias of Udaipur and their allies continued to fight as guerillas in Rajasthan's mountains and forests. Their new leader, Rana Pratap, also took a vow: he and his successors would never sleep in a proper bed or eat off plates until Chittor had been recovered. Since then, succeeding Maharanas of Udaipur have slept with grass under their mattresses and eaten off platters of leaves in remembrance of those long years in the wilderness – a period now regarded as their years of glory and which earned them the title of 'ornament of the thirty-six royal races'.

pages 68 and 69: ROYAL CHILDREN OF MYSORE (19TH CENTURY): H. H. SRI KRISHNA RAJA WODEYAR BAHADUR IV, PRINCE KANTIRAVA NARASIMHARAJA WODEYAR AND PRINCESS CHELUVAJAMMANNIAVARU. THE WODEYARS RULED OVER THE THIRD LARGEST OF THE INDIAN PRINCELY STATES. THE ADMINISTRATION OF THE STATE BY THE RULERS OF MYSORE WAS ALWAYS AN EXAMPLE TO THE OTHER STATES AND SOMETIMES, YOUNG PRINCES FROM NORTHERN STATES WERE EVEN SENT TO MYSORE TO OBSERVE AND BENEFIT FROM THEIR PROCEDURES.

DURING THE FESTIVAL OF DUSSEHRA, MAHARAJA SAWAI BHAWANI SINGHJI OF JAIPUR PERFORMS *SHASTRA* (ARMS) PUJA IN CHANDRA MAHAL WITH ROYAL PRIESTS IN ATTENDANCE. FOR THE KSHATRIYA, HIS WEAPONS ARE HIS LIFELINE AND, THEREFORE, WORSHIPPED. IN THE FOREGROUND ARE SEEN ARMS, ARMOUR, BATTLE STANDARDS AND INSIGNIA.

top right: PRINCESS DIYA KUMARI OF JAIPUR GREETS HER FATHER MAHARAJA BHAWANI SINGHJI IN THE ZENANA *DEODI*, LADIES' WING, ON HIS BIRTHDAY. TRADITIONALLY NO OTHER MEN ARE ALLOWED ENTRY INTO THIS PART OF THE PALACE. IN THE FOREGROUND STANDS A FEMALE RETAINER CARRYING A SILVER GARLAND HOLDER. THE WALLS ARE ADORNED PROFUSELY WITH PAINTINGS AND GLASS-COVERED MINIATURES.

The Legend of Padmini

•

In 1275 CE, the minor Lakumsi ascended the throne of Chittor. His uncle, Bheemsi, who had married the beautiful Padmini, became his protector. Tales of Padmini's beauty and accomplishments spread far and wide, resulting in Allauddin Khilji's demand to possess her. After a long, arduous siege of Chittor fort by Allauddin's forces, Padmini relented to allow him to look at her, but only in the reflection of a mirror.

Having sated his desire, Allauddin was accompanied back to the foot of the fortress by Bheemsi. There Bheemsi was ambushed and captured, and the surrender of Padmini made the condition for his release.

Padmini agreed, while simultaneously planning a strategy to fool Allauddin. The latter was informed that Padmini would go to him, but would be accompanied by her attendants and a large retinue who desired to pay their last respects to her. Seven hundred covered litters reached Allauddin's camp, each litter containing one valiant from Chittor and six soldiers as litter-bearers.

Bheemsi was allowed to meet Padmini for half an hour to bid her farewell. After the half hour was over, seated in a litter, with Padmini, he started to return with a small band of followers. But Allauddin ordered pursuit, and though Bheemsi and Padmini reached the fort, the others perished to the last man.

Lying low for some years, Allauddin plotted his revenge and finally entrenched him at the southern end of the fort in 1290. Realising that they would be no match for Allauddin's army, the Rana and his men decided to defend Chittor to their death.

Another horrible sacrifice, however, preceded their fight to death. With Queen Padmini in the lead, all the women of Chittor committed *jauhar*, self-immolation, to prevent captivity.

And so fell Chittor, its queen and its people.

•

Jodhpur was the second Rajput kingdom to follow Amber's example. Maharao Udai Singh of Jodhpur outdid his Amber rival by giving a sister in marriage to Akbar and a daughter to Akbar's son, Prince Salim. This did much to improve Marwar's fortunes. Two later rulers of Jodhpur distinguished themselves as the Mughal's best generals, most notably, Maharao Jaswant Singh, who first led Emperor Shah Jehan's army against his rebel son Aurangzeb, then switched sides to become Aurangzeb's leading general. By then Rajput resistance to the Mughals had all but ended. In 1615, after years of struggle, Rana Amar Singh of Udaipur finally agreed to submit to Emperor Jehangir, but asked to be excused from the humiliation of making his homage in person before the emperor. In recognition of his status as first among Rajputs, Jehangir allowed his request and in this way Amar Singh — now elevated to the status of Maharana — and those who followed him avoided the humiliation of having to bow down before another power. In later years, when called upon by the British to make their submissions before the visiting King-Emperor or his Viceroys, the Maharanas of Udaipur always contrived to make some excuse to avoid doing so, usually by pleading sudden illness.

Emperor Akbar and his successors laid the foundations for modern government across much of India, providing the administrative framework both for the British and their successors in independent India and Pakistan. This was based on the division of the Mughal empire into provinces, divisions and districts, and the establishment of an imperial civil and military service made up of *mansabdars* or civil administrators, divided into thirty-three grades. An accurate settlement of all land was made and assessed for revenue annually. Local fiefdoms in the form of *jagirs* of land were also granted as rewards. In the military field many Rajput princes served the Mughal empire as its most able *mansabdars,* amassing enormous wealth and war booty

facing page: Fabric armour was most commonly used for ordinary soldiers. Quilted fabric of linen or cloth made it economical and light, though certainly not the safest.

in the process – two exceptions being the Sisodias of Udaipur and the Hadas of Bundi, whose independence cost them their land and prosperity.

As part of his efforts to integrate different philosophies, Akbar sought to fuse the Hindu concept of kingship based on the ideal of *Ramrajya*, the perfect state as exemplified by the hero Lord Rama, with the Muslim concept of *Mahdi*, the servant of God who follows the rules of *sharia* as set down by the Prophet Mohammed. During his long rule architecture and all the arts flourished throughout Islamic and Rajput India. The magnificent, richly decorated and painted palaces of Rajasthan and elsewhere, which fuse Indian and Islamic architecture into one Indo-Saracenic style are, in large part, Akbar's legacy.

The Decline of the Mughals

Towards the end of the seventeenth century the Mughal empire began to break up, weakened within by the rise of the Hindu Marathas in the Deccan and without by new invasions from Afghanistan and Persia. This process was hastened by Aurangzeb, Emperor Shah Jehan's younger son, who abandoned the Mughal policy of religious tolerance. In doing so, he provoked the last great uprising of the Rajputs, led by the Rathores of Jodhpur from their great rock fortress of Meherangarh.

In 1678 Maharao Jaswant Singh died while leading Aurangzeb's army on a military campaign. One of his widows was pregnant and as her husband had died without a surviving male issue, the succession now depended on her giving birth to a boy. A boy named Ajit Singh, was duly born, and was at once made a prisoner of Emperor Aurangzeb and brought to Delhi. Here the queen, her infant son and her escort were installed in a large mansion ringed by armed guards.

The officer charged with looking after Prince Ajit was Durga Das Rathore – to this day a hugely popular folk hero in northern India, the subject of street ballads and their modern-day equivalent, comic-strips and TV drama. Fearing that Aurangzeb intended to keep the infant as his hostage and bring him up as a Muslim, Durga Das organised a daring rescue. The baby prince's place in his cradle was taken by the child of his wet nurse, Gora Dai, and he was lowered out of a window of the mansion hidden in a snake-charmer's basket. As the boy was being smuggled out Durga Das and his men charged out through the gate of the mansion shouting the Rathore war cry, 'Rar banka Rathor' – We are the Rathores, invincible in battle! Meanwhile, all the women left behind gathered together and applied a burning torch to a large pile of gunpowder – blowing themselves and half the building to pieces. These self-sacrificing diversions allowed the infant prince to escape Delhi undetected.

For the next three decades Durga Das and the Rathores conducted a guerilla war against Aurangzeb's armies, keeping their prince hidden in the Aravalli hills until he was old enough to take his place in battle alongside the men. But it was not until the death of Aurangzeb in his eighty-second year that they were able to reclaim Jodhpur. Just one week later, on 10 March 1707, Maharao Ajit Singh, his aged general Durga Das and their troops entered the city in triumph.

The wet nurse Gora Dai, who had sacrificed her son to save the life of Ajit Singh, was not forgotten. Her name was inscribed in the state anthem and her memorial can still be seen in a street in Jodhpur. Ajit Singh himself outlived seven Mughal emperors but was less than a model prince. Death came to him in 1724 as he lay asleep in his bedchamber, fatally stabbed by his second son on learning that his father was having an affair with his wife. However he did not die alone.

A Bikaner State medal from the time of Maharaja Sadul Singhji.
top left: A 19th century portrait of a group of princes from Jaipur.
top right: Tukoji Rao Holkar, Maharaja of Indore in the late 19th century. The Maharaja abdicated over his involvement with a mistress, which led to a shoot-out in Bombay. The Holkars were the aides of the Peshwas and made a kingdom for themselves during the decline of the Mughals. Their domain became the centre of western India's foreign trade.

He was joined on his funeral pyre by no less than six queens and fifty-eight concubines.

Among the Rajputs only the kingdom of Amber came out of the war against Aurangzeb stronger and larger, largely due to the diplomatic skills of the young Maharaja Jai Singh II, who was astute enough to keep on good terms with Aurangzeb, winning for himself and his successors the curious title of *Sawai,* meaning one and a quarter. After becoming ruler in 1700 Jai Singh II ruled for forty-three years, transforming his state into the wealthiest in central India, expanding his territories and building a new capital modelled on a grid-system, which he named Jaipur. Although known today as the 'pink city', it was originally multicoloured, and was only painted uniform pink as part of the clean-up that preceded the state visit of the Prince of Wales in 1876.

In 1806 a young lieutenant of the British East India Company's Bengal Army was attached to the army of the Maratha warlord Madhavrao Scindia of Gwalior as it advanced through Rajputana. 'Nothing but ruin to the eye', the twenty-three-year-old James Tod recorded. 'Deserted towns, roofless houses and uncultured plains. Wherever the Mahratta encamped annihilation was ensured.' The Maratha army halted at a place which Tod was always to remember as 'the most romantic spot on the continent of India', beside Lake Pichhola and the city of Udaipur, dominated by the ancient palaces of the Ranas of Mewar. Here he witnessed the final humiliation of Maharana Bhim Singh, who besides having his land ravaged by the Marathas, was also caught up in a quarrel between his two powerful neighbours, the rulers of Jodhpur and Jaipur. Both had demanded the hand of his sixteen-year-old daughter, Princess Kishna Kumari Bai, described by Tod as 'sprung from the noblest blood of Hind and justly proclaimed the "flower of Rajasthan" '. The Maharaja of Jaipur had the prior claim but the impoverished Maharana of Udaipur was in no position to favour either prince, so the two rivals had gone to war. Aided by a Pathan general named Amir Khan, the Marwar army defeated that of Jaipur and Amir Khan was sent to Udaipur to claim the prize. But Amir Khan gave the Maharana of Mewar a stark choice: he could give his daughter to one of the two rival maharajas and be attacked by the other – or he could kill his daughter and 'by her death seal the peace of Rajwarra' (Rajasthan).

Had the Maharana been stronger he would have heeded the tradition of a thousand years and chosen death before dishonour. Instead, he ordered his brothers to kill his daughter. One refused and the second, when faced with his intended victim, found himself unable to do the deed – whereupon the young princess took the matter into her own hands by declaring that if her father's welfare and the safety of his kingdom required her death then she was ready to kill herself. Accordingly, a bowl of poison was prepared and brought to her: 'As the Rana's messenger presented it in the name of her father, she bowed and drank it, sending up a prayer for his life and prosperity.'

This act of royal infanticide was judged such an affront to Rajput honour that it was taken to herald the end of the royal line of Mewar (Udaipur). It is said that a curse was laid on the Maharana's family by which no male heir would be born to a ruler – an unhappy circumstance which has prevailed to this day. One happier consequence of this tragedy was that it won the sympathy of the young English officer, James Tod, who witnessed it, and became a champion of the Rajputs and a keen promoter of political alliances between the Rajput states and the British Government, which he saw as the only means to their survival.

BEAUTY-IN-ARMS – THIS BEJEWELLED DAGGER AND SHEATH TYPIFIES THE JEHANGIRESQUE STYLE OF CRAFTSMANSHIP. INLAYS OF TREES, BIRDS, ANIMALS, FLOWERS AND ARABESQUE IMAGES IN IVORY, RUBIES, EMERALDS, DIAMONDS, GLASS AND ENAMEL MERGE IN THIS EARLY 17TH CENTURY SCABBARD AND HILT. WHILE THE SCABBARD IS MADE OF WOOD, OVERLAID WITH GOLD, THE HILT IS SHEER GOLD. THE BALUSTER AND POMMEL FORM THE TREE OF LIFE. JUST ABOUT TOUCHING THE END OF THE POMMEL ABOVE IS A STYLISED HORSE'S BUST. RESTING ON THE OTHER SIDE OF THE SCABBARD IS THE GROWLING FACE OF A TIGER, WITH TEETH OF IVORY AND A TONGUE COMPRISING A SINGLE RUBY.

The Bri
and Princ

tish Raj
ely States

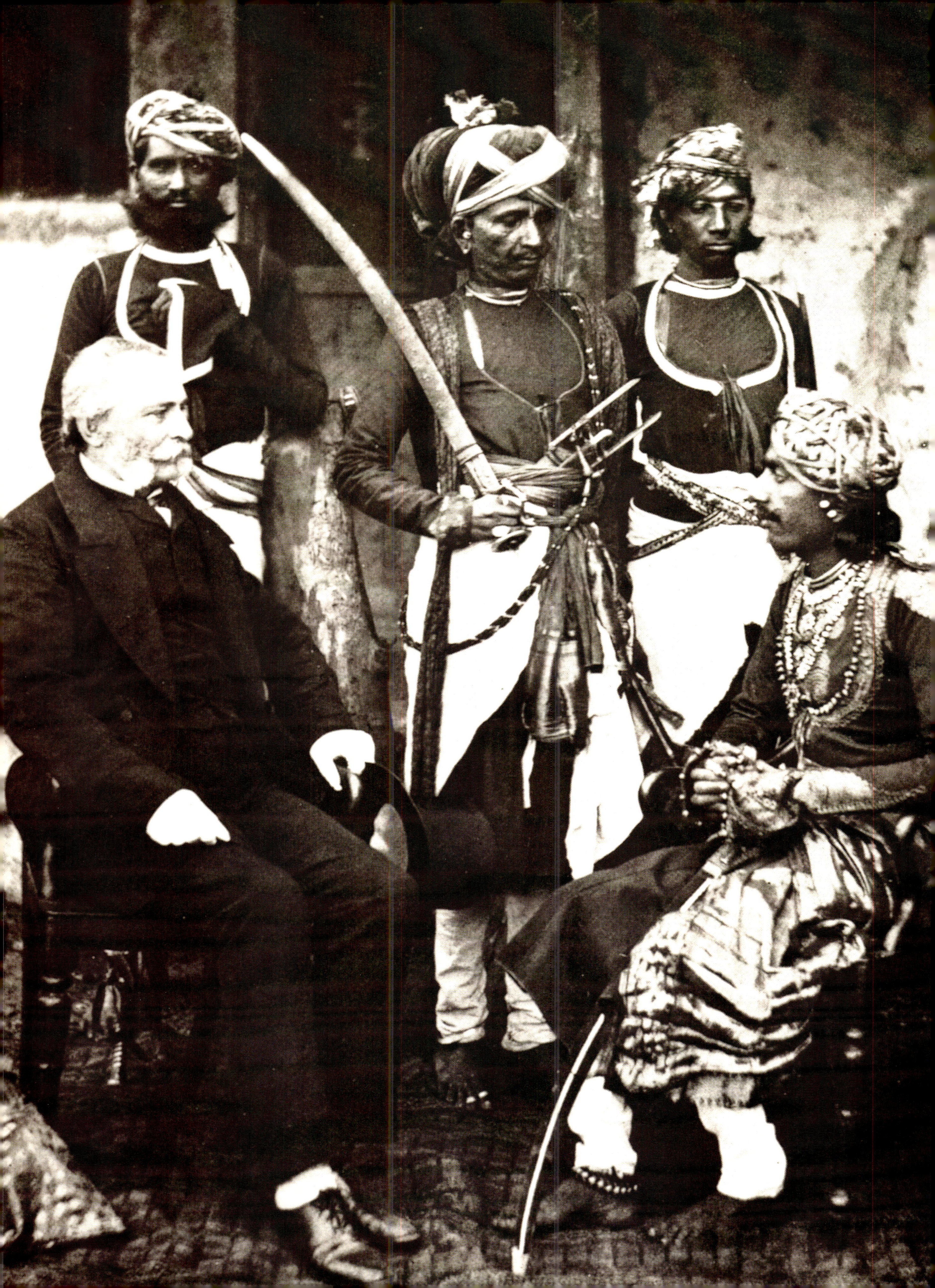

The continuing decline of Mughal power in the centre now allowed former viceroys of provinces to break away to form their own Muslim states, such as Hyderabad and Berar in the south-east. In the north the Sikhs rose to found their own kingdom and in western India Afghan freebooters moved in to establish Palanpur, Bawalpur and other Muslim states. In central and western India the Hindu Marathas formed a loose confederacy under a number of warlords, who advanced northwards to overrun the weakened Rajput kingdoms and set up their own dynasties and kingdoms on the Rajput model: the Gaekwads of Baroda, the Holkars of Indore and the Scindias of Gwalior. Only Jaipur and Jodhpur remained strong enough to fight off these new invaders. By the nineteenth century every remaining Rajput kingdom in central India was forced to pay huge sums in tribute to the Marathas or to Pathan freebooters in central India.

The British East India Company, founded in 1600 with a monopoly to trade in the so-called East Indies, had also exploited the vacuum in Delhi to form alliances with Indian states and to play one off against another, nearly always winning new territories. In their struggles for survival many Indian rulers now turned to 'John Company', entering into treaties of 'perpetual friendship, alliance and unity of interests' in return for military protection. Others, after seeing how powerful rulers like the Nawabs of Bengal had been reduced by the British to the status of mere zamindars or landowners, did so for fear of following suit. A third category was made up of rulers like the Jat Maharaja of Bharatpur who fought the British and lost but was allowed to retain his powers after acknowledging the suzerainty of the British monarch. Gradually scores of semi-independent kingdoms which had hitherto acknowledged the emperors of Delhi transferred their loyalties to the East India Company. So did the several hundred small feudatory principalities which had hitherto pledged their loyalties to these larger semi-independent monarchies.

From Kings to Princes

The penultimate phase for the maharajas began in November 1858, when government by a commercial trading company gave way to British Crown rule and the division of India into British India and the Native or Princely States. These were made up of no less than five hundred and sixty-five so-called Princely States, all enjoying direct political relations with the Government of India but with their rulers exercising various degrees of independence according to their size and importance. At one end of the scale were the dominions of the Nizam of Hyderabad and Berar, occupying 214,000 square kilometres of the Deccan plateau; at the other were a score of minute landholdings in western India, each taking up less than two and a half square kilometres. The British dealt with this multiplicity by dividing them into three categories. At the top were the Salute States, numbering one hundred and eighteen, whose rulers were accorded the title of Maharaja or Raja (or its Muslim equivalent, usually, Nawab), enjoyed full jurisdiction with their boundaries and were ranked according to the number of gun salutes they merited, descending by odd numbers from twenty-one to nine (as compared to the Queen-Empress Victoria's one hundred and one gun salute). In the middle were the one hundred and seventeen Non-salute States, who enjoyed limited jurisdiction as Chiefs, and at the bottom of the pile

Maharana Arvind Singhji of Udaipur and Maharani Vijayraj of Udaipur. Mewar was the leading state of Rajasthan, with its capital Chittorgarh. After it was captured by Ala-ud-Din Khilji, Udai Singh II built the new captial at Udaipur.

facing page: Lieutenant Churchill seen with a ruling prince and his men in the 1860s.

pages 76-77: A gold, enamelled and jewelled watch and watch-chains gifted by the Maharaja of Patiala to H. H. The Prince of Wales in 1867.

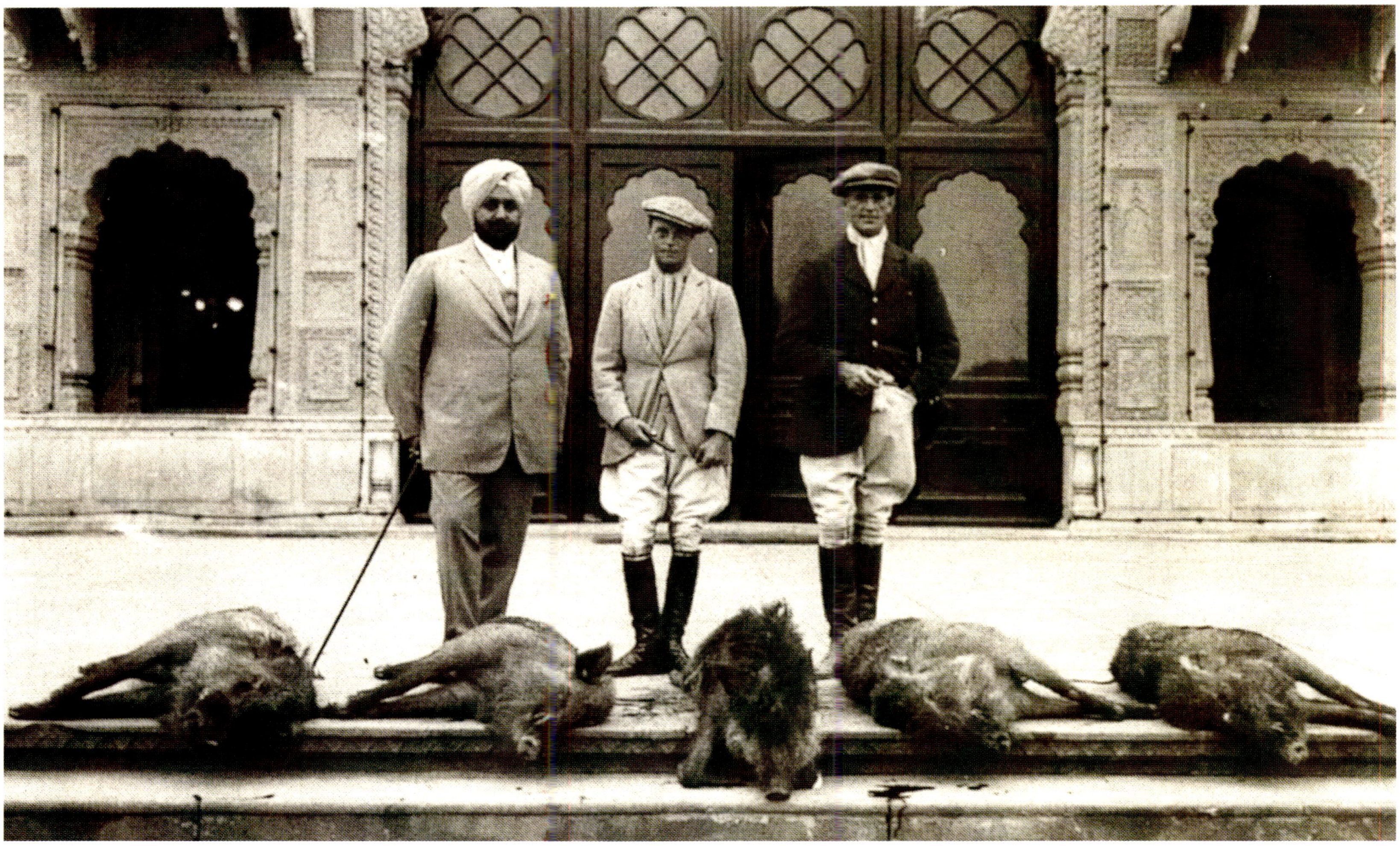

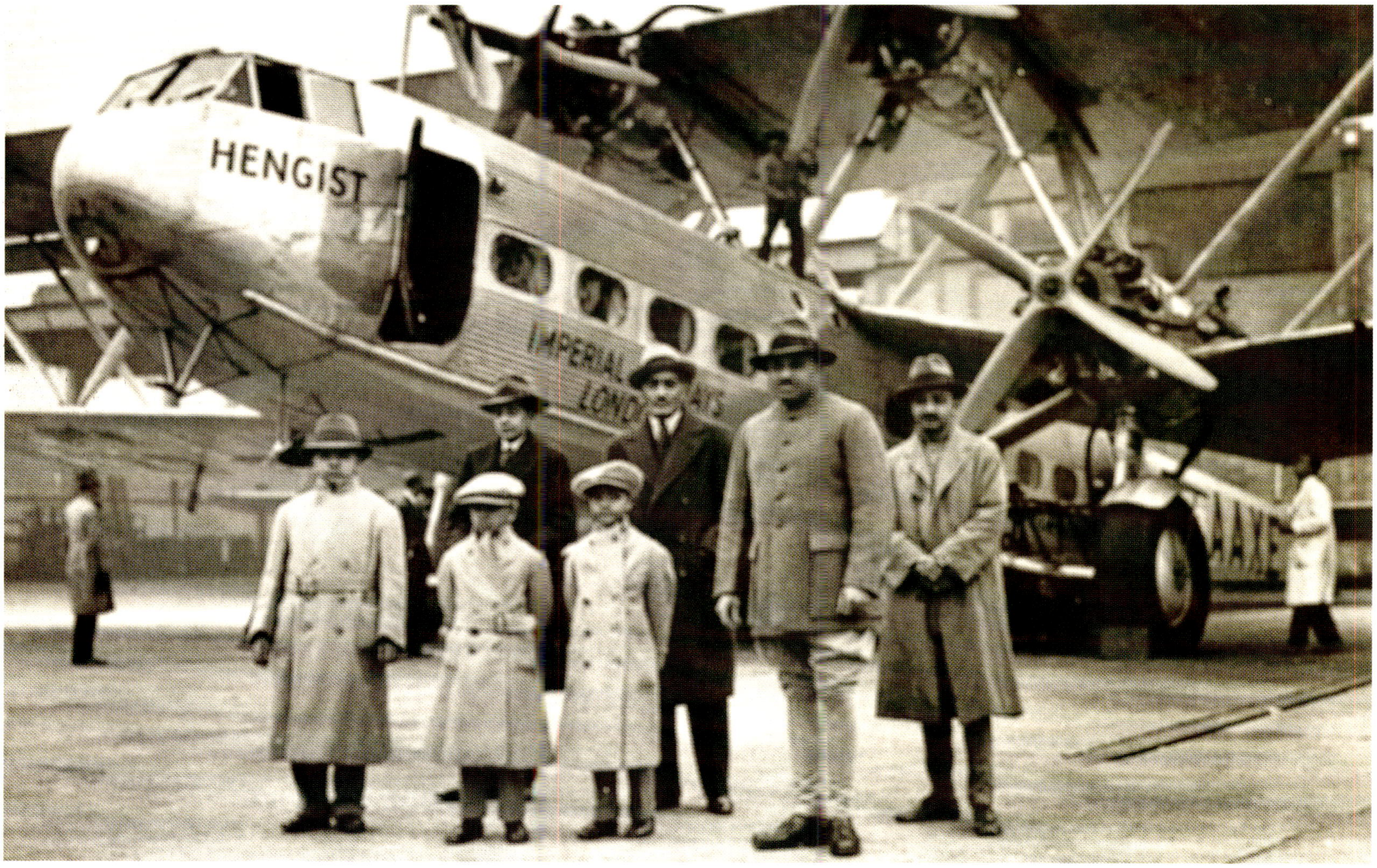
HENGIST
IMPERIAL

were three hundred and twenty-seven non-jurisdictional Estates whose rulers carried titles such as *Thakur* or *Taluqdar*.

The Royal Proclamation of November 1858 guaranteed the 'rights, dignity and honour' of the Princes and their futures as rulers of Princely States, but also divested them of their chief duty, which was to protect their people. It was the moment, according to one of their number, when 'we ceased to be kings and became princes'. The *raja-praja* link had been broken. 'Whereas the Indian Princes, when they were kings were answerable and responsive to local sanctions, as they became responsible to the superior power – here always called the Paramount Power – so they paid less attention to internal sanctions.' Despite the British administration's declared aim of treating the Princes 'not as relics, but as rulers; not as puppets, but as living factors in the administration', the maharajas were effectively barred from entering the mainstream of Indian political life. Encouraged to rule their states on modern lines by bringing in chief ministers and councils of ministers, many rulers did just that, abandoning the cares of state completely and giving themselves over to a life of indulgence. Others went the other way and continued to rule as autocrats, making no effort to adapt to modern ways.

Under the eyes of the Viceroy and his Political Agents, the princes continued to rule, some well and some badly. Any moves on their part to introduce words associated with sovereignty such as royal, crown, his majesty or throne were vigorously opposed by the British. At the same time those princes who showed the greatest loyalty to the Crown were showered, on the Mughal principal, with titles, honours, more gun salutes and all the outward pomp and trappings of rule. They were also exhorted to Anglicise themselves and their states in ways that increasingly isolated them from their subjects. They were encouraged to employ English nannies, tutors and guardians for their children and to employ British experts who would help them to run their states on modern lines. Beginning with the Rajkumar (Princes) College set up in Rajkot in 1870,

top: YOUNG PRINCES WHO ACTED AS PAGES TO KING GEORGE V AND QUEEN MARY AT THE DELHI DURBAR OF 1911. MAHARAJA GANGA SINGH'S ELDEST SON, SADUL SINGH, IS ON THE EXTREME RIGHT. THE DURBAR WAS ONE OF THE MOST MAGNIFICENT AND MEMORABLE OCCASIONS IN PRINCELY INDIA WITH A TENTAGE OF 233 CAMPS OF RULERS SPREAD OVER TWENTY-FIVE SQUARE MILES. facing page, bottom: MAHARAJA UMAID SINGH OF JODHPUR AND HIS SONS GETTING READY TO LEAVE FOR EUROPE FROM CROYDON AIRPORT, 1932. THE ELDEST SON OF THE MAHARAJA, SEEN ON THE EXTREME LEFT IN THE PICTURE, WAS KILLED IN AN AIRPLANE CRASH IN 1952.

facing page, top: MAHARAJA BHUPINDER SINGH OF PATIALA WITH THE PRINCE OF WALES AFTER A SESSION OF PIG STICKING, 1922. THE MAHARAJA WAS INFAMOUS FOR HIS SEXUAL MARAUDING AND HAD AN ASSOCIATION WITH ONE OF THE VICEROY'S DAUGHTERS, WHICH EVENTUALLY LED TO HIS BEING BANNED BY THE BRITISH FROM THE HILL STATION OF SIMLA. AS A RESULT OF THE BAN HE BUILT A PALACE IN CHAIL WHERE HE HOSTED SOME VERY FANCY CRICKET MATCHES, ONE OF WHICH REQUIRED ALL MEN TO DRESS UP AS WOMEN. THE HUGE MAHARAJA HIMSELF APPEARED AS A NUN. THE MAHARAJA HAD A PENCHANT FOR A RICH LIFESTYLE AND OWNED TWENTY-SEVEN ROLLS-ROYCES AND SOME HUNDRED OTHER CARS. HE ALSO INDULGED HANDSOMELY IN HIS PURSUIT FOR COLLECTING THE WORLD'S MOST SPECTACULAR JEWELS. ON ONE OCCASION HE BOUGHT A LOT OF PRESENTS FROM FINNEGANS AND HIS SPREE IN SUITCASES COVERED THE ENTIRE FIFTH FLOOR OF THE RITZ, INCLUDING THE CORRIDORS.

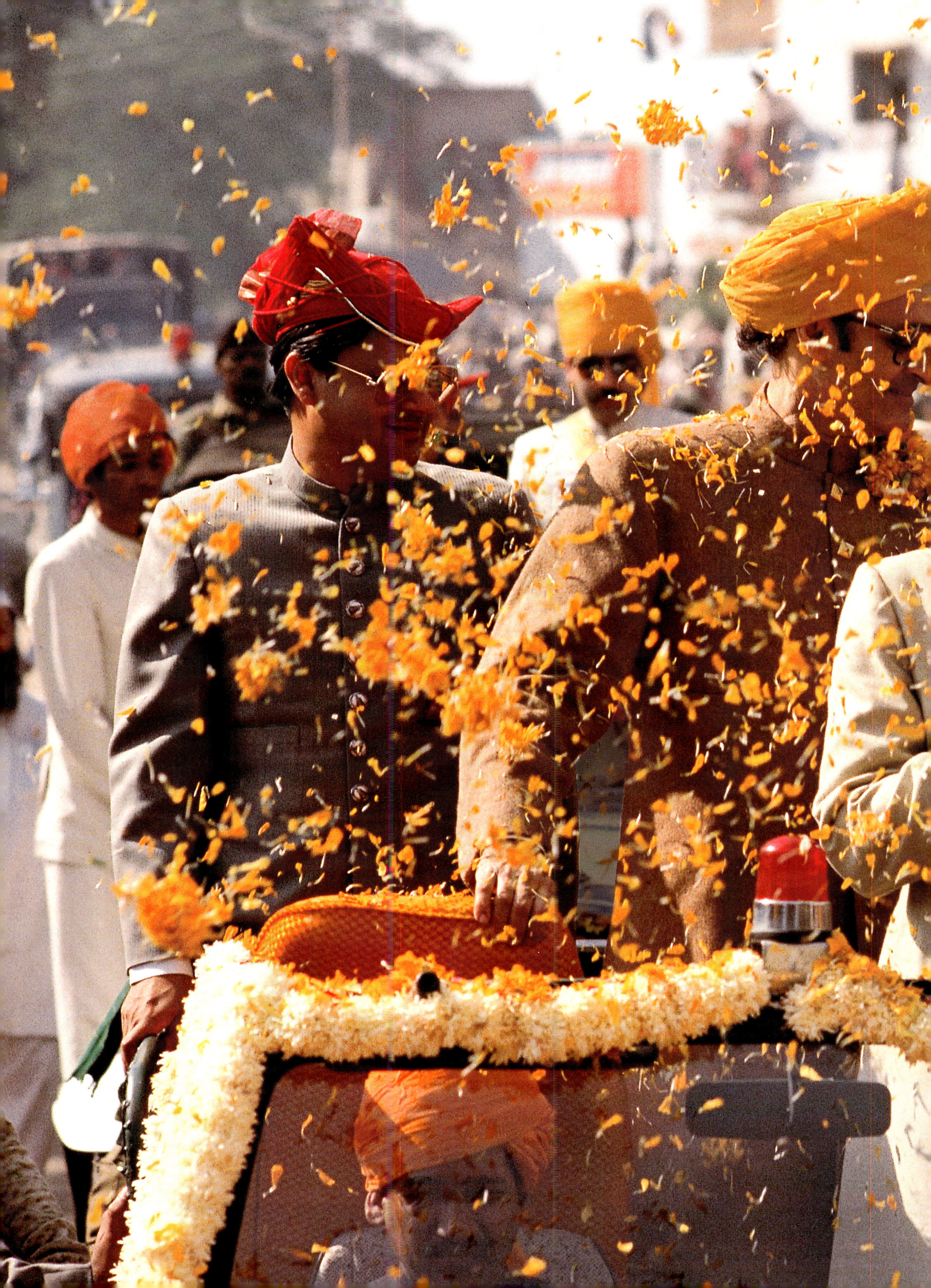

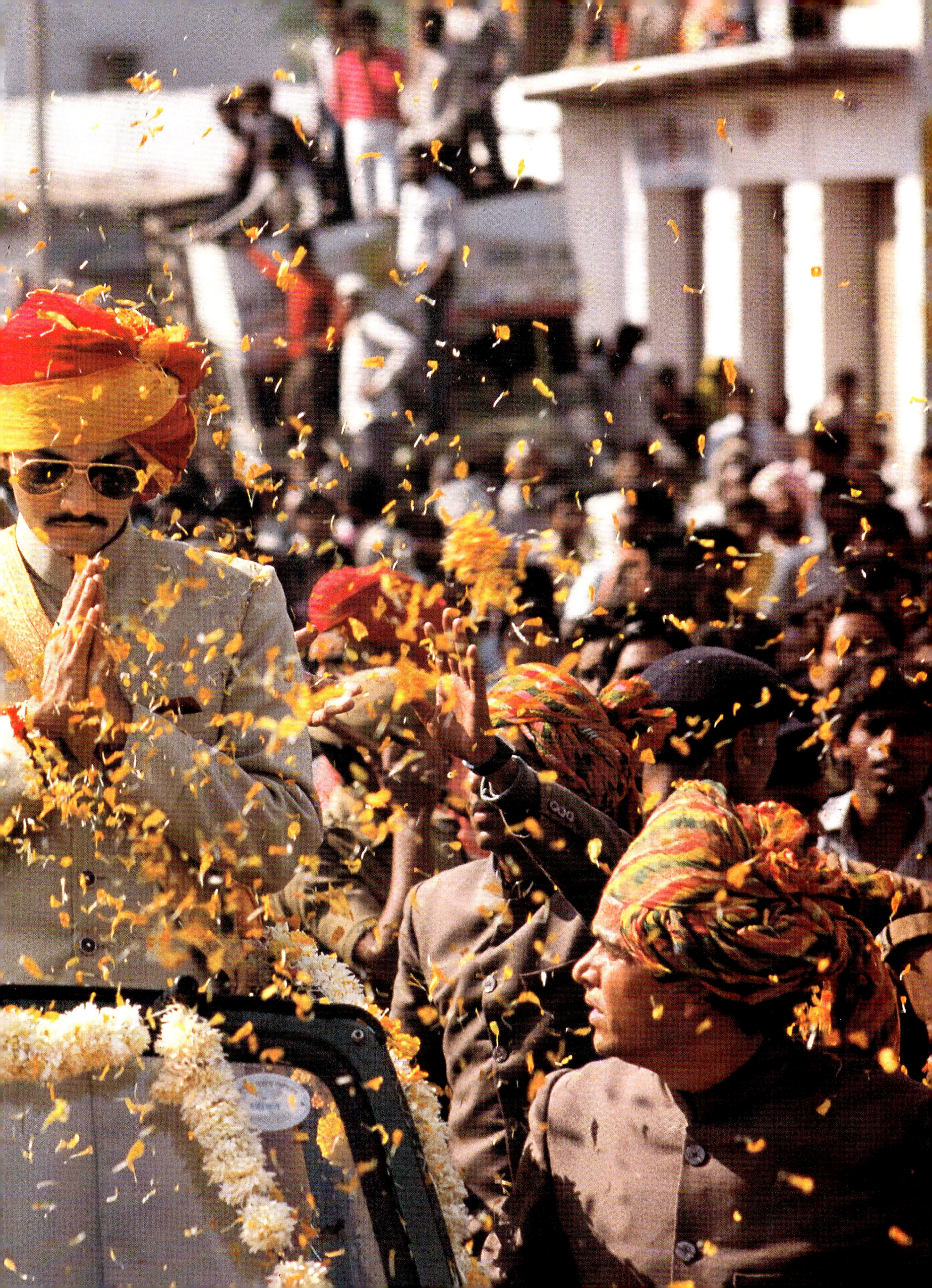

pages 82-83, left to right: The late Maharaja Madhavrao Scindia of Gwalior, Maharaja Dr Karan Singh of Kashmir and Yuvraj Vikramaditya Singh of Kashmir are showered with flowers by the people of Gwalior as they drive through the city after the Yuvraj's marriage to Princess Chitrangadaraje Scindia. The Late Maharaja Of Gwalior is wearing his traditional headgear known as the *Shindeshahi Pagdi*. He was a very successful politician who served as a Cabinet minister. Even till this day he is remembered for his excellent performance as the Minister of Railways. The Maharaja of Kashmir is a well-known scholar and statesman. He has also served as India's ambassador to the United States.

A *turra*, turban jewel, worn by the Nizam of Hyderabad in the 19th century as a symbol of loyalty to the British. Shaped like a crown with diamonds, emeralds and faceted rubies, the top has seven vertical wire-sprays set with the same stones.

top: With the Red Fort in the background, a procession of Indian rulers on elephants makes its way into Delhi on the occasion of the last imperial durbar in 1911. The first of such durbars was held when Queen Victoria was proclaimed Empress of India in 1877. The order in which the princes entered the Durbar Hall was a serious affair and officers were posted on different routes to get the rulers into the durbar in the right order. The princes entered with their ceremonial pomp, greeted the king and the queen and presented them with items of jewellery and other gifts.

boarding schools were set up for the sons of the aristocracy which were intended to inculcate in them the virtues of the English public school, including a love of outdoor games such as cricket.

Inevitably, the effect was to drive a cultural wedge between the rulers and the ruled, epitomised by the widespread removal of the former from their ancient palaces sited at the hearts of their capitals to new palaces outside the city built by British architects in European or Indo-Saracenic design. In effect, they moved from what were essentially citadels into glorified stately homes, which for many became pleasure domes. As Rudyard Kipling wrote, the only function left to them was to 'offer mankind a spectacle', so it was hardly surprising that a number of rulers embarked on spending sprees in Europe, built themselves grandiose palaces (including one modelled on Versailles), indulged in sexual excesses or simply found solace in drink or opium. Many would have agreed with the sentiments of the Maharaja of Vizagapatam who, on being admonished by the local British Resident for his heavy drinking, replied, 'I know, sir. I am an idle drunken fellow . . . but what can I do? Your *pax Britannica* has robbed me of my hereditary occupation. What is my hereditary occupation? It is fighting'. It was in those states where the rulers were hostile to change and which the British Government in India regarded as the most 'backward' – most notably in Rajasthan and Hyderabad – that Hindu and Muslim culture and arts flourished.

Lord Curzon set out to address these issues when he came to India as Viceroy in 1899. However, he had first to change Queen Victoria's romantic notions of the princes. Many, he wrote to her, were 'frivolous and sometimes vicious spendthrifts and idlers'; the Maharaja of Patiala was 'little better than a jockey'; the Rana of Dholpur was 'fast sinking into an inebriate and a sot'; the Maharaja of Bharatpur had shot his servant; Maharaja Holkar of Indore was half mad and 'addicted to horrible vices'. The Francophile Maharaja of Kapurthala was 'a third class chief of fifth rate character', only happy when philandering and gambling in Paris; the Nizam of Hyderabad was 'wrapped up in the sloth of the seraglio', and the Nawab of Rampur was 'a sensual and extravagant debauchee'.

Progressive Rulers

But that was only one side of the coin. A number of rulers were thoroughly enlightened and patriotic and set up local administrations on the European model, often employing large numbers of British administrators and leaving the running of the state to an enlightened dewan or chief minister. Lord Curzon was particularly impressed by Maharaja Madhavrao Scindia of Gwalior, who provided an excellent model for other rulers to follow. According to his grandson, he was 'a down-to-earth, practical type of man, full of common sense . . . He mixed continually with the public and, unlike some rulers, he went abroad only twice in his life. For six months of the year he used to be under canvas or in small inspection bungalows, where the poorest of the poor could approach him'. He also introduced a degree of local government almost unheard of elsewhere in India: directly-elected municipal councils, a five-man panchayat council, a nominated upper chamber and a partially-elected lower chamber. Here was someone who was 'the servant as well as the master of his people', Curzon declared in a speech, and he was proud to claim him 'as my colleague and partner'.

Madhavrao Scindia was also extremely skilful in maintaining good relations with the British. The Gwalior tiger-shoots were the best organised in India, with the largest tigers always appearing in front of the right shooting platform at the right time, so ensuring that the Maharaja dealt directly with Viceroys rather than the Viceroys' Political Agents. He also ensured that he had the ear of the British monarch, asking the Prince and Princess of Wales to be godparents to his two children – and naming them George and Mary. He is remembered today as the

A MUGHAL-STYLE BRONZE TABLEAU MADE IN LUCKNOW DEPICTS THE CAVALCADE OF THE KING OF AVADH AND THE BRITISH RESIDENT. THE TABLEAU REPRESENTS THE STATUS OF MANY RULERS UNDER BRITISH RULE IN THE 19TH CENTURY. TO BELITTLE AND ABOLISH THE TITLE OF THE MUGHAL EMPEROR, THE EAST INDIA COMPANY BESTOWED THE TITLE OF KING ON GHAZI-AD-DIN HAIDAR, THE NAWAB OF AVADH, WHO HAD LENT THE COMPANY ENORMOUS AMOUNTS OF MONEY. HOWEVER, TO KEEP HIM IN HIS PLACE, THE BRITISH RESIDENT AT LUCKNOW WAS ACCORDED THE SAME STATUS AS THE KING OF AVADH ON FORMAL OCCASIONS. THE BRITISH RESIDENT IS SEEN HERE WEARING A *CHAPEAU*, AND THE NEWLY APPOINTED KING, HIS CROWN. THE ELEPHANTS SYMBOLISE POWER.

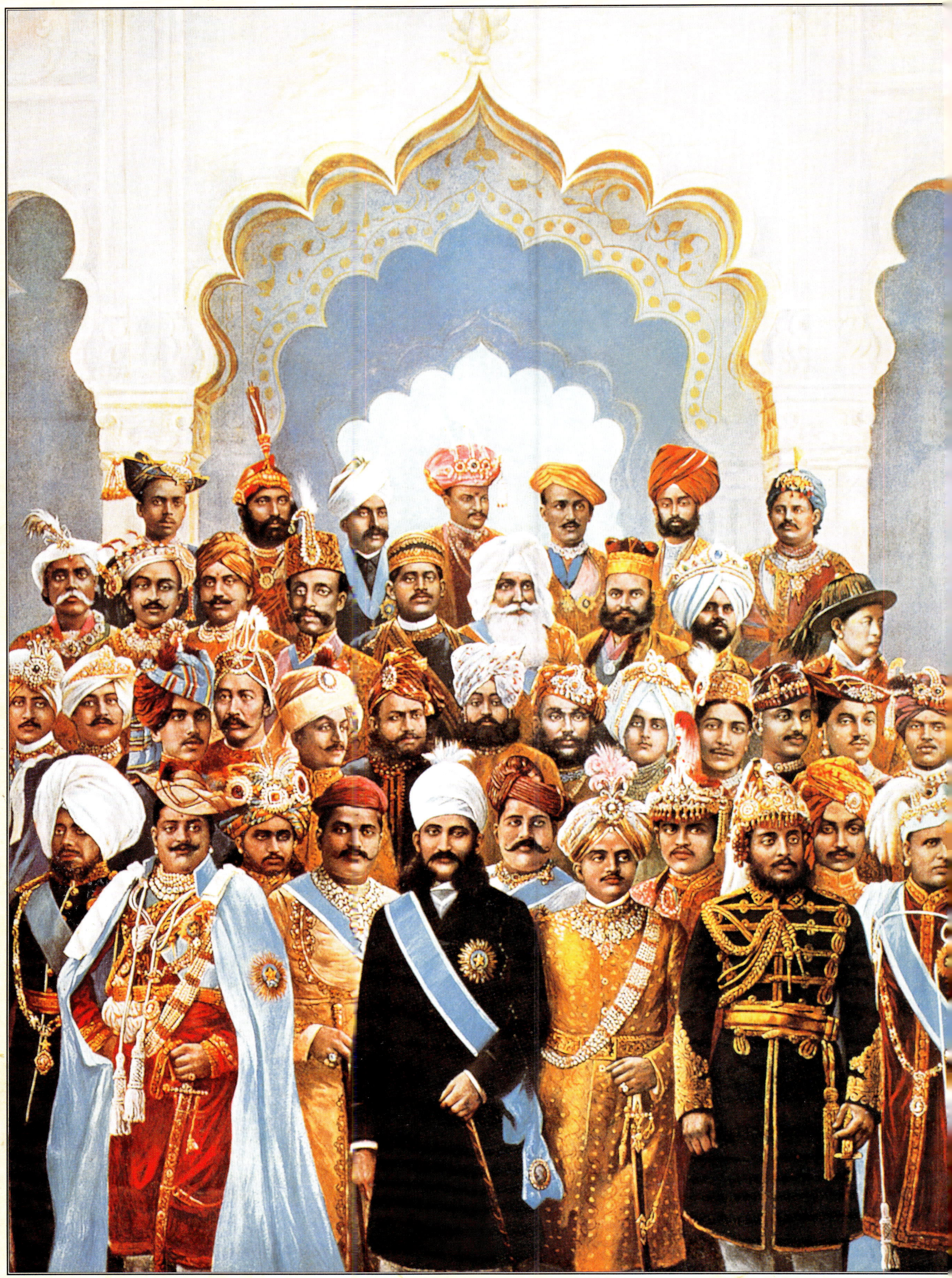

Salute States

**It was with gun salutes being fired on formal occasions
that the British accorded respect to their king, viceroy and the Princely States.**

King Emperor	101 gun salutes
Viceroy	31 gun salutes

League of Princes
First Division States or Salute States: 118
Enjoyed complete jurisdiction within their states and full relations with the Government of India.

Maharaja Gaekwad of Baroda	21 gun salutes
Maharaja Scindia of Gwalior	21 gun salutes
Nizam of Hyderabad and Berar	21 gun salutes
Maharaja of Jammu and Kashmir	21 gun salutes
Maharaja of Mysore	21 gun salutes
Nawab of Bhopal	19 gun salutes
Maharaja Holkar of Indore	19 gun salutes
Khan of Kalat	19 gun salutes
Maharaja of Kohlapur	19 gun salutes
Maharana of Mewar	19 gun salutes
Maharaja of Travancore	19 gun salutes
13 states	17 gun salutes
17 states	15 gun salutes
16 states	13 gun salutes
31 states	11 gun salutes
30 states	9 gun salutes

- Rulers with 13 gun salutes or more were recognised as Maharajas (Great Kings)
- Rulers with 11-9 gun salutes were recognised as Rajas (Kings)

Note. Rulers with 11 gun salutes were also referred to as His Highness.
This caused ill feeling among the 9-gun salute states, and they too had to be given the same honorific.
The exception was the Nizam of Hyderabad (11-gun salute state): he was always addressed as His Exalted Highness.

Second Division States or Non-salute States: 117
- Their rulers were called Chiefs and had limited jurisdiction and full relations with the Government of India.
- The Chiefs were represented or elected in the Chamber of Princes from 1921 onwards.

Non-jurisdictional Estates: 327
- Their rulers were the *Talukdars, Thanedars, Thakurs, Jagirdars*.
- They were hereditary landowners.
- Criminal and civil jurisdiction was carried out 'on their behalf' by Political Agents of the Government of India.

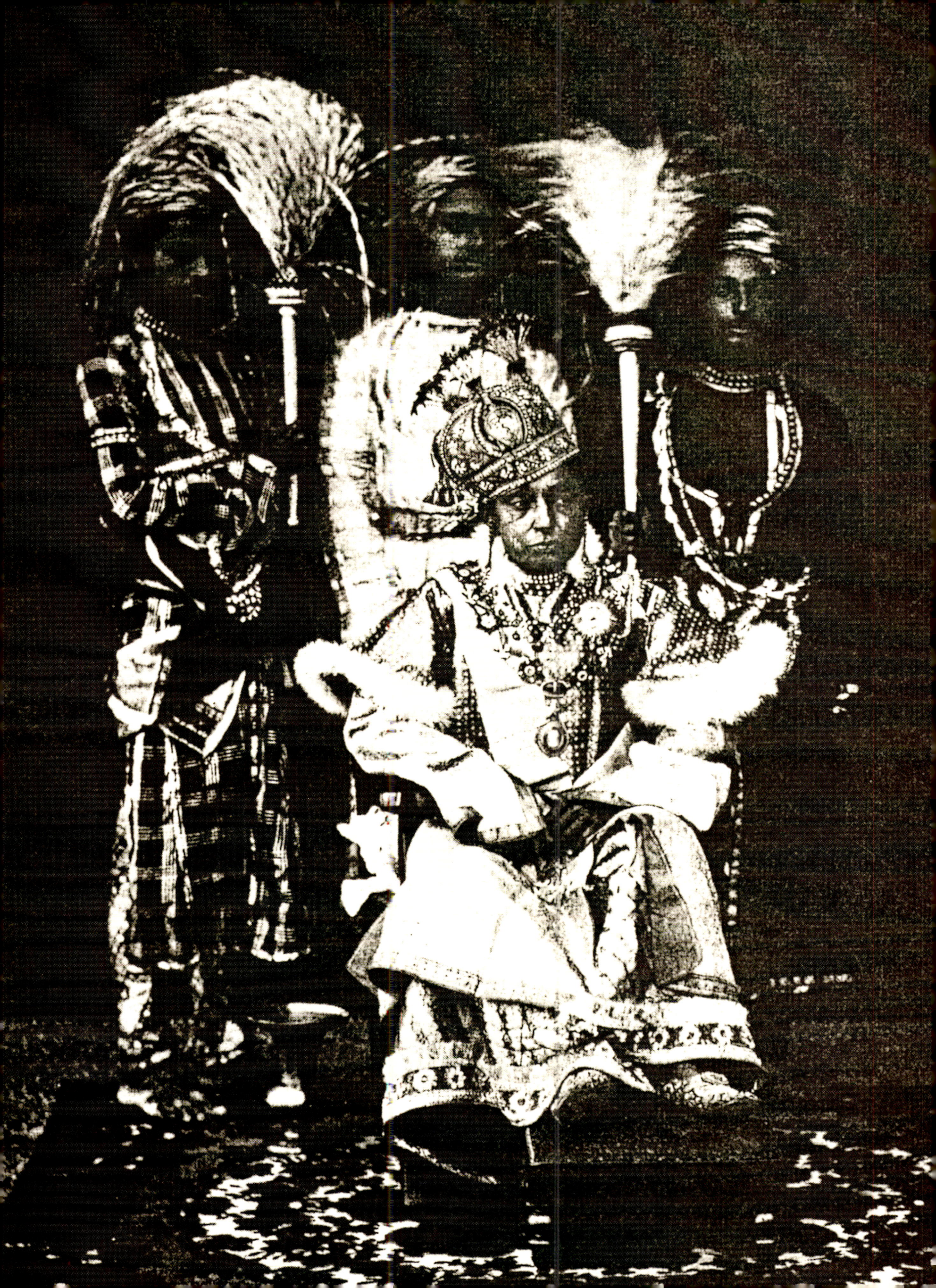

THE ONLY WOMAN RULER OF THE TIME IN ASIA, NAWAB SULTAN JEHAN BEGUM OF BHOPAL WALKS WITH THE PRINCE OF WALES AS SHE WELCOMES HIM IN FEBRUARY 1922. COMPLETELY HIDDEN UNDER A PALE BLUE *BURQA*, SHE WAS, NEVERTHELESS, A PROGRESSIVE AND STRONG RULER WHO ACHIEVED A LOT FOR HER STATE AND THE EMANCIPATION OF WOMEN.

below: MADE FOR MAHBOOB ALI PASHA WHO ASCENDED THE THRONE OF HYDERABAD WHEN HE WAS TWO AND A HALF YEARS OLD, THIS *SARPECH*, TURBAN ORNAMENT, HAS A UNIQUE DESIGN OF DIAMONDS, EMERALD BEADS AND CABOCHON RUBIES SET IN GOLD. ATOP THE CENTRAL PEAR-SHAPED DIAMOND SITS A DIAMOND-STUDDED BIRD WITH A DIAMOND *TAVEEZ* HANGING FROM THE BEAK.

facing page: THE BEGUM OF BHOPAL WITH HER ATTENDANTS. IT WAS NOT EASY FOR A WOMAN TO RULE OVER A STATE, BUT DESCENDING FROM THE AFGHAN ROYAL FAMILY, SHE TOOK HER RESPONSIBILITIES SERIOUSLY, EVEN TOURING THE RURAL AREAS AND LISTENING TO THE COMMON MAN'S PROBLEMS.

maharaja who liked to drive his own state railroad engine at enormous speed, while shouting to his alarmed guests, 'Never fear! Scindia is driving'!

Two other rulers of the late Victorian period regarded as remarkable were the Begum Sahiba of Bhopal, Shah Jehan, and Maharaja Ram Singh II of Jaipur. The Begum was unique in being the only woman ruler in India, although it was a position established by force of personality rather than right by a succession of strong women regents. What made the Begums of Bhopal even more remarkable was that they ruled over a Muslim state, where all women remained in purdah and only appeared in public when covered from head to toe in a *burqa*. Begum Shah Jehan was a widow who became the effective ruler of Bhopal in 1868 at the age of forty-three following the death of her mother. Although there were whispers about the early death of her husband, she ruled extremely effectively, presiding over council meetings from behind a screen and taking a particular interest in women's education.

By Rajput standards Maharaja Ram Singh II of Jaipur was dangerously progressive. Although in many respects a traditionalist who followed Rajput customs and religion, he abolished slavery, the infanticide of girls, the ancient custom of sati and the immolation of Rajput wives on the funeral pyres of their husbands. He ensured that the administration of his kingdom was run on modern lines and he did much to modernise Jaipur itself by introducing gas lighting, waterworks, sanitation and new roads. As well as being a great patron of the arts, he was also an enthusiastic amateur photographer who enjoyed taking self-portraits as well as photographing the women of his zenana, and he encouraged the photographic recording of the activities of Jaipur State. His first marriage was to the daughter of the rival state of Jodhpur, but to reinforce this alliance he also married his bride's sister and first cousin.

In 1900 Lord Curzon sent out a circular defining the princes' duties and encouraging them to follow the paths taken by Gwalior and other 'model rulers'. Significantly, the one enlightened ruler whom he failed to put forward as an example was Gaekwad Sayaji Rao III, Maharaja of Baroda. The Gaekwad had been adopted and placed on the

Durbar Hall of Gwalior Palace. Opulence and splendour marked the interiors of palace halls. Magnificent chandeliers, engraved and embossed ceilings and custom-made carpets spoke volumes of a glory that was . . . top: Maharaja Jayajirao Scindia with his courtiers. He built his city-palace between 1872 and 1874 when the British were still occupying the Fort.

Gwalior

top: The facade of Man Mandir, the Kachhawa ruler Raja Man Singh's palace in Gwalior fort. In his memoirs Babar called this fort the 'pearl in the necklace of Hind'. The fort was first captured by the Maratha general Mahadaji Scindia in 1784. *bottom:* The traditional headgear of the Maratha court of Gwalior – the *Shindeshahi Pagdi*. This headgear is made of nearly twenty yards of specially woven chanderi fabric. It takes the *pagadbandh*, headdress maker, a minimum of two days to make the *pagdi*. The craft of the *pagadbandh* still survives only due to the patronage of the present Maharaja Jyotiraditya Scindia. *top right:* H. H. Maharaja Rao Scindia of Gwalior, whom the British earmarked as one of the most progressive rulers of princely India.

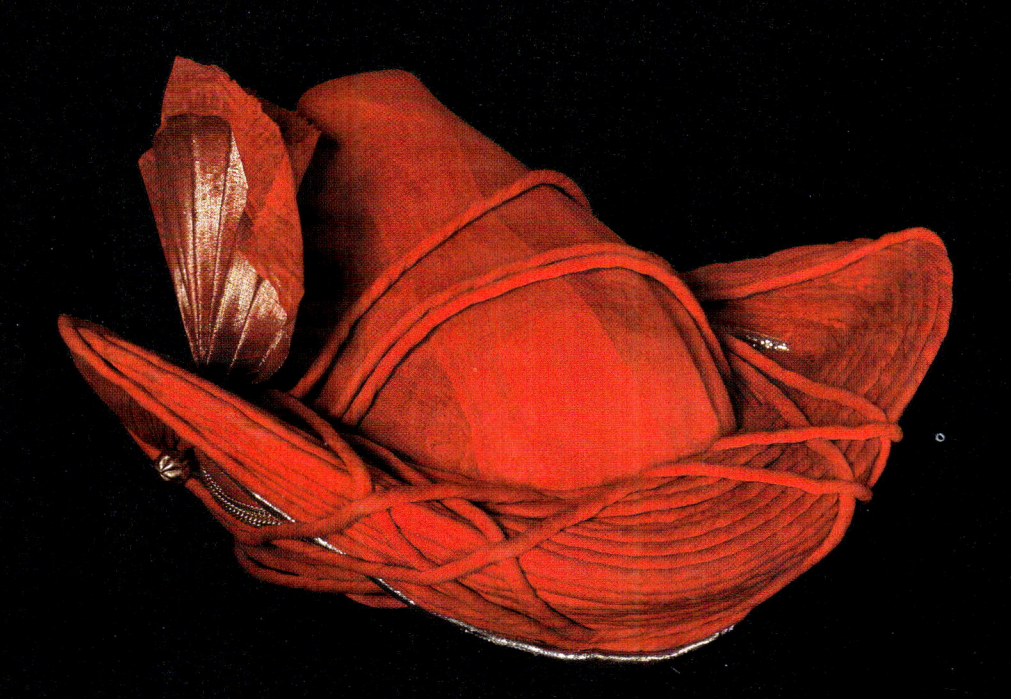

8th century
The fort was built by a Rajput chieftain.

12th century
Captured by Mahmud Ghazni.

13th century
Captured by Muslim raiders.

Taken by a Hindu chieftain.

16th century
Captured by Muslim invaders.

1526
Captured by Mughals.

1770s
Occupied by Scindia family.

Twice captured by British in Maratha wars.

1845
Gwalior troops in Maratha army rebelled.

1857
Gwalior troops joined the Indian Mutiny.

British reclaimed the fort.

1885
Scindias got back the fort.

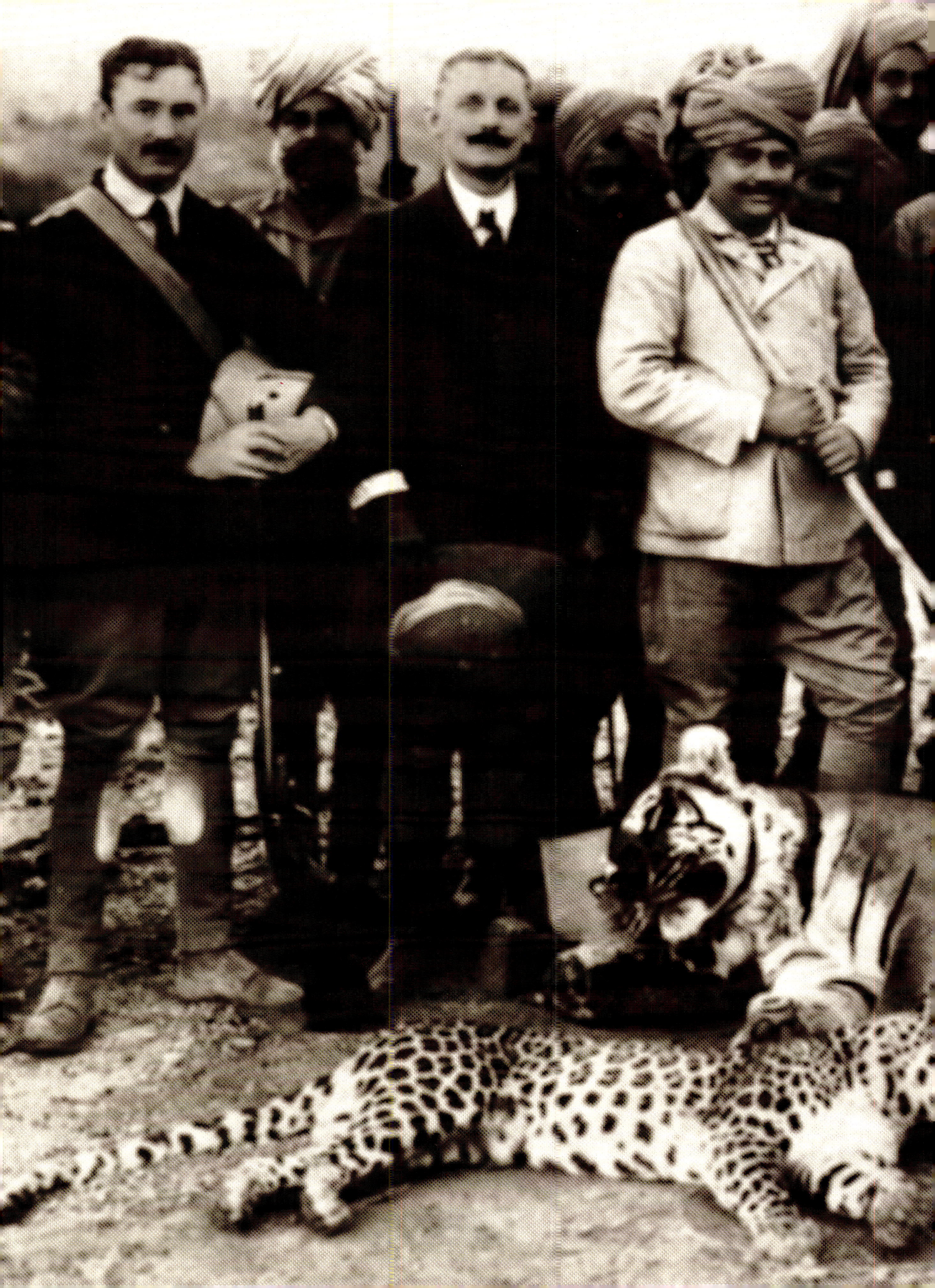

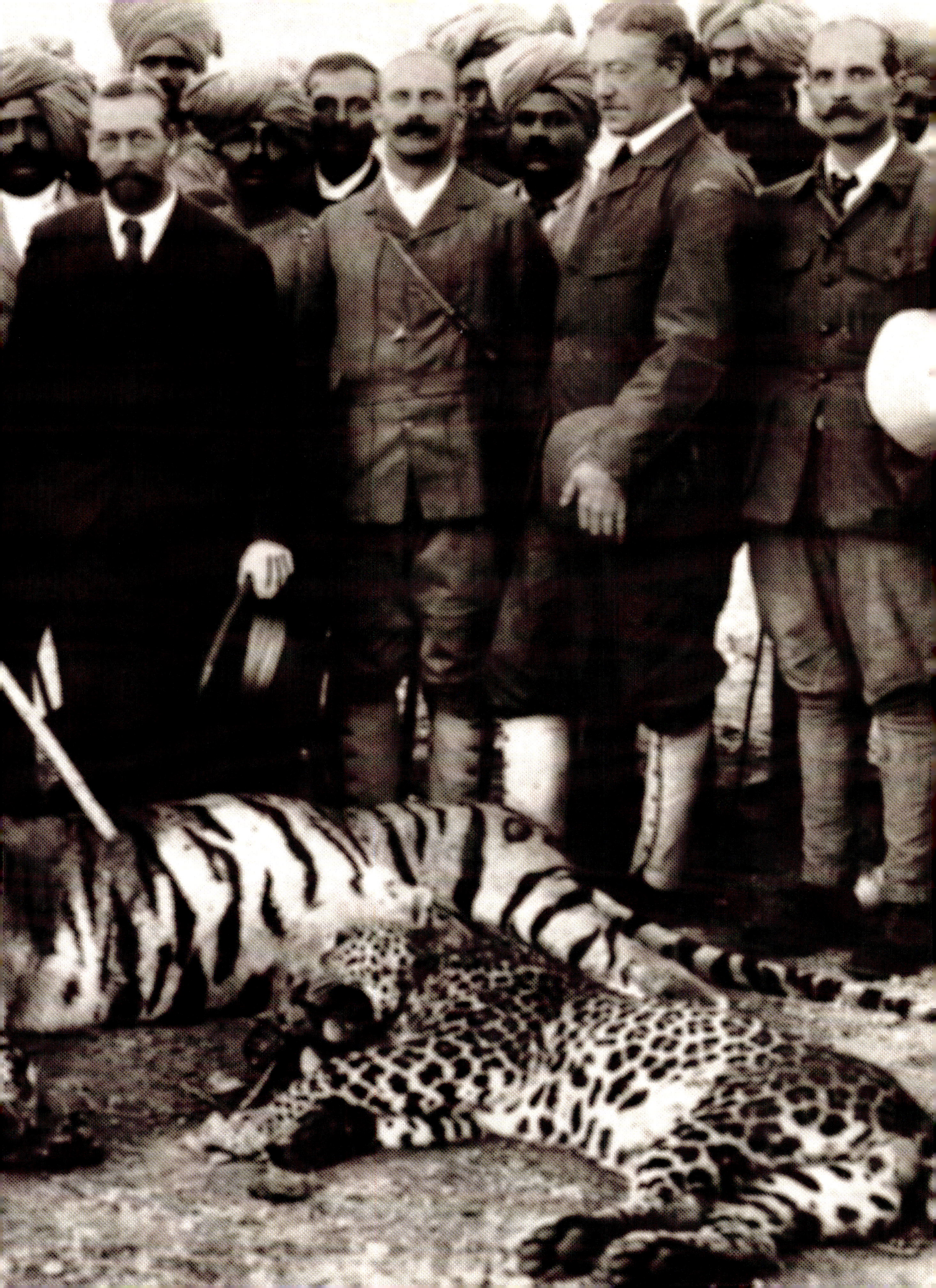

pages 92-93: A prize catch! Maharaja Madhav Rao Scindia of Gwalior points with a stick to a large tiger shot by the Prince of Wales (later King George V) in 1905. Shooting tigers was a prestigious outdoor activity among the Indian royals. The Maharaja himself had eight hundred killings to his credit.
He took military training seriously and believed that both boys and girls of royal families should undergo training and should accompany the state forces on military manoeuvres. The Maharaja also encouraged development of infrastructure and industry in his state.

royal throne of Baroda in 1872 at the age of thirteen following the deposition of the previous ruler for gross misrule. Thanks to an enlightened chief minister and tutor, he developed into a wise and humane ruler, eager to seek out and implement the best aspects of the two cultures. This liberalism brought him into contact with Indian nationalism and the Indian National Congress, which he discreetly supported and funded while at the same time assuring the Viceroy of his loyalty as a subject of the Crown. The Government of India remained deeply suspicious of him – suspicions amply confirmed by the Gaekwad's behaviour at the 1911 Durbar. The princes were all required to advance one after another in order of precedence towards the royal dais, bow three times to the seated figure of the King-Emperor George V and then retire by stepping backwards. All were dressed in their full regalia, richly bedecked with jewels and decorations – except for the Gaekwad, who wore a simple white robe. Instead of following the protocol, he gave no more than a nod before walking back to his seat. Later, he was unable to give a satisfactory explanation for his discourtesy, which was probably due to

nothing more than his absence from the rehearsals. But his actions had been recorded by the newsreel camera and to many delighted Indians and outraged British, the message was crystal clear.

Living in the Past

While Jaipur and Marwar were among the most progressive of the Rajput states at this period, two of the oldest, Udaipur and Bundi, remained resolutely old-fashioned. In Bundi the magnificently bewhiskered Maharao Raja Ragubhir Singh lived very much in the past, following the ancient customs of his forefathers and busying himself in his vast and magnificent medieval palace. Significantly, both he and his neighbour in Udaipur refused to move out into modern quarters. In Udaipur, Maharana Fateh Singh went to enormous lengths to avoid appearing before the Viceroy. Forced by Lord Curzon to attend the Delhi Durbar of 1903 to celebrate the coronation of the new King-Emperor Edward VI, he arrived with a large retinue by train but returned to Udaipur without setting foot in Delhi due to 'sudden ill-health'. The

A 20th century helmet of curved iron plates enjoined with mail in a European style. Coated with black lacquer, with golden creeper and floral designs, it is flanked by two iron ear-guards. The spike is missing. The neck attachment comprises four curved iron sheets lacquered in brown.

top: The young Maharaja of Bharatpur with his courtiers, c. 1865. The Jats of Bharatpur claimed descent from the moon, but were never accepted by the Rajputs. The lakes of Bharatpur were famous for the duck shoots arranged by the Maharaja.

facing page, top: A broad torque or neck collar made of gold and set with white sapphires in a jaali design.
facing page, bottom: Considered to be the holiest of Hindu states (and now cities), the young son of the Maharaja of Benares performs a religious ceremony with him, c. 1973.

process was more or less repeated at George V's Durbar in 1911, although on this occasion he was received at the railway station by the King-Emperor, before again heading back to Udaipur without attending the actual Durbar ceremonies. When the Prince of Wales visited Udaipur in 1920, the Maharana refused to meet him at the railway station, as demanded by protocol. His explanation was: 'He (the Prince of Wales) is like a son to me. Would you expect a father to receive his own son?' This annoyed the British and the following year he was formally deposed in favour of his adopted son.

In Jodhpur, his contemporary, Maharao Jaswant Singh II, might have suffered a similar humiliation had the British known of a youthful indiscretion. As a prince he had been secretly entertaining one of his father's courtesans in his room when the ruler arrived unexpectedly at his door. To conceal the woman's presence the young man grabbed her by the hair and held her suspended outside his window. Puzzled by his son's behaviour, the Maharao advanced across the room – whereupon his son released his grip and the girl fell more than two hundred feet to her death. Whether because of this fatal tryst or for more practical reasons, this prince was the last of the line to live in the ancient Meherangarh fort. After ascending the marble *sringar chowki,* seat of anointing, in Meherangarh's Moti Mahal in 1873 as Maharao Jaswant Singh II, he had a new palace built on the plains below. Not one to care about the state, he left the government of Jodhpur to his half-brother, Pertab Singh – an extremely capable administrator who later became a great favourite of Queen Victoria's, although best remembered today as the inventor of the riding breeches known as jodhpurs.

THE MAHARAJAS IN RETREAT

Loyalty to the British Crown guaranteed the maharajas their place in the sun and throughout British rule in

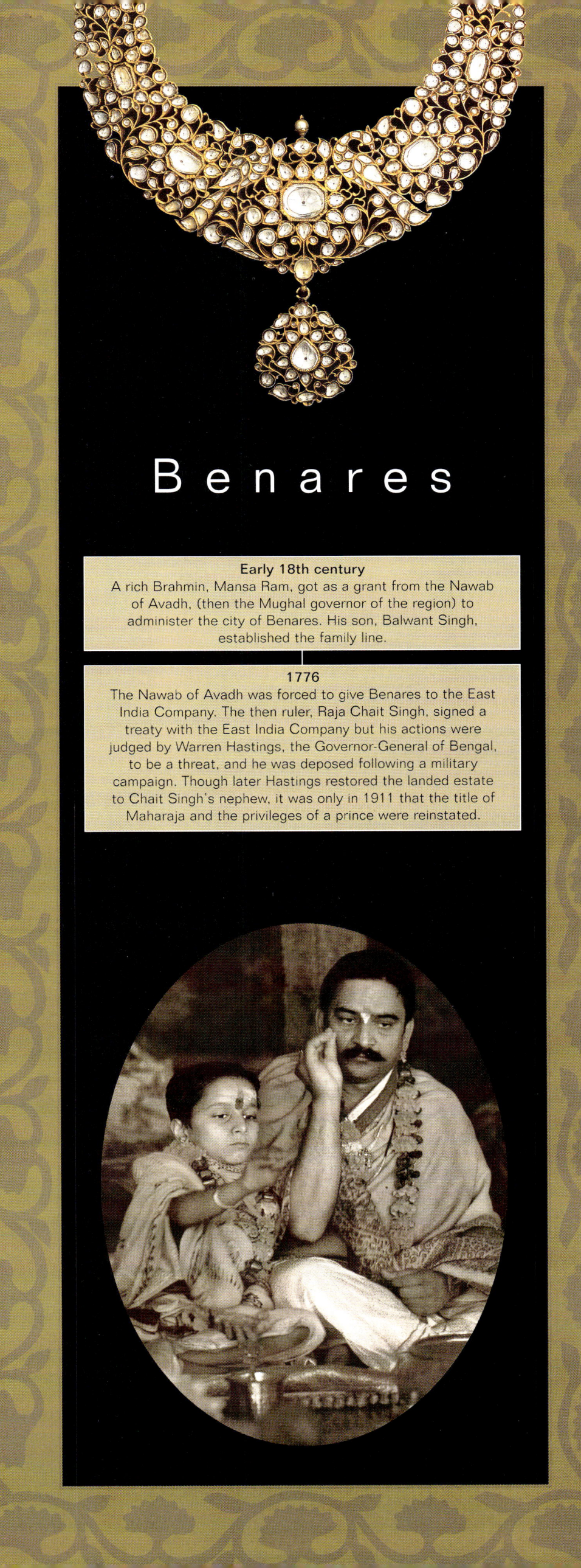

Benares

Early 18th century
A rich Brahmin, Mansa Ram, got as a grant from the Nawab of Avadh, (then the Mughal governor of the region) to administer the city of Benares. His son, Balwant Singh, established the family line.

1776
The Nawab of Avadh was forced to give Benares to the East India Company. The then ruler, Raja Chait Singh, signed a treaty with the East India Company but his actions were judged by Warren Hastings, the Governor-General of Bengal, to be a threat, and he was deposed following a military campaign. Though later Hastings restored the landed estate to Chait Singh's nephew, it was only in 1911 that the title of Maharaja and the privileges of a prince were reinstated.

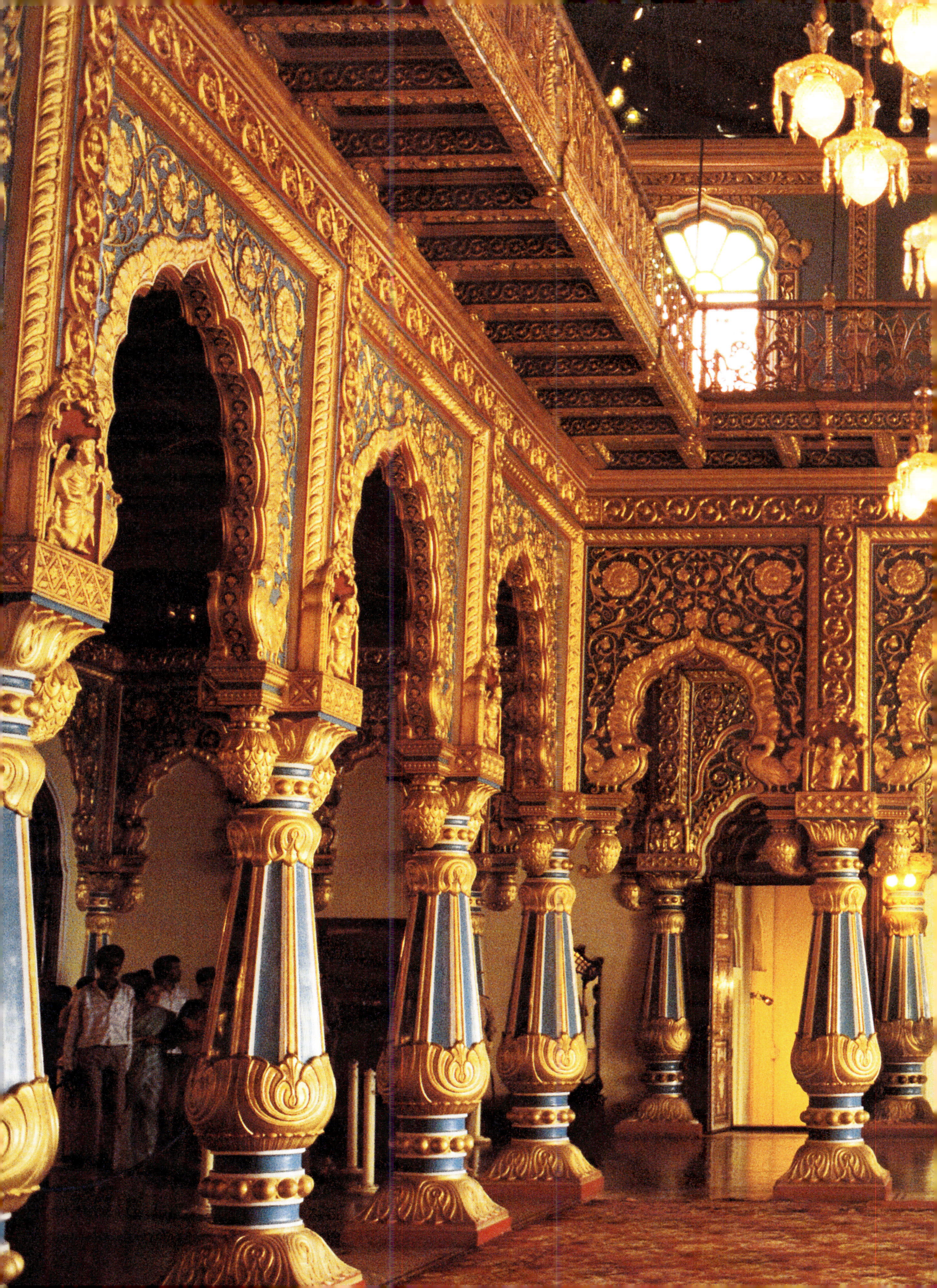

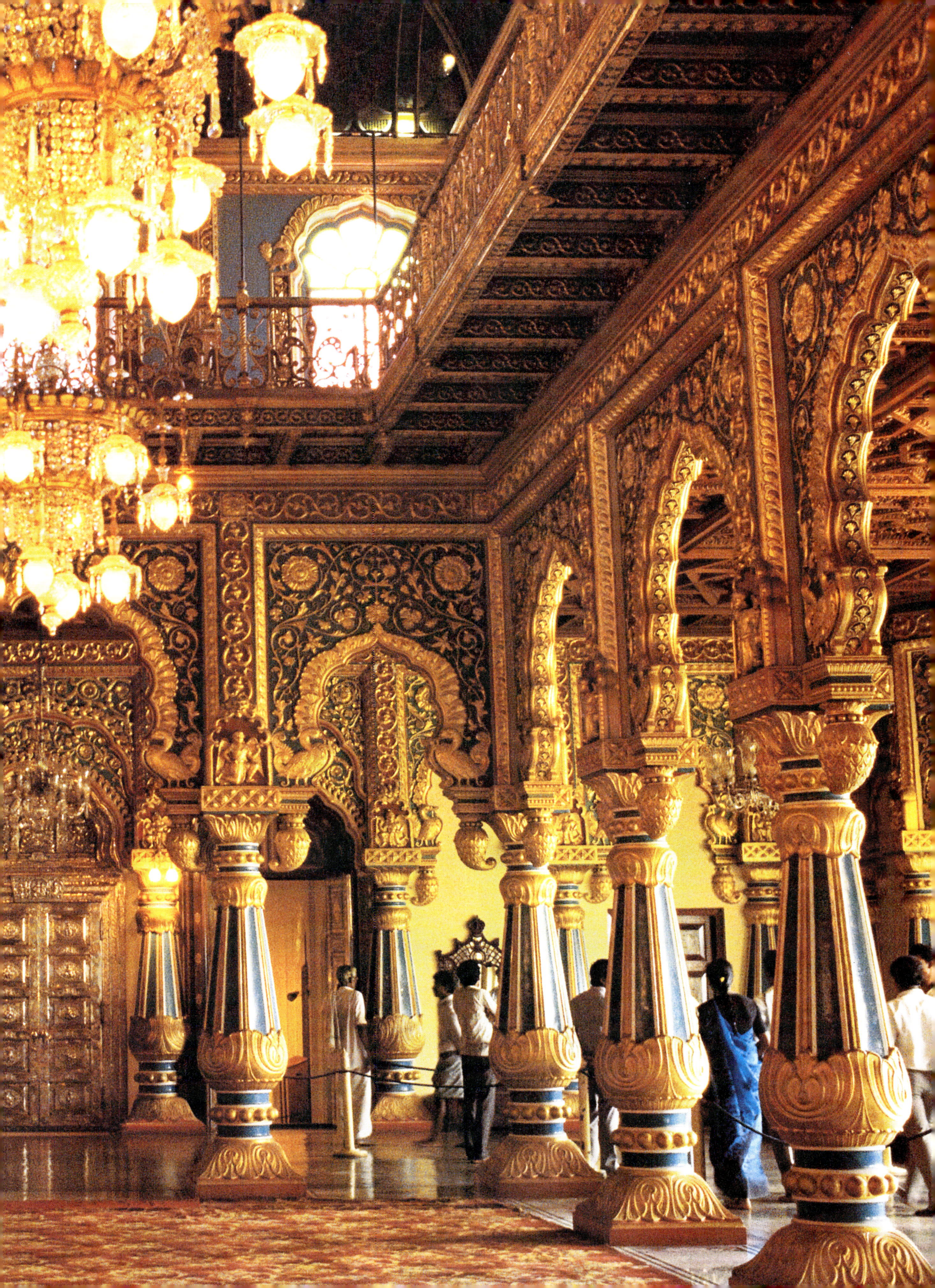

independence from Britain as a threat to their survival.

The maharajas refused to read the writing on the wall, continuing to live as their forefathers had done. Encouraged to spend no more than ten per cent of their annual revenues on themselves, most continued to use these revenues as they wished. Some, like the charismatic polo-playing Maharaja Jai Singh II of Jaipur, continued to modernise their states and implement modest political reforms. But many more behaved as if there were no tomorrow, living and spending with ostentation and extravagance.

THE WINDS OF CHANGE

When independence came to the subcontinent in 1947, the princes were unprepared and unable to present a common front to the challenges facing them. The best acted in the greater public interest and, when British paramountcy lapsed, urged their colleagues to ally their states and principalities with either India or Pakistan. A year later all but a handful voluntarily surrendered their sovereignty and their states, and in return were granted certain constitutional rights such as the retention of their titles and pensions. Had they then abstained from politics their new honorary status might have remained unaffected, but the decision by a number of ex-rulers or members of their families to stand for election to parliament was a fatal mistake. The maharajas' successes in the polls in elections from 1952 onwards, nearly always standing in opposition to the governing Congress Party, was seen by the leaders of

India, all but a few princes toed the line. Their loyalty was exemplified by strong local rulers such as Maharaja Ganga Singh of Bikaner, among the first to show his support for Britain at the start of the First World War. Many fellow-maharajas followed suit and their reward was the setting up of the Chamber of Princes in 1921, a debating body that offered advice to the Government of India but had no real powers of its own. But as the nationalist movement gained strength in the 1920s, the princes found themselves under ever-growing pressure to modernise and democratise, and to remain loyal supporters of the British, or to align with the new political parties demanding independence. A few rulers offered covert support to the nationalists but the great majority remained hostile or indifferent, viewing

top: A YOUNG WESTERN INDIAN PRINCE STANDS COCKILY – IS HE ALREADY AWARE OF HIS STATUS AND RESPONSIBILITIES? BORN WITH A SILVER SPOON IN THEIR MOUTH, ROYALTY IN DRESS AND MANNERISMS CAME NATURALLY TO THE MANOR BORN.

right: A *KARCHOBE* WORK *TOPI*, CAP, ADORNED WITH SEED PEARLS FROM GWALIOR (EARLY 20TH CENTURY).

pages 96-97: MYSORE PALACE. THE EXQUISITELY PAINTED WALLS AND COLUMNS IN GOLD LEAF AND BLUE NEED NO FURTHER EMBELLISHMENT TO PRESENT A PICTURE OF GRANDEUR.

that party as a challenge to democratic government. Although she was not the first to enter politics, Maharani Gayatri Devi of Jaipur won a landslide victory against a Congress opponent in her home state in 1962. In December 1970 a bill derecognising the princes and removing their privileges was passed in India's Lower House but voted out in the Upper House. It was then pushed through by Presidential Order. There was a brief stay of execution when this Order was declared unlawful but a second bill, passed by both houses, saw the maharajas pass into history.

The derecognition of the maharajas and the end of their privy purses was a deathblow for most ancient royal houses. Government legislation limiting landownership meant the break-up of the landed estates. Drastic changes of lifestyle had to be made and for some this was infinitely harder than the withdrawal of their ancient titles, for even though no longer officially in use, these titles are now regarded as honorary and are still widely used out of respect to their owners.

The first to go were the retainers and staff, who in some cases had been linked to the royal house for centuries and often had no other source of employment. Many chose to stay on without pay so long as a roof remained over their heads. The process of selling off the family assets had begun long before 1970 but was now accelerated. All objects of value were supposed to have been declared but, of course, a great deal had not and many discreet visits abroad to jewellers and art houses in London, Paris and New York took place in the years that followed, greatly to India's loss. However, the most valuable assets that the maharajas had been allowed to retain proved in many cases to be the greatest headaches: their royal palaces and properties. To many these vast buildings seemed nothing less than white elephants, impossible to keep and maintain. As a result many were offered to the government in lieu of taxes, today serving as government offices and schools.

The first to see their true potential was Maharaja Sawai Jai Singh II of Jaipur, who in the 1960s planned to convert one of his many Jaipur palaces into a hotel

top left: A MAHARASHTRIAN NOSE-RING, MADE OF PEARLS, DIAMONDS AND EMERALDS STRUNG ON GOLD WIRE. SUCH NOSE-RINGS WERE POPULAR IN THE 19TH CENTURY AND FORMED A DEFINITE PART OF A BRIDE'S JEWELLERY.
top right: MAHARANI JAMNA BAI OF BARODA. THE MAHARANI IS WEARING A *PAITHANI*, NINE-YARD SARI, GOLD ANKLETS AND TOE RINGS. IT WAS UNUSUAL FOR ROYAL WOMEN TO BE PHOTOGRAPHED IN THOSE DAYS. THIS PICTURE BY HANSAJI RAGHUNATH, TAKEN IN 1878, IS AN EXCEPTION. A VERY FAMOUS PAINTING MADE FROM THIS PHOTOGRAPH ADORNS THE WALLS OF THE PALACE ART GALLERY AT BARODA.
pages 100-101: THIS PHOTOGRAPH FIGURED IN THE ALBUM PRESENTED TO THE MAHARAJA OF DHARANGDHARA BY THE MAHARAJA OF RATLAM IN 1880. IT WAS PROBABLY TAKEN BY BOURNE AND SHEPHERD, CALCUTTA.

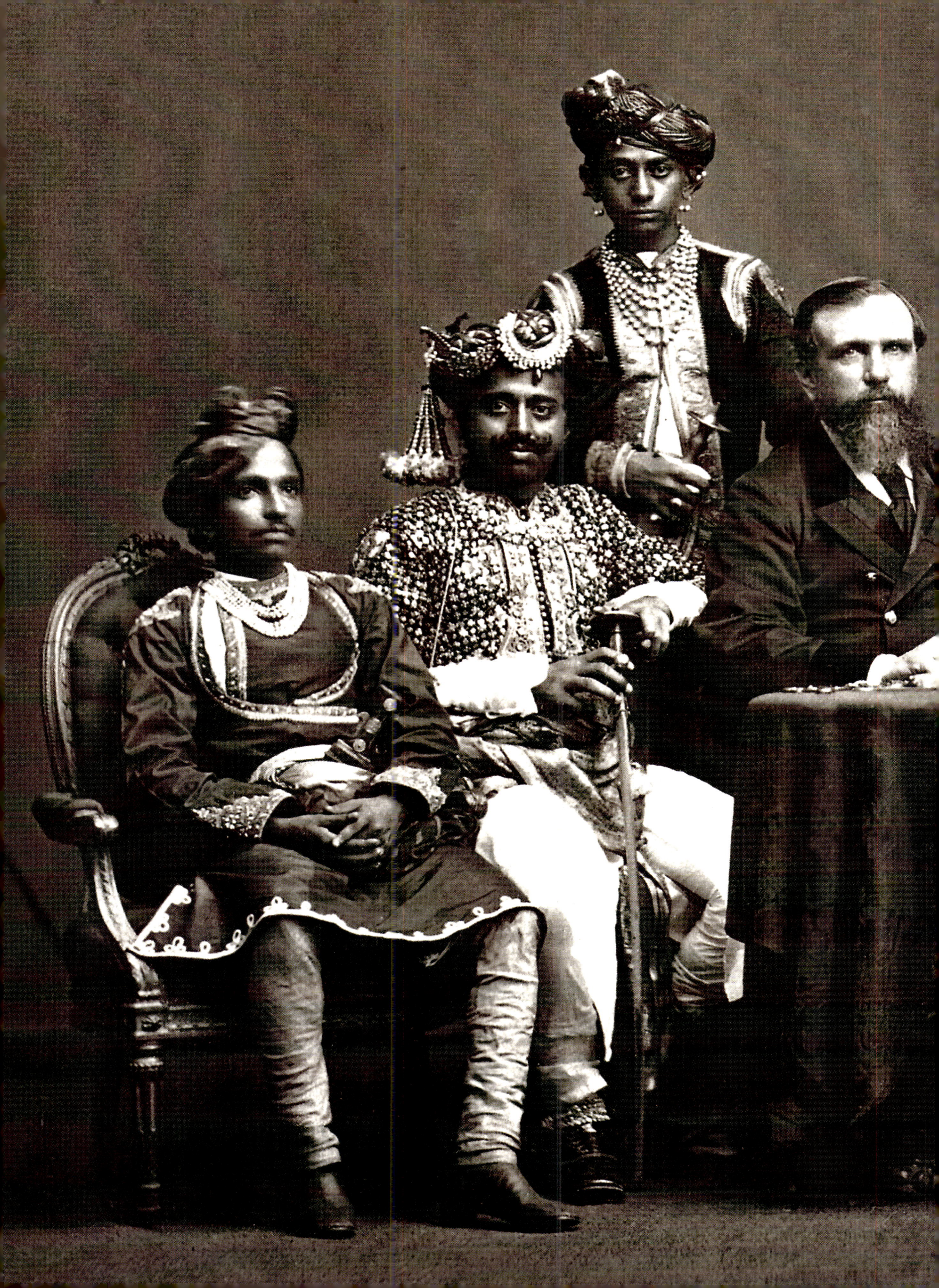

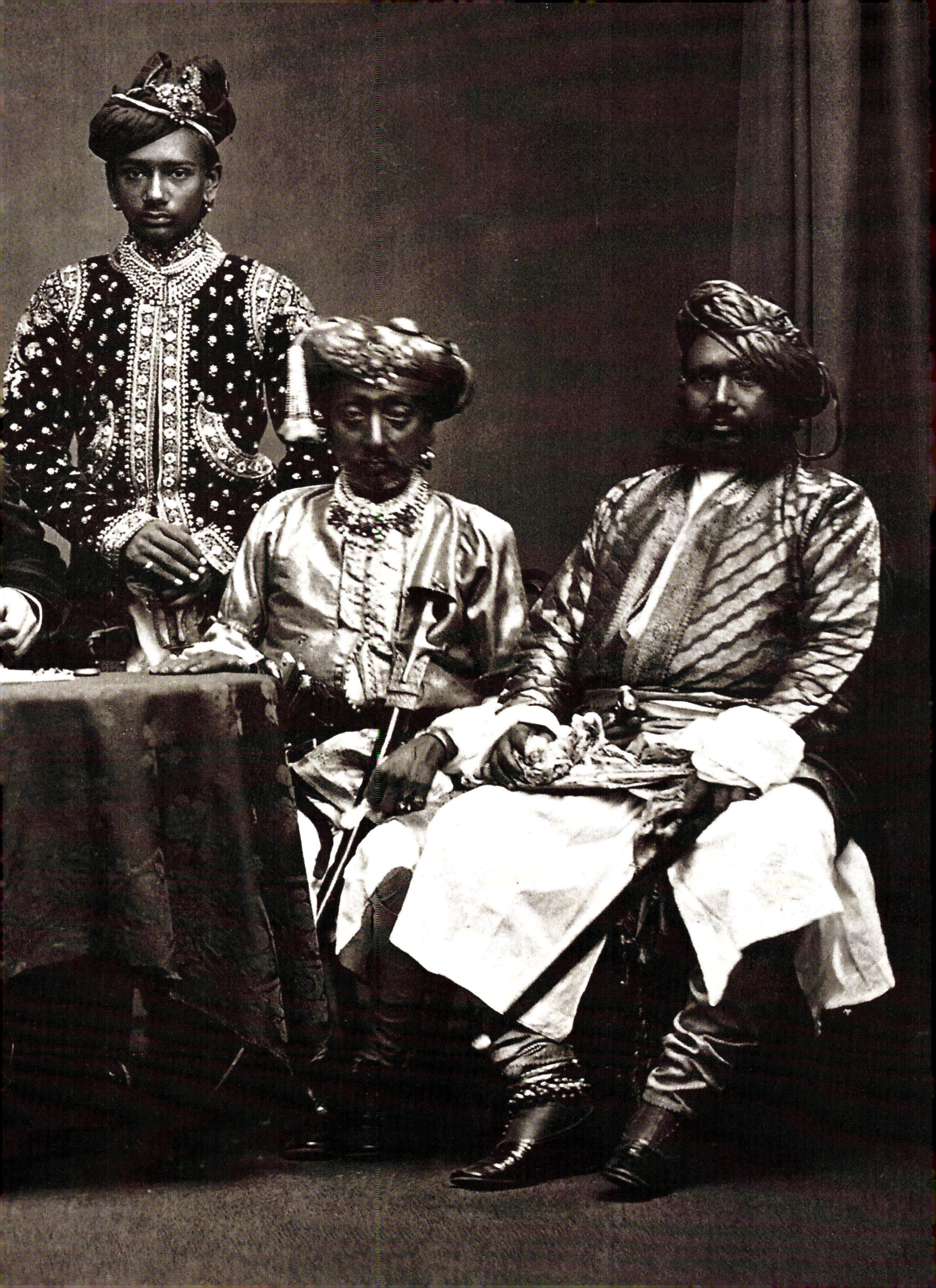

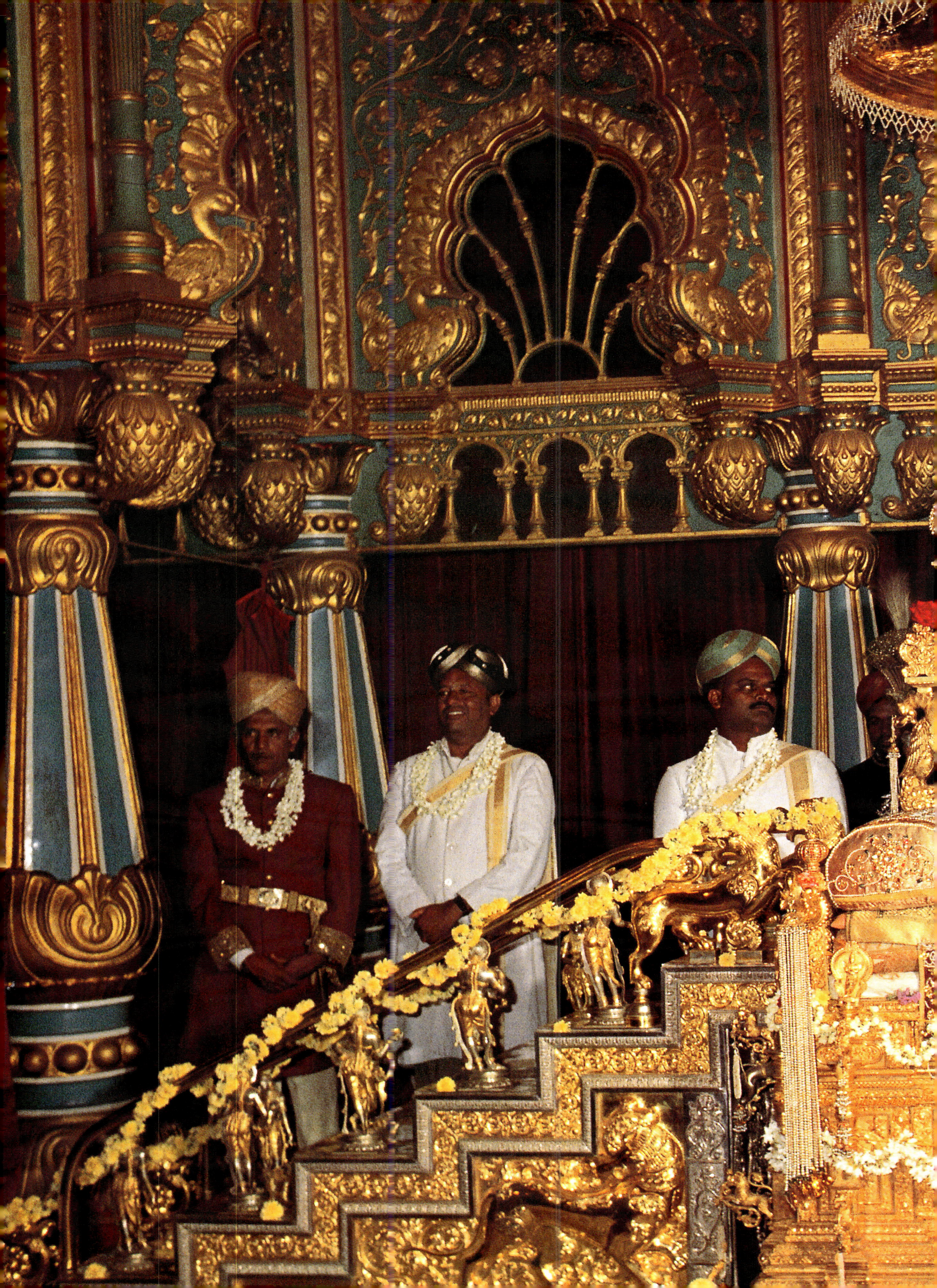

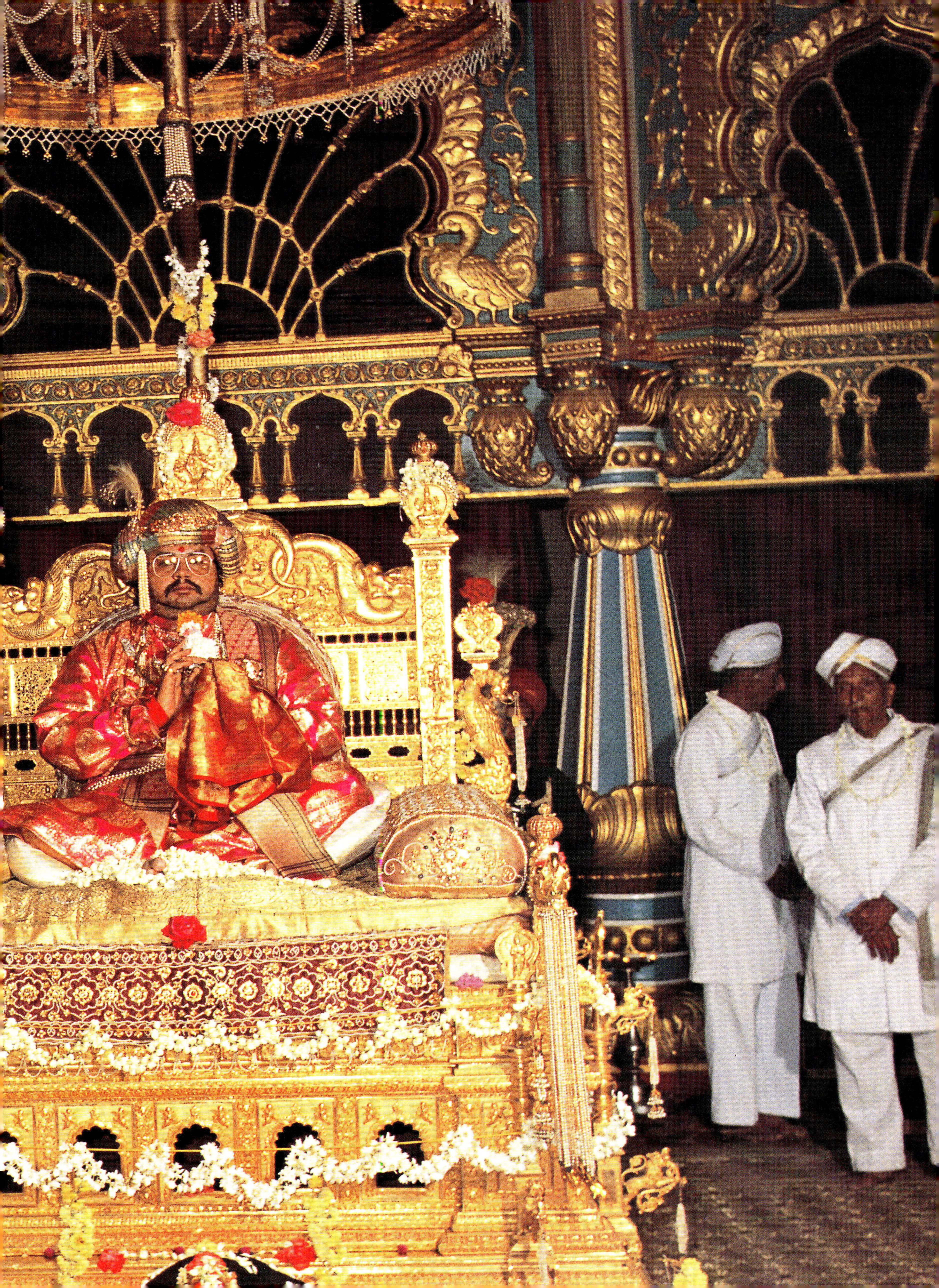

for the growing numbers of international air-travellers who now saw India as a tourist destination. This was not the City Palace but the Rambagh Palace, where he and his third wife Maharani Gayatri Devi had spent their married lives. Although the popular Jai Singh died of a heart attack on the polo field before his plans could fully fructify, the Rambagh became the first of scores of palace hotels – in many cases crumbling palaces or *havelis*, restored and revitalised under the management of hotel chains such as the Taj Group. Undoubtedly the most internationally famous was Udaipur's marble Lake Palace, formerly the water palace of Jag Nivas, whose picturesque setting on Lake Pichhola, with the ramparts and turrets of Udaipur's ancient City Palace, has made it the archetypal image of Rajasthan. 'Here,' wrote James Tod of its original occupants, 'they listened to the tale of the bard and slept off their noonday opiate amidst the cool breezes of the lake, wafting delicious odours from myriads of lotus flowers.' Today these palace hotels in India have not only given their owners and many of their former retainers a new lease of life but have also played an important role in keeping alive traditional arts and crafts such as fresco painting and stone-carving.

Indeed, it can be said that one of the most positive legacies of the maharajas is the continuing tradition of patronage: many of the former Princely States continue to be bastions of culture, attracting tourists and so helping to keep traditional arts and crafts alive. The old royal schools of classical music known as *gharanas* that were once a feature of many states in Rajasthan and central India, continue to flourish. In many cases members of the old royal families continue to promote and support local traditional crafts – few more tirelessly than the widow of Maharaja Sawai Jai Singh II of Jaipur, Rajmata Gayatri Devi, who has revitalised the famous blue pottery of Jaipur and seen it and other crafts grow into major industries. Many have turned their palaces and their contents into trusts, converting them into repositories of culture in the form of museums and libraries open to the public and scholars. After years of neglect by the central government many such buildings are being recognised as part of India's national heritage and given protected status under such organisations as the Indian National Trust for Art and Cultural Heritage (INTACH), India's equivalent of Britain's National Trust and National Heritage schemes. Here, too, many princes and their descendants continue to play leading roles.

Politics and diplomacy continue to attract many of the maharajas and their families: many entered the diplomatic services of India and Pakistan and continue to serve their respective republics with distinction; others entered politics and a number have enjoyed distinguished careers as government ministers, including the late Madhavrao Scindia of Gwalior and Dr Karan Singh of Kashmir – although it has to be said that an equal number failed as politicians, expecting

pages 102-103: Maharaja Srikantdattanarsimharaja Wodeyar of Mysore seated on a golden throne during Dussehra celebrations. The state of Mysore under the Wodeyars was one of the most efficiently administered states in India. It was famous for its spectacular religious ceremonies and its patronage of a high calibre of musicians. The Amba Vilas Palace in Mysore built at the beginning of the 20th century is a unique blend of South Indian temple, Mughal and European Baroque architecture. It has a magnificent Durbar Hall with numerous thick columns. The interior is profusely decorated in bright colours with exquisite metal and woodwork.

automatic election and re-election without accepting that politics is a two-way street. A number of the more forward-looking princely states and their rulers, notably the Gaekwads of Baroda and the Scindias of Gwalior, long ago invested in commercial interests with the result that today their families are successful business leaders. To many Rajputs, however, the idea of going into business is an offence to their pride and it seems they would sooner eke out a modest living as petty landowners than dirty their hands with money. Some of these Rajputs have failed to adapt to the modern world and found solace in drink and dreams of past glories.

In Udaipur, the Sisodia clan is riven in a family quarrel that began with the bitter legacy left by the fifty-fifth Maharana, Bhagwat Singh, who turned his family against him by abandoning his wife for an Englishwoman. His eldest son Maharana Mahendra Singh has the royal title, while his younger brother, Arvind Singh, has the palaces and the revenues. Whereas in the past such quarrels might have been resolved in the battlefield, today they are fought in the law courts over decades, with the lawyers as the only winners. Their neighbours in Jaipur, the Kachhawas, have been luckier for Jaipur has been one of the great success stories of international tourism. Here too there has been dissension with the once powerful family adjusting to a new role as entrepreneurs. Much of the success in the selling of the 'pink city' is due to the present Maharaja, Colonel Bhawani Singh, and his family, greatly aided by his stepmother, Rajmata Gayatri Devi, who has done a lot in the last sixty years to promote a modern image of Indian royalty.

Jaipur has been both a bastion of tradition and an agent for change. Maharaja Bhawani Singh's sole heir, Princess Diya Kumari, was undoubtedly the most eligible bride in India, and ought to have been betrothed to the most eligible Rajput prince in India. Instead, she broke with centuries of tradition and made history by marrying a Rajput commoner, a humble aide of her father's.

Perhaps the ideal balance between the royal past and the democratic present can be found in Jodhpur. Maharaja Gaj Singh II or Bapji, as he is widely known, acceded the royal throne of Jodhpur at the age of four after his father was killed in an aeroplane crash in 1952. After his education in England and a period of diplomatic service overseas he returned to Jodhpur determined to preserve the best of the past and to improve the living standards of ordinary Jodhpuris. He plays a central role in Jodhpur's annual round of colourful ceremonies and has encouraged the growth of tourism. His social welfare programmes range from women's education to the improvement of the status of widows. In doing so he has returned to act as the *mabaap* or father and mother of his people and their *annadata*, giver of food. The wheel, in fact, has turned full circle.

SEATED ON HIS GOLD THRONE DURING DUSSEHRA CELEBRATIONS, THE MAHARAJA OF MYSORE RECEIVES GREETINGS FROM A COURTIER. DUSSEHRA, SIGNIFYING VICTORY OF GOOD OVER EVIL IS THE MOST IMPORTANT FESTIVAL OF THE KSHATRIYA, WARRIOR CASTE, AND IN FORMER TIMES, IT WAS CELEBRATED ON A VERY LARGE SCALE. TODAY MYSORE IS ONE OF THE FEW STATES THAT CONTINUE THIS ROYAL TRADITION. THE FESTIVAL LASTS A TOTAL OF TEN DAYS AND EACH EVENING A ROYAL DURBAR IS HELD IN WHICH THE MAHARAJA WEARS PRICELESS ROBES AND JEWELS. ON THE TENTH DAY OF THE CELEBRATIONS THE MAHARAJA SITTING IN A GOLDEN *HOWDAH*, RIDING AN ORNATELY DECORATED ELEPHANT AND SURROUNDED BY HIS ATTENDANTS AND THRONGED BY THOUSANDS OF PEOPLE, GOES OUT IN A CEREMONIAL PROCESSION FROM THE PALACE TO THE PARADE GROUND. THE PROCESSION IS ACCOMPANIED BY HUNDREDS OF CAMELS, HORSES AND ELEPHANTS. THE RICHLY ILLUMINATED PALACE IS ALSO A SIGHT TO BEHOLD.

facing page, top left: THE MAHARANI OF MYSORE ADJUSTS HER HUSBAND'S JEWELLERY AS HE GETS READY FOR DUSSEHRA PUJA, WHILE AN OLD RETAINER HOLDS A TRAY FULL OF PRECIOUS ORNAMENTS IN THE FOREGROUND. THE MAHARAJA HAS BEEN IN POLITICS FOR A LONG TIME AND IS A MEMBER OF PARLIAMENT.

DRESSED IN TRADITIONAL SOUTHERN STYLE, THE MAHARAJA WEARS A HEAVY BENARASI BROCADE *ACHKAN* OVER A BROCADE *SIDHA PYJAMA*. A YELLOW *PATKA* IS TIED AROUND HIS WAIST AND SHOULDER. HIS *JUTTIS*, SLIPPERS, ARE EMBROIDERED AND A PLUMED *KALGI* ADORNS HIS TURBAN.

THE MAHARANI IS WEARING A GOLD BELT IN MYSORE STYLE. **pages 104-105, top centre:** AFTER VISITING A FAMILY TEMPLE DURING DUSSEHRA, THE MAHARAJA OF MYSORE IS HELPED BY A RETAINER TO PUT ON HIS SLIPPERS. HIS FAMILY MEMBERS ARE SEEN IN WHITE, ALONG WITH *CHOBDARS*, MACE BEARERS.

Lives of
All Rem

Great Men
ind Us....

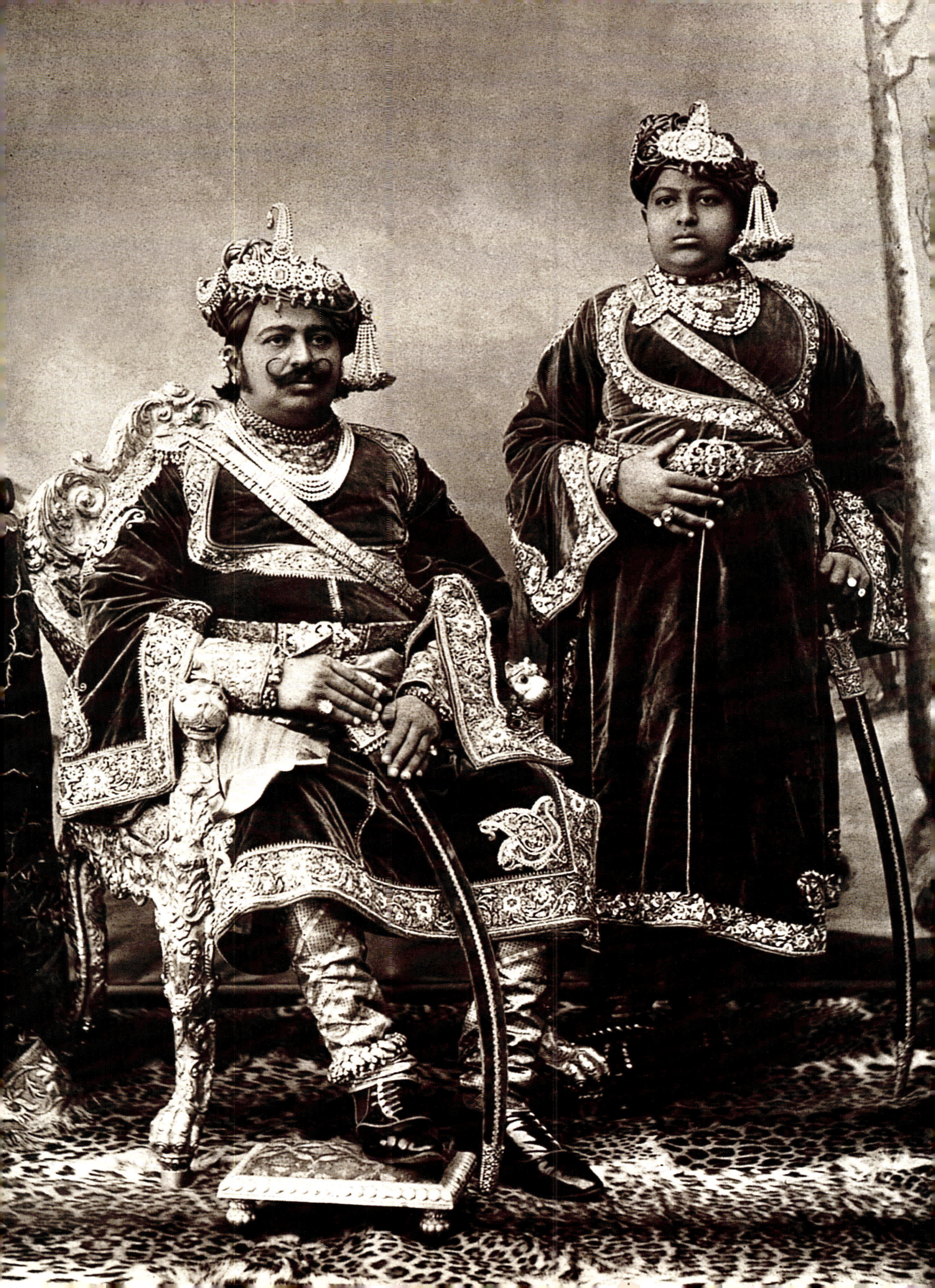

In his classic history, *Annals of Rajasthan*, the British political officer-turned-historian James Tod wrote that, firstly, 'The Rajput worships his horse, his sword and the sun, and attends more to the Martial Song of the Bard than the Litany of the Brahmin'; and secondly, 'Fidelity to the chief is the climax of all virtues. The Rajput is taught from his infancy, in the song of the bard, to regard it as the source of honour here and of happiness hereafter'. These two elements – the warrior ethic and loyalty to the clan – became the essence of Rajput culture, which developed into a warrior cult that was a cross between the code of bushido evolved by the samurai in Japan and knightly chivalry in medieval Europe. This same culture was adopted by the non-Rajput Maratha warlords and others such as the Sikh clan-leaders who came to power in their wake in the eighteenth and early nineteenth centuries. They too had a strong martial tradition that adapted itself well to the ancient traditions of Indian kingship, reflected in the vibrant cultures of the societies that grew up in their respective kingdoms. A lifestyle soon evolved around this twin code, centred on the figure of the clan chief or raja, whose nobles attended him at his court or durbar and paid tribute in gold coins. These same nobles were powerful men with their own estates where homage was paid to them by their knights, who in their turn, had their own small manorial estates where they too ruled as local chieftains.

Forts and Palaces: Bastions of Royal Power

The first act of a new ruler was to strengthen his defences, so that the legacy of India's maharajas comprises the scores of forts and citadels to be found throughout central India, many now in ruins and all but swallowed up by jungle. With its foundations laid in the seventh century, Ajmer's Taragarh or Star Fort (from the star-like shape of its bastions) is arguably the oldest stone fort in India. But these forts also had to house their ruler's family and followers. As each succeeding chief did his best to strengthen, enlarge and beautify his fortress, these buildings were transformed into huge fortified palaces. Nowhere is this better displayed than at the great, rambling palace at Bundi, which the writer Rudyard Kipling was moved to describe as 'such a palace as men build for themselves in uneasy dreams – the work of goblins more than the work of men. It is built into and out of hillside, in gigantic terrace on terrace, and dominates the whole of the city ... Looking at it from below, the Englishman could readily believe that nothing was impossible for those who had built it. The dominant impression was of height – height that heaved itself out of the hillside and weighed upon the eyelids of the beholder.' With success and greater security came additional structures that reflected the ruler's growing power: summer palaces, pleasure palaces, hunting lodges, memorial cenotaphs and temples – and a style of living that reflected their culture. The men lived in the world of the *mardana*, the more open part of the palace-fort. Its focal point was the Durbar Hall, modelled on the Mughal Diwan-i-Am, Hall of Public Audience, and decorated to make it as visually impressive as possible. This was where the maharaja met his courtiers, received petitions from his subjects and accepted *nazar*, tribute, usually in the form of silver coins, at impressive public ceremonies. These durbars took place on such occasions as the ruler's birthday or at the end of important festivals of the year.

Seven-year-old Princess Rajkumari Setu Laxmibai of Travancore. The Maharaja adopted her and her cousin Parvatibai as his nieces: the child born first to either of them was to become his heir. Travancore was a matriarchal state where succession passed through the ruler's eldest sister to her son. Setu Laxmibai's childhood was spent in the beautiful Sundervilas Palace. At the age of ten she selected her husband from one of two brothers who were shown to her from one of the palace windows. She selected the younger brother.

facing page: The Raja of Bansda and his heir to be. Dressed in the royal regalia of the late 19th century, the raja ruled over an area of 348 square miles.
pages 106-107: A Nepalese turban of diamonds, emeralds and rubies.

top: A TABLE MADE OF BELGIAN CRYSTAL IN THE CRYSTAL ROOM OF SHIV NIWAS PALACE, UDAIPUR. THE WALLS AND PILLARS ARE PROFUSELY INLAID WITH COLOURED GLASS DEPICTING ANIMAL AND BIRD SCENES FROM BOTH AFRICA AND INDIA. LIKE MANY OTHER PALACES IN INDIA, SHIV NIWAS IS RUN AS A LUXURY HOTEL BY MEMBERS OF THE UDAIPUR ROYAL FAMILY.

pages 110-111, top centre: A BEAUTIFULLY PAINTED CEILING OF THE PHOOL MAHAL PALACE IN JODHPUR'S MEHERANGADH FORT. PURE GOLD LEAF AND RICH EARTH COLOURS HAVE BEEN USED RESULTING IN THE BRIGHT, FRESH LOOK EVEN CENTURIES LATER.

The fortress of Amber, the first citadel of the Kachhwahas, overlooks the Maota Lake and modern-day Jaipur. Probably named after the goddess Amba Mata, its entry is through the Suraj Pol, the Sun Gate, that faces the east to catch the first rays of the sun. The two subsidiary forts of Najafgarh and Jaigarh add further grandeur to the surroundings overlooking Jaipur. It is averred that when Sawai Jai Singh started to renovate the Najafgarh Fort, the newly built walls collapsed every night till religious rites were conducted to appease the spirit of Nahar Singh, an old warrior whose cenotaph it was stated to be. Jaigarh Fort houses the world's largest cannon on wheels which boasts a six-metre long barrel. Ironically, apart from a trial run, the cannon was never used in battle.

No less imposing are the walls of Meherangarh which have borne silent witness to many acts of loyalty to the ruler. On the walls of the Loha Pol, Iron Gate, at the northernmost point of the fortress, can still be outlined in stone six rows of handprints. Each print marks the final blessing of a widowed queen, made by pressing her tumeric-covered palm and jewelled wrist against the stone as she bade farewell to her home. The top six belong to the wives of Maharaja Man Singh, who died in 1843. They mark the last royal sati in Marwar — the end of a tradition which over the centuries saw

CITY PALACE, JAIPUR. BRASS-STUDDED DOORS GUARDED BY A PAIR OF ELEPHANTS CARVED IN WHITE MARBLE, ADORN THE SPLENDID GATEWAY TO CHANDRA MAHAL. THE DIWAN-I-KHAS HOUSES THE TWO ENORMOUS SILVER URNS USED BY MADHO SINGH II TO CARRY HOLY WATER FROM THE GANGES ON HIS VISIT TO LONDON. EACH URN WEIGHS 242 KILOGRAMS. CHANDRA MAHAL IS A SEVEN-STOREYED BUILDING, ON TOP OF WHICH IS THE MUKUT MANDIR, A STYLISH ROOF WITH A CURVILINEAR 'BENGAL' ROOF. EACH FLOOR OF THE PALACE HAS BEEN DONE UP IN A DIFFERENT STYLE.

hundreds of wives and concubines die in the flames of their lord's funeral pyres at Mandore, the ancestral funeral grounds of the Marwar rulers.

Honour lay at the heart of Rajput sacrifice and no one took this more seriously than Rajput women. One Rathore ruler who learned this the hard way was the great general, Maharao Jaswant Singh, who is probably best remembered today for the famous rebuff he received from his seniormost queen, the formidable Hadi Rani, from the battlements of Meherangarh. He had just led Shah Jehan's largely Rajput army against his two rebel sons, and after fighting with great gallantry, had been defeated with heavy losses. The five hundred survivors had struggled back to their capital where, to their dismay, the gates of the fortress were closed on them. The queen had learned of her husband's defeat and was furious that he had retreated rather than died on the battlefield. From the battlements she declared that the man below could not be her husband – and then began to prepare for her sati. Although dissuaded from killing herself, she never forgave him for his 'cowardice'. Even so, when in 1678 the news was received that Maharao Jaswant Singh had died leading the army of Emperor Aurangzeb on a military campaign, Hadi Rani dutifully committed sati with her late husband's second wife and a dozen concubines.

top: The African room in Udai Bilas Palace, Dungarpur. On display are immaculately kept trophies shot by the late *Maharawal* Lakshman Singhji. He was not only a very keen shikari, but also a fine cricketer and a politician. He converted the palace into a fine hotel which his family runs today.

bottom: The throne room, Anoop Mahal, in Bikaner's Junagadh Fort, Where the rulers of Bikaner held court. The walls and pillars are richly painted in pure gold leaf and profusely inlaid with mirrors. The decoration was done by craftsmen from the Usta community originally brought from Persia. Their descendants still live in Bikaner.

pages 112-113: During a royal celebration, Maharani Padmini Devi and Princess Diya Kumari of Jaipur watch ladies performing the *ghoomar*, which is one of the most popular dance forms of Rajasthan, in the Sheesh Mahal of the City Palace in Jaipur. The pillars and arches of the Sheesh Mahal are richly decorated with mirror and glass inlay and gold leaf work. Such palaces of mirrors, probably Persian in influence, were invariably used for dance and entertainment and also exist in other major palaces in Rajasthan.

111

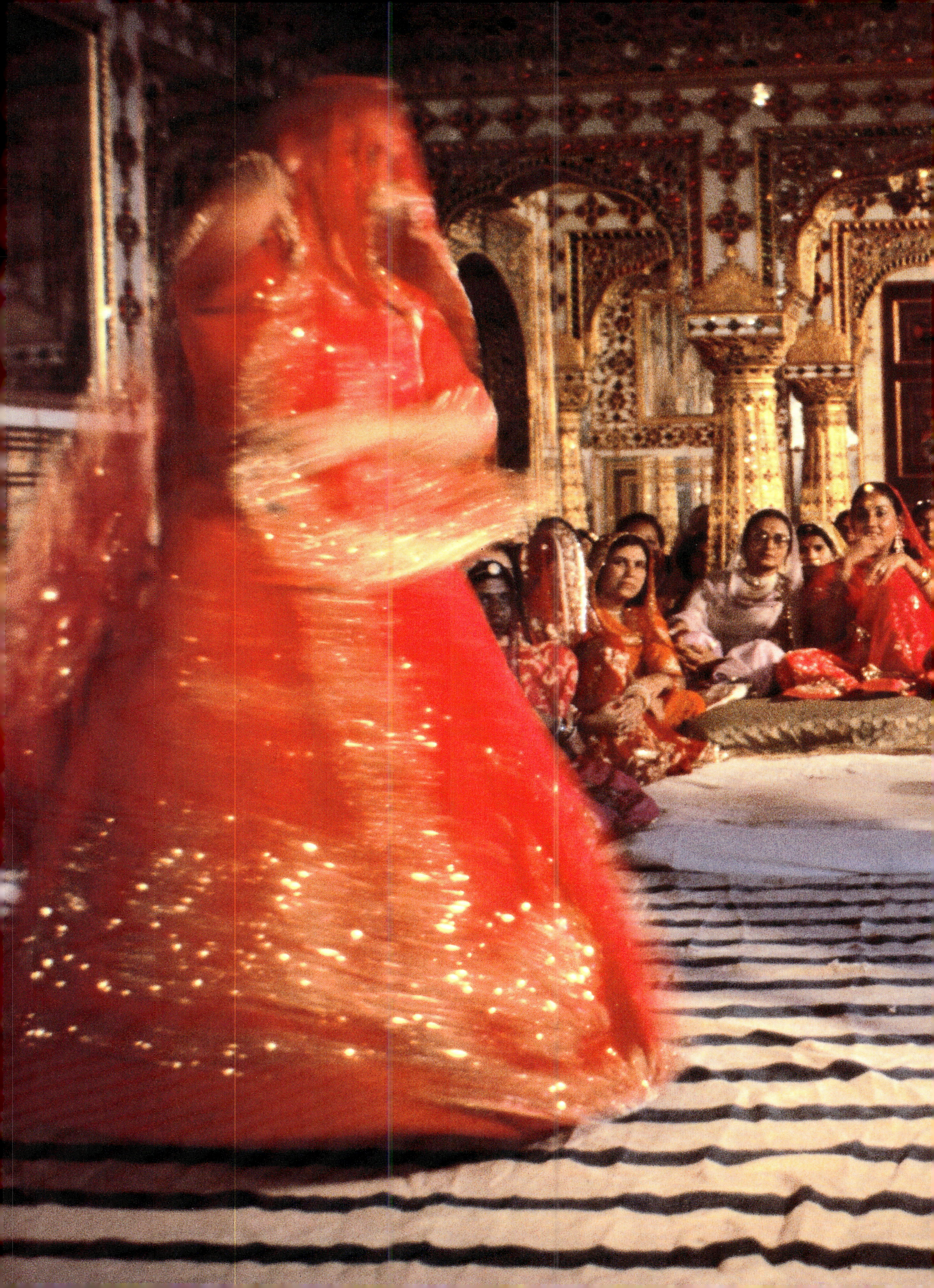

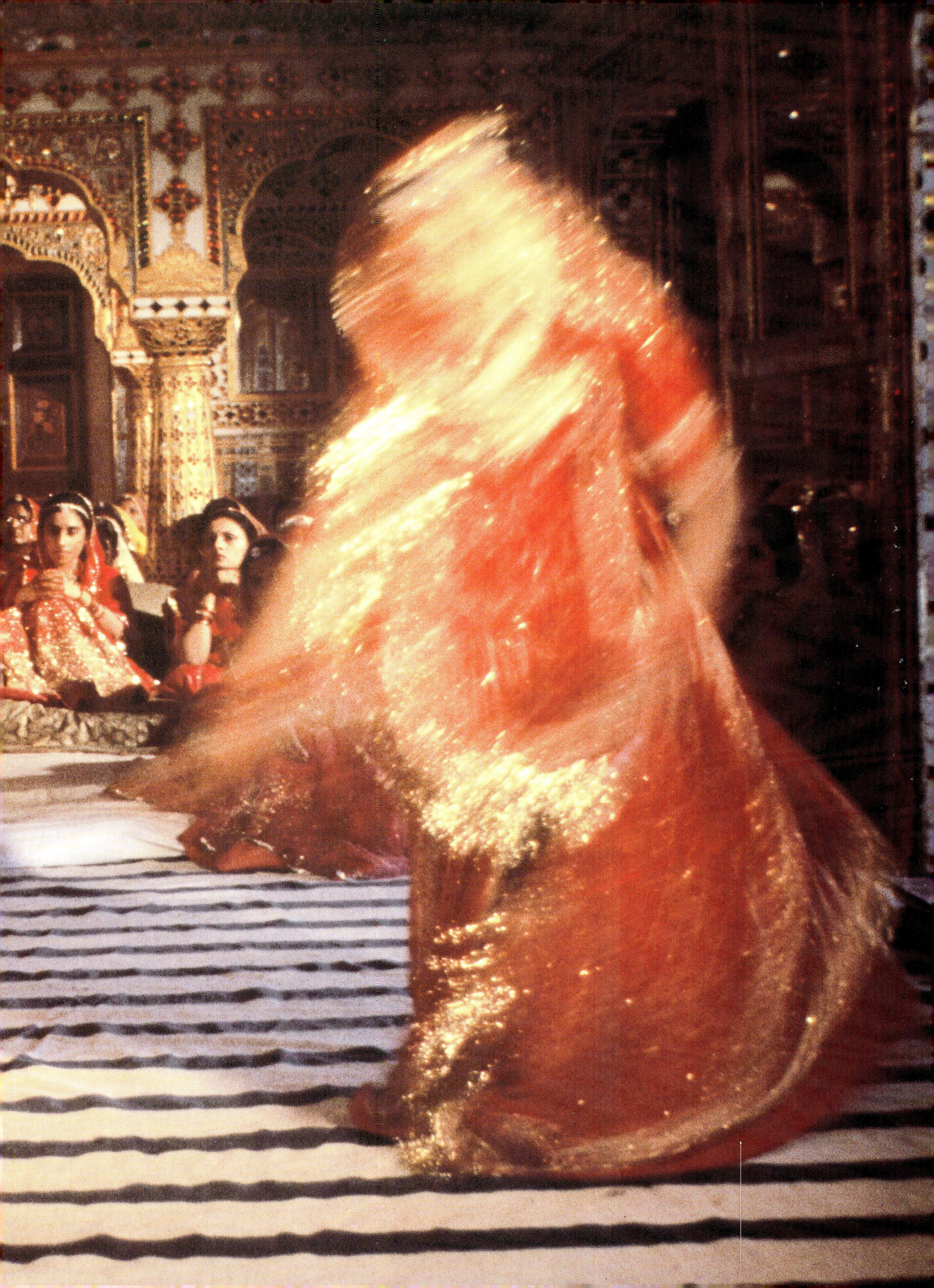

Kapurthala

18th century
Sardar Jassa Singh, the head of a Sikh *misl*, lost his *misl* to Patiala. As a reaction he ousted the old Mughal commander of the Kapurthala fort and took it over.

1808
Fateh Singh co-signed the treaty made by Ranjit Singh with the British, fixing the Sutlej river as the boundary between the Sikh and the British states. Acknowledging Ranjit Singh as a brother, he assisted him in his campaigns.

1845
His successor, Nihal Singh, decided not to take sides in the war between the British and Ranjit Singh's descendants but his troops sided with the Sikhs. The British captured the southern parts of Kapurthala.

1857
Kapurthala sent troops to assist the British in the Indian Mutiny and was rewarded with titles and territory.

1890
Jagatjit Singh ascended the throne. A passionate Francophile, he turned Kapurthala into 'a scrap of Paris'.

The great fortress of Kumbhalgarh, called the Eye of Mewar, is famed for never having been captured. The walls were broad enough for eight horsemen to ride abreast on. Built by Rana Kumbha, it witnessed the latter's death by his own son.

Equally magnificent is the fortress of Gwalior. Built on an enormous sheer rock, its walls were originally raised by a Rajput chieftan in the eighth century. Over succeeding centuries this most valuable prize passed through many hands – Rajput, Muslim and Marathas – until it was taken by the Scindias in the 1770s. Although held by the British after the Maratha wars, it was returned to the Scindias in 1885.

The Jai Vilas Palace in the plains below, was built by the ostensibly simple Maharaja Jayaji Rao between 1872 and 1874 while the British were still occupying the Fort. Designed by Lieutenant-Colonel Sir Michael Filose for the forthcoming visit of the Prince of Wales, the exterior was an eclectic mix of pristine white marble in the style of Italian provincial architecture and Gujarati domes. The most striking feature of the palace was its Durbar Hall or the Victorian Diwan-i-Am, lit by two three-ton glass and crystal chandeliers, each carrying two hundred and fifty candles and said to be the largest in the world.

Sawai Jai Singh's City Palace in Jaipur is today only partly occupied by the erstwhile royal family. The rest comprises museums and pleasure pavilions interconnected by gateways and courtyards. The Chandra Mahal is entered through an imposing gateway with magnificent brass-studded doors guarded by two elephants in white marble. The Diwan-I-Khas, Hall of Private Audience, boasts two mammoth silver urns used by Madho Singh II to carry holy water from the Ganges when he travelled to London. The museum's display of miniature paintings, textiles, manuscripts, costumes, Persian carpets and palanquins is a tourist's delight. The Rambagh Palace was the only palace to have its own exclusive polo ground; it is today one of the most favoured luxury hotels in India.

Jodhpur's Umaid Bhavan took fifteen years to build and was the last palace to be constructed in India. Though the layout is traditionally Indian, it is decorated in the Beaux Art and Art Deco style of early twentieth-

THE INTERIOR OF THE BASHIR BAGH PALACE IN HYDERABAD. PROBABLY THE LAST REMNANT OF THE MUGHAL ERA, A BRITISH OFFICER COMMENTED, 'IT IS MORE PERSIAN THAN INDIAN'.

top: A DURBAR BEING HELD TO CONFER BIRTHDAY HONOURS TO THE MAHARAJA IN THE MARATHA STATE OF BARODA IN 1947, SHORTLY BEFORE THE STATE WAS MERGED INTO THE INDIAN UNION. MAHARAJA PRATAPSINH GAEKWAD IS SEATED ON THE THRONE IN LAXMI VILAS PALACE.

facing page, extreme left: H. H. MAHARAJA JAGATJIT SINGH OF KAPURTHALA (1872-1949). THE MAHARAJA WAS ONE THE MOST WIDELY TRAVELLED OF INDIAN PRINCES AND TOOK PRIDE IN THE ARTIFACTS AND PIECES OF FURNITURE, AS ALSO THE COMPANY OF ATTRACTIVE YOUNG WOMEN THAT HE BROUGHT FROM HIS TRIPS ABROAD. HE WAS ALSO THE PROUD OWNER OF A LARGE COLLECTION OF ROLLS-ROYCES. IN 1910 HE MARRIED THE SPANISH DANCER ANITA DELGRADA.

facing page, top: RANI KANARI, THE FOURTH WIFE OF MAHARAJA JAGATJIT SINGH, SEATED IN A FRENCH GOWN. BOTH SHE AND HER HUSBAND WERE ENAMOURED OF ALL THINGS FRENCH.

facing page, bottom: JAGATJIT SINGH, ASCENDING THE THRONE IN 1890, MADE A NEW PALACE AND GARDENS ON THE MODEL OF VERSAILLES. NAMED THE ELYSEE PALACE, IT WAS FILLED WITH SÈVRES ORNAMENTS AND AUBUSSON CARPETS.

LORD MINTO, HIS DAUGHTER LADY EILEEN ELLIOT AND LADY MINTO (STANDING) WITH MAHARAJA GANGA SINGH AT THE END OF A BLACKBUCK SHOOT.

pages 116-117, centre:
AN ELEPHANT FIGHT REGALES ONLOOKERS DURING LORD READING'S VISIT TO BARODA IN 1926. AS IN ROMAN TIMES, ANIMAL FIGHTS PROVIDED LIVELY ENTERTAINMENT IN PRINCELY INDIA. AREAS WERE SPECIALLY BUILT TO SUPPORT THIS ACTIVITY. IN ELEPHANT FIGHTS THE MALE PACHYDERMS WERE FED WITH DOSES OF INTOXICANTS TO MAKE THEM OVERLY AGGRESSIVE, AND ATTENDANTS STOOD WITH BALAMS, SPEARS, AND GOADED THE ANIMALS INTO A FEROCIOUS FRENZY. THE AREAS WERE ALSO PROVIDED WITH ESCAPE DOORS FOR THE ATTENDANTS IN CASE THE ANIMALS TURNED ON THEM.

century Europe. With a gigantic central dome 59.4 metres high, its marble staircases are juxtaposed with an indoor swimming pool, a billiards room, a ballroom and three hundred and eight kitchens.

The Junagadh Fort in Bikaner houses several palaces. Durga Niwas was like an oasis in the desert, with its beautifully carved pool with an open-pillared marble pavilion. Lal Niwas is the oldest palace; its bejewelled hall has walls and ceilings which are painted in red and gold floral designs. The Badal Mahal's (Cloud Palace) ceiling is painted in aquamarine with motifs of clouds. The idea was that royal children would know what clouds looked like if it ever rained in the desert.

The Chitran ki Burj (Painted Turret) in Udaipur's City Palace glitters with mirrors, mosaics and frescoes. The two most beautiful palaces in Udaipur are located on Lake Picchola. In the eighteenth century Jagat Singh was not allowed by his father to take a party of women to Jag Mandir. Infuriated, he constructed Jag Niwas, filling it with prismatic stained glass, delightful frescoes and breathtaking inlays. This is today the famous Lake Palace Hotel. Jag Mandir, a seventeenth-century palace, was immortalised by providing shelter to the legendary lovers, Emperor Shah Jehan and his queen, Mumtaz Mahal. It also gave refuge to British officers and their families in 1857, the year of the Indian Mutiny.

COL. BRIJENDRA SINGH, THE LATE MAHARAJA OF BHARATPUR, SEEMS LOST IN THOUGHT AS HE STANDS IN FRONT OF THE LAST OF THE ENVIABLE COLLECTION OF THE STATE'S ROLLS-ROYCES. A NUMBER OF THEM WERE FITTED WITH ATTACHMENTS AND CONVERTED AND USED TO TAKE GUESTS TO THE FAMOUS DUCK-SHOOTS. BY THE MID-1970S, THEY HAD ALL BEEN SOLD. THE ROYAL GARAGES OF INDIA'S MAHARAJAS BOASTED OF AN AMAZING COLLECTION OF CARS. THE ROLLS-ROYCE WAS A FAVOURITE AMONGST MOST. SOME MAHARAJAS HAD FLEETS OF MERCEDES, CADILLACS, HISPANO SUIZAS AND DUISENBERGS. VERY OFTEN THEY ORDERED CUSTOM-MADE MODELS DIRECTLY FROM MANUFACTURERS. SOME OF THEM WERE SPECIALLY FITTED WITH DARKENED WINDOWS AND CURTAINS FOR ROYAL LADIES IN PURDAH.

On the plains of Malwa, in Indore, the reigning Holkar family, having endured a rocky relationship with the British, built the New Palace next to the Old Palace. Inspired by the wife of the then ruler Shivaji Rao Holkar, said to be, 'very up to date in fashions of dress', its gateway resembled that of Buckingham Palace. The interior too was decidedly 'British' in design: 'like a modern English country house' with electric heating, electric kitchens and a cocktail bar. The only room in the nearby Lal Bagh Palace which was not English in character, was the hall where the *nautch* girls performed.

The nineteenth-century Nizams of Hyderabad lived within the dull brown walls of their palace, King Kothi. Their chambers were separated from the other buildings by huge courtyards, while the outer buildings were uncomfortable abodes for their relatives, wives, concubines and servants. Mir Osman Ali, Hyderabad's last Nizam, did not use Falaknuma, the palace on the hill, overlooking the city, described as having a 'Grecian facade with the cornice resting on Corinthian columns'. One of the striking features was an ornate marble staircase with beautifully carved balustrades supporting marble figures bearing candelabra.

Before the eighteenth century temples dominated southern architecture. The Amba Vilas Palace in Mysore, designed by an Englishman named Irwin, was

THE TIGER AT HER FEET SYMBOLISES MAHARANI CHIMNABAI OF BARODA, WHO APART FROM BEING A CRACK SHOT, BELIEVED IN WOMEN'S EMANCIPATION. THOUGH SHE GAVE UP THE PURDAH, SHE INSISTED ON YOUNG GIRLS KEEPING THEIR HEADS COVERED WITH THEIR SARIS IN PUBLIC PLACES.

below: YOUNG OSMAN ALI PASHA OF HYDERABAD SHOWS HIS SKILL AT RIDING AS HE CUTS A GOAT IN HALF WHILE GALLOPING. HORSE RIDING WAS THE FIRST STEP IN THE EDUCATION OF EVERY CHILD OF A ROYAL FAMILY.

pages 118-119: MAHARAJA SAWAI BHAWANI SINGHJI OF JAIPUR PLAYING HOLI WITH THE PEOPLE OF JAIPUR OUTSIDE THE GOVIND DEVJI TEMPLE. HOLI WAS AND STILL IS A VERY POPULAR SPRING FESTIVAL. THE MAHARAJA JOINS HIS PEOPLE IN CELEBRATING AND THROWING GULAL, COLOURED POWDER, ON THEM. IN BHARATPUR ON HOLI EVERYONE WORE WHITE, INCLUDING THE POLICE CONSTABLES ON DUTY. THE MAHARAJA CAME OUT INTO THE CITY, RIDING HIS ELEPHANT, WITH A BIG TANKER FILLED WITH COLOURED WATER FOLLOWING HIM. HE USED A HOSEPIPE TO SHOWER THE WATER ON HIS PEOPLE, WHO ALSO THREW COLOUR ON HIM, USING PICHKARIS, HAND PUMPS.

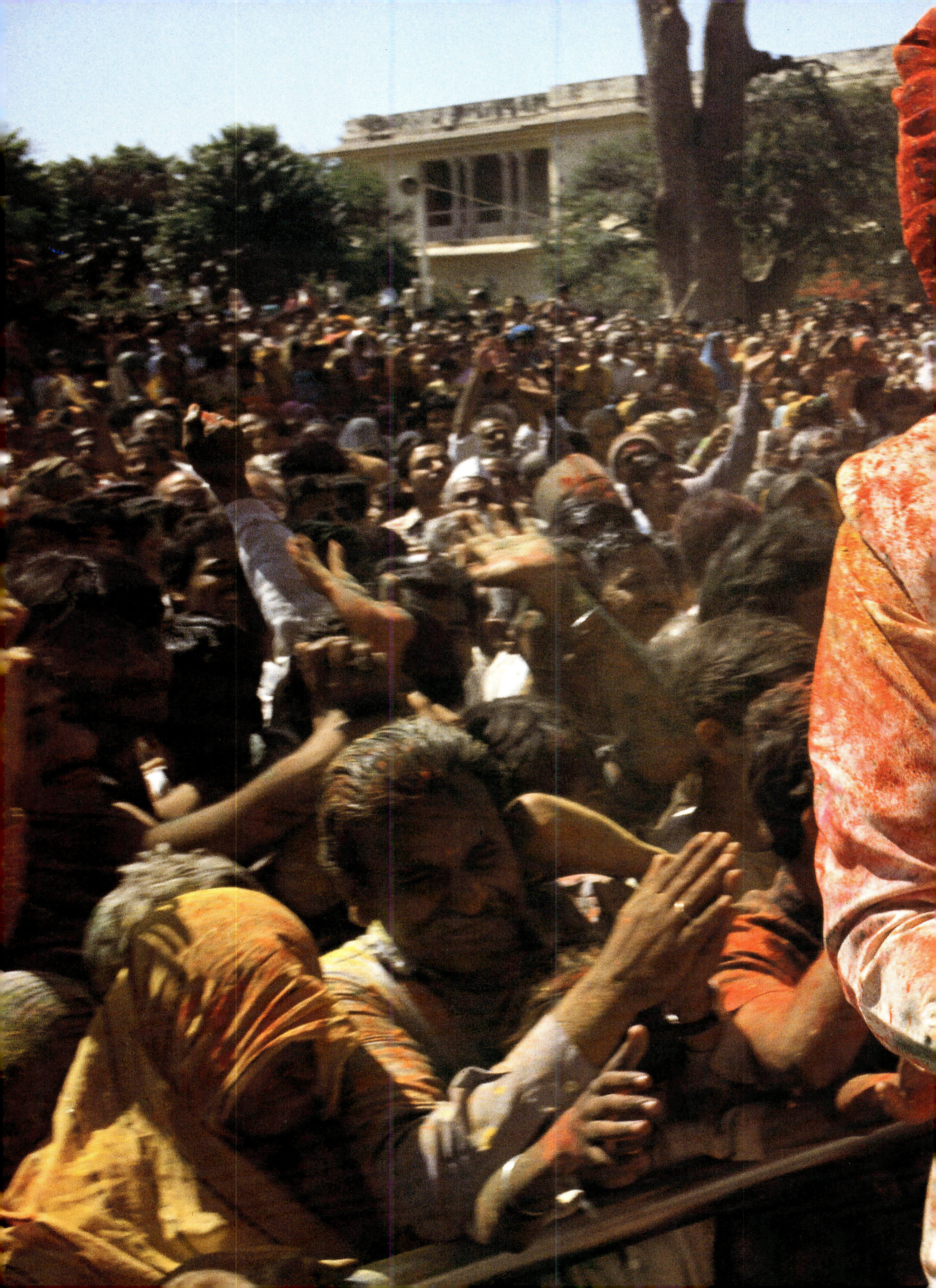

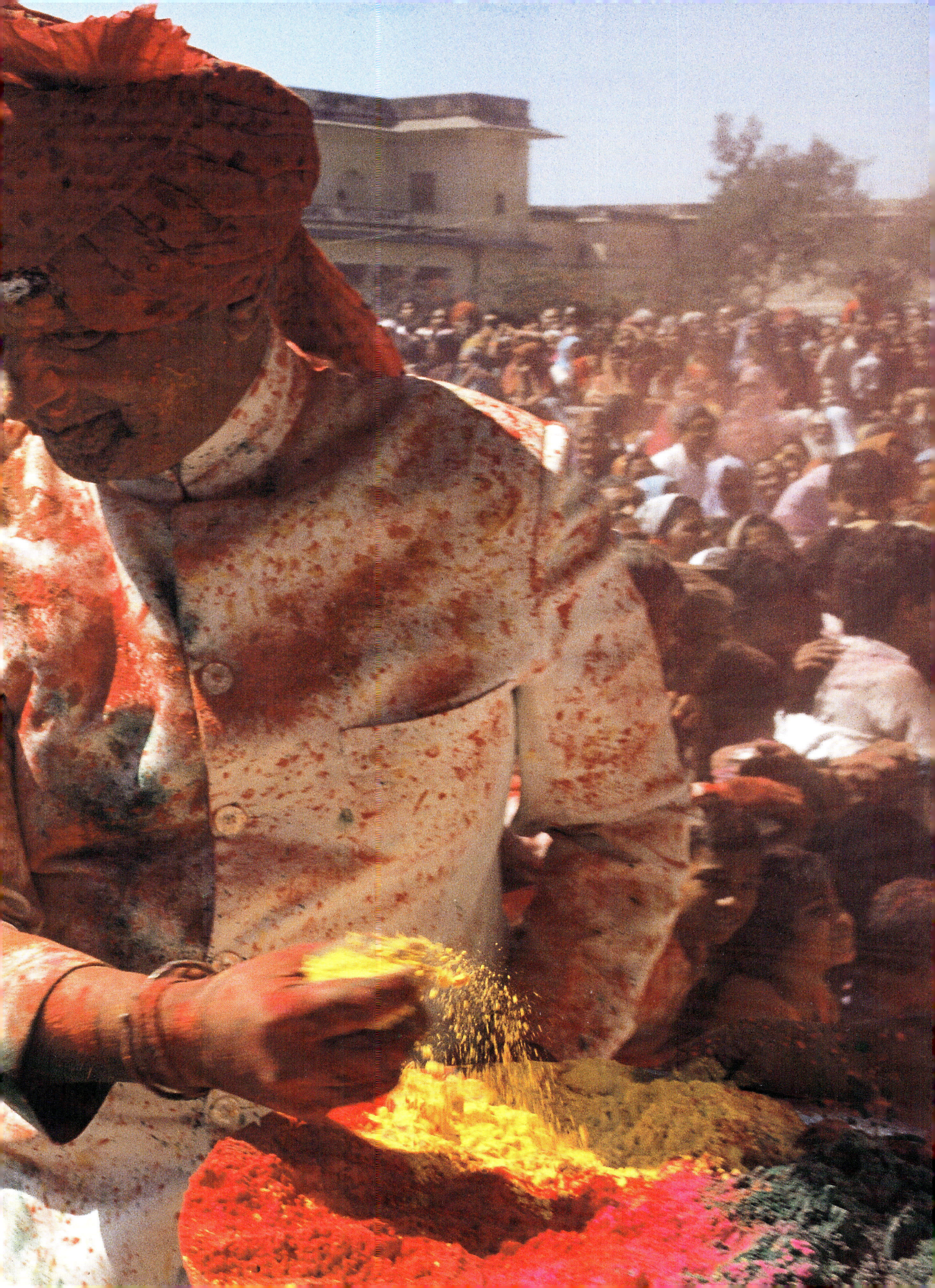

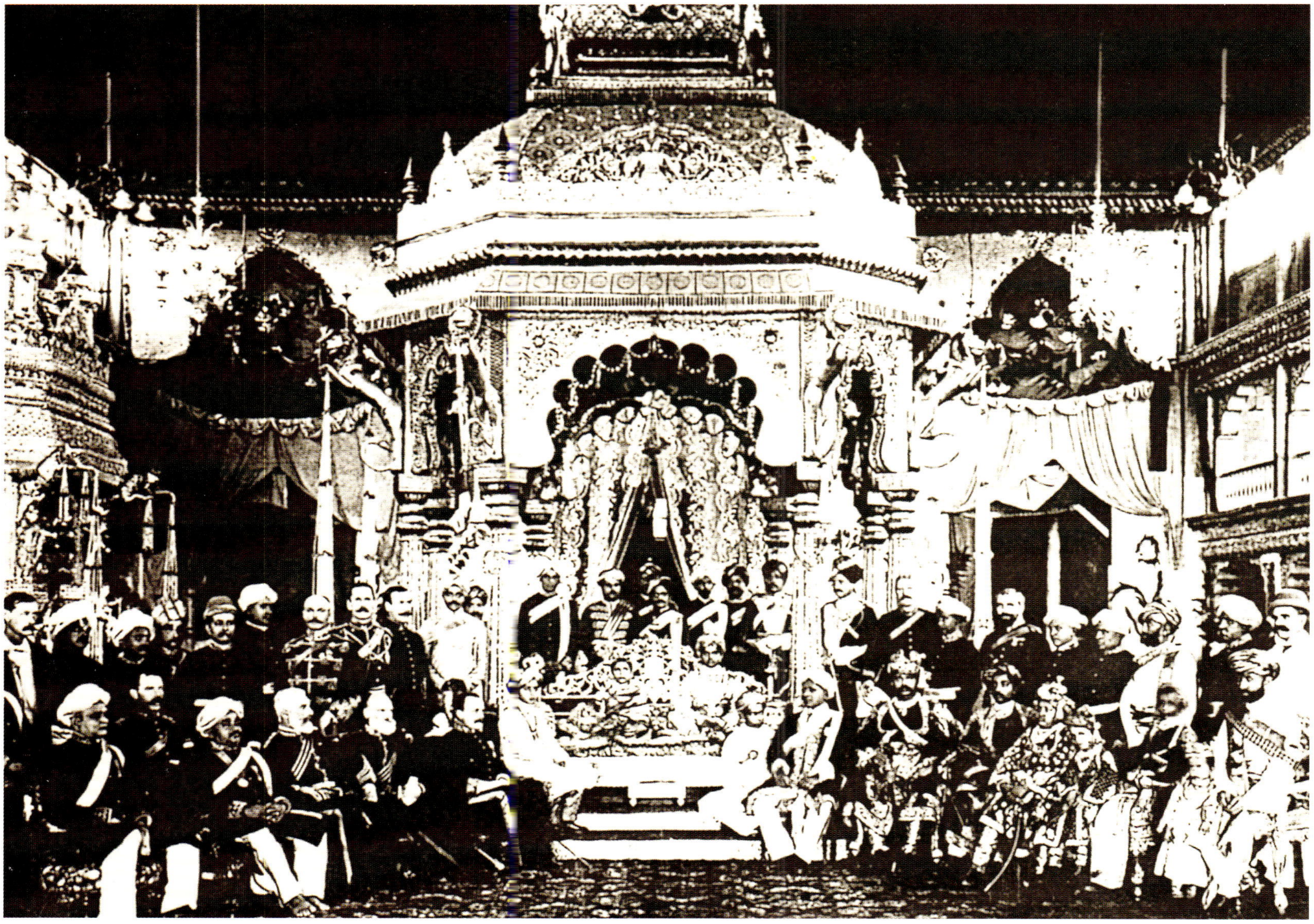

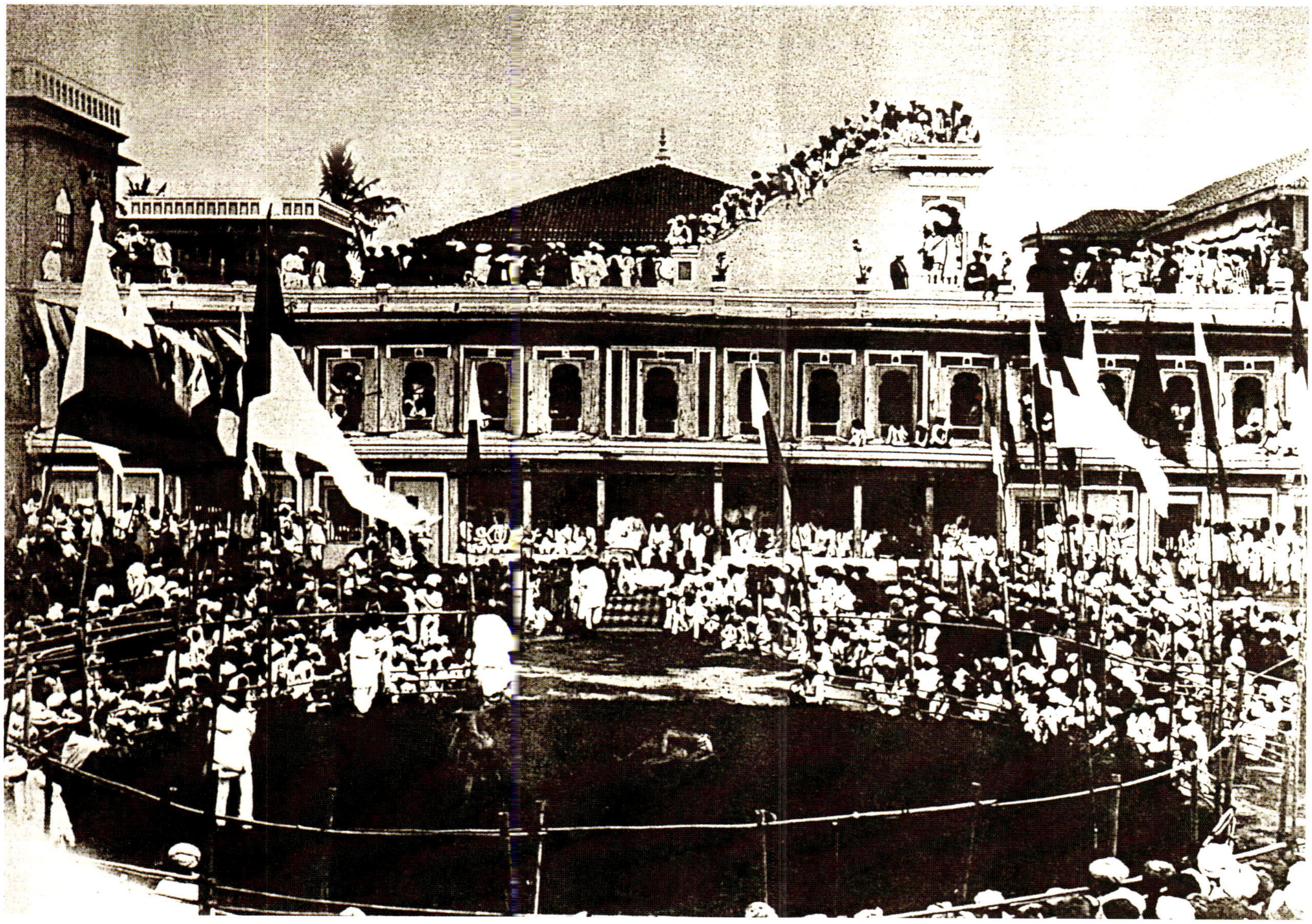

a combination of Muslim, Indian and British styles. Fluted pillars and foliate capitals from the Delhi fort, domes from the Taj Mahal and canopies from Rajput palaces adorned the exterior. Inside, ceilings with temple-like stone carvings, jostled with European-styled halls and Mughal interiors. Stained-glass windows were set off with early twentieth century European furnishings. The Diwan-i-Khas was a spectacular sight, decorated throughout with gilt and lapis lazuli.

Baroda's Sayaji Rao III discarded the old Nazar Bagh Palace which was built on damp soil and built the Laxmi Vilas Palace. Completed over a period of twelve years at a cost of £ 180,000, it was divided into three parts: the public rooms, the Maharaja's private apartments and the zenana. The Western touch was added by incorporating impressive dining rooms, billiard rooms and guest apartments for visiting European dignitaries. The East-West blend continued further. While the main construction was brick and red sandstone from Agra, blue trapstone from Poona and marble from Rajasthan, Venetian mosaic covered the floor of the Durbar Hall. English gardens and Italian sculptures vied with stained-glass windows, Old masters, Period furniture and Venetian chandeliers.

Patiala's Motibagh Palace 'would make Versailles look like a cottage', said the author Maud Diver. A combination of Rajput, Mughal and Venetian architecture, one hundred chandeliers hung from the Durbar Hall ceiling and fifteen dining rooms in which were employed one hundred and forty-three cooks. The Sheesh Mahal, Hall of Mirrors, outside the main building, housed the family's senior ladies. In the nineteenth century Bhupinder Singh expanded the area of his palace since he was finding it difficult to accommodate his growing number of wives. Story has it that he sired eighty-seven children! After Independence Maharaja Yadavindra Singh built a new Motibagh Palace, more modest than the earlier one,

facing page, top: THE EUROPEAN DURBAR HELD AT THE MARRIAGE OF THE MYSORE MAHARAJA IN 1900.
facing page, bottom: WRESTLING MATCHES WERE COMMONLY HELD IN THE OLD *RAJWADA* IN KOHLAPUR. HUNDREDS THRONGED TO WITNESS THESE MATCHES.
right: A LADY'S COSTUME – THE *FARSHI PYJAMA* OF RAMPUR. THE PANTS OR THE MAIN BODY OF THIS COSTUME IS OF GOLD AND PURPLE BROCADE AND THE *GOTE*, OR THE LOWER PORTION, IS MADE UP OF YELLOW, GREEN, RED AND PURPLE PATCHED RIBBONS WITH *ZARDOZI* EMBROIDERY. THE *NEFA*, WAISTBAND, IS OF PURPLE SILK THROUGH WHICH A DECORATIVE TASSEL RUNS.

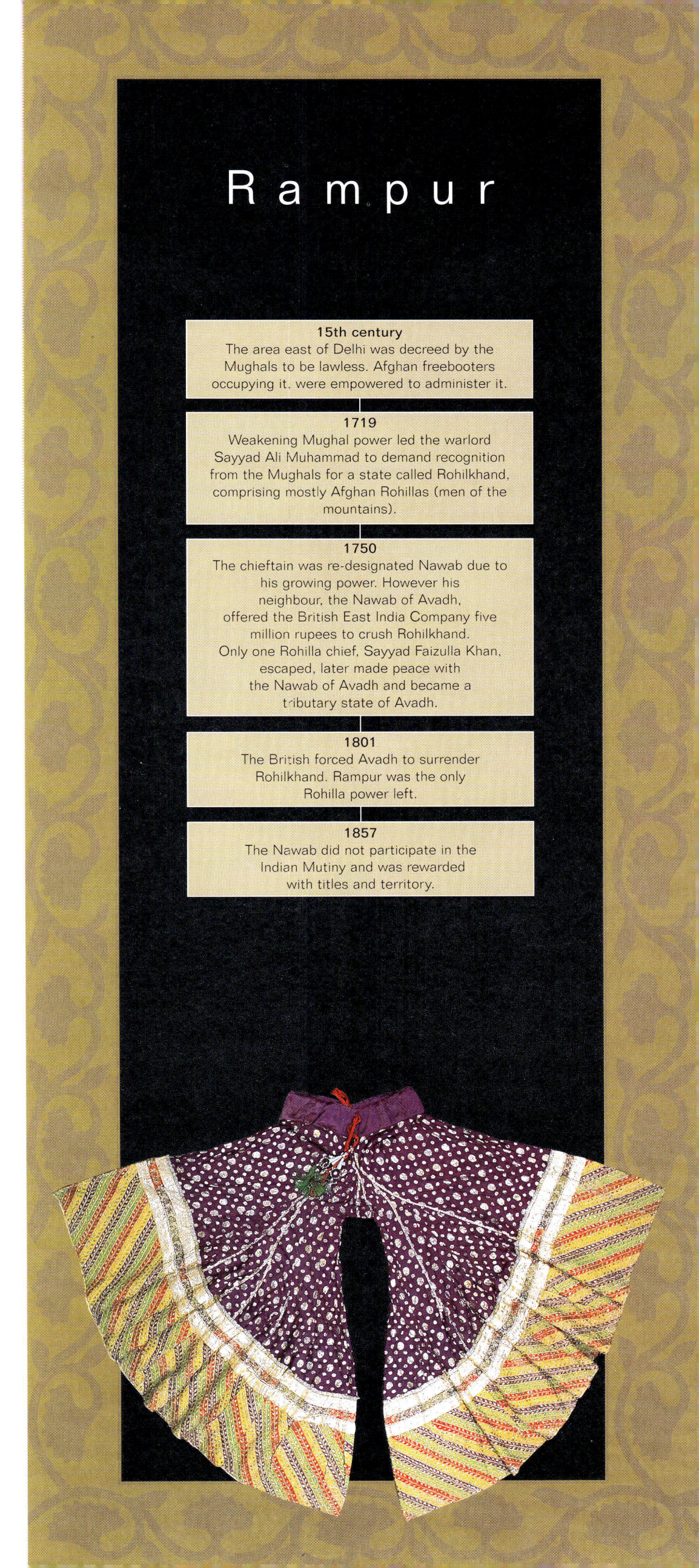

Rampur

15th century
The area east of Delhi was decreed by the Mughals to be lawless. Afghan freebooters occupying it, were empowered to administer it.

1719
Weakening Mughal power led the warlord Sayyad Ali Muhammad to demand recognition from the Mughals for a state called Rohilkhand, comprising mostly Afghan Rohillas (men of the mountains).

1750
The chieftain was re-designated Nawab due to his growing power. However his neighbour, the Nawab of Avadh, offered the British East India Company five million rupees to crush Rohilkhand. Only one Rohilla chief, Sayyad Faizulla Khan, escaped, later made peace with the Nawab of Avadh and became a tributary state of Avadh.

1801
The British forced Avadh to surrender Rohilkhand. Rampur was the only Rohilla power left.

1857
The Nawab did not participate in the Indian Mutiny and was rewarded with titles and territory.

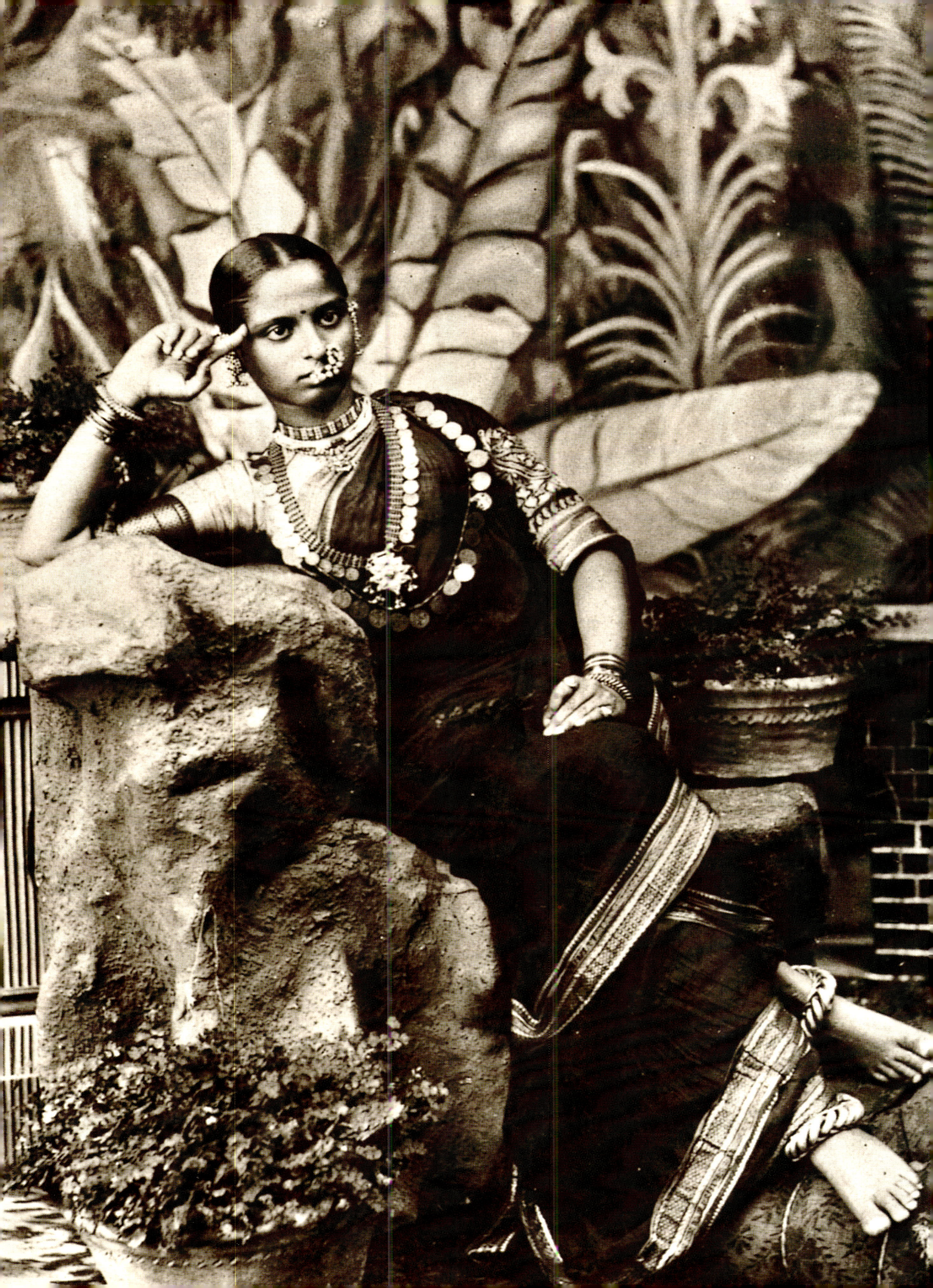

but still covered with two acres of carpetting. The old palace is today the National Institute of Sports.

In 1890, Jagatjit Singh ascended the throne of Kapurthala. A Europhile, influenced by English and French tutors in his youth, he hired a French architect, M. Marcel, to design a palace modelled on Versailles, and named it the Elysée Palace. The Mansard roof with its *oeil-de-boeuf* windows and the coupled columns running along the arcade were copied from the Louvre in Paris. Sculptures of nymphs on vaulted ceilings, Sèvres ornaments and objets d'art, lapis lazuli pillars from Italy and customised Aubusson carpets flooded the interiors, while artists were brought especially from France to paint the ceilings. The main reception hall was named after Louis XIV. The Grand Cross of the Legion of Honour was bestowed on Jagatjit Singh for his dedication to France. The Elysée Palace is now a boys' school run on military lines.

The British described Kashmir as 'an earthly paradise'. In the wake of the First Sikh War, it was sold by the conquering British to Gulab Singh of Jammu to become the combined state of Jammu and Kashmir in 1846. Making Srinagar his summer capital, Gulab Singh had the Baradari Palace constructed on the banks of the Jhelum river. The walls and ceilings were covered with *papier maché* paintings. His son built the Mondi Palace on the wooded hills overlooking the Tavi river, after which Maharaja Sir Pratap Singh built the Amar Singh Mahal. Later still Maharaja Hari Singh built a palace like an English country club on a hill beside the Dal Lake, now a luxury hotel.

In Rampur Nawab Hamid Ali Khan remodelled his fort and palace complex at the beginning of the twentieth century. The Rang Mahal, the Machchi Bhawan, the Imambara and the old Benazir and Badri-Muni palaces were electrified with lights and fans. A new palace, Khas Bagh, was constructed over twenty-five years on an old part of the Fort. Here the Nawab built a huge zenana, sealed off

top: An 800-carat necklace comprising two rows of polished spinel beads and seed pearls. The central pendant is also of spinels and diamonds. Though spinels are found in the same mines as rubies, they are lighter in colour and weight. Pinkish-red is the most sought after colour in spinels.

A zenana carriage made of silver from Baroda, which was one of the richest princely states. Such beautifully decorated carriages pulled by bullocks were used in many Indian states. The bullocks here are caparisoned in heavily embroidered brocade and velvet *zhool*. Royal animals like elephants, camels, horses and bullocks, and used in carriages, were opulently decorated in keeping with the ruler's status, and this produced a number of skilled craftsmen specialising in decoration of animals for the royals.

facing page: A Hindu princess in the late 19th century. Adorned with an elaborate nose-ring, tiers of necklaces, bangles and heavy anklets, this portrait-photograph is reminiscent of the Raja Ravi Varma style of paintings.

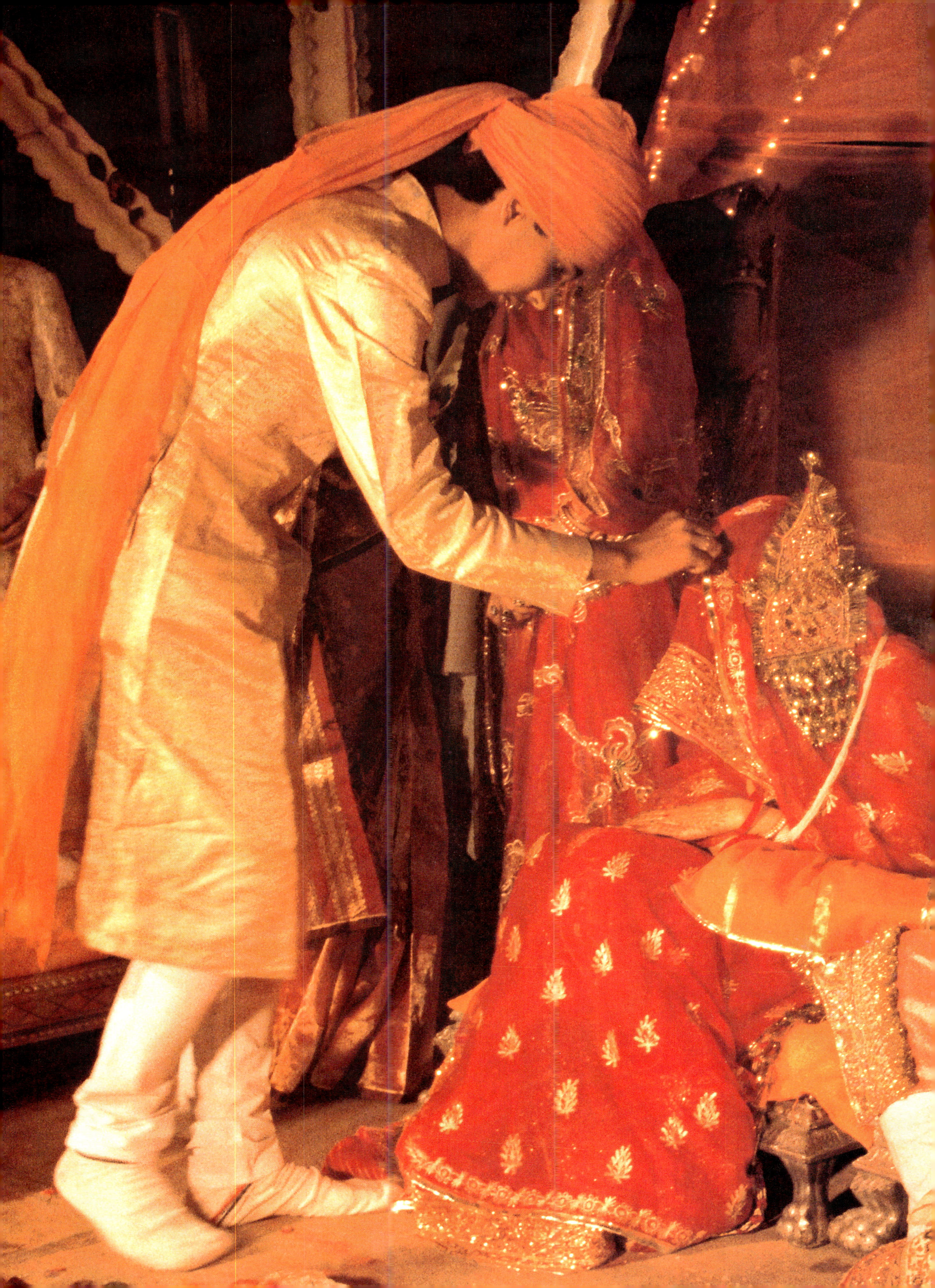

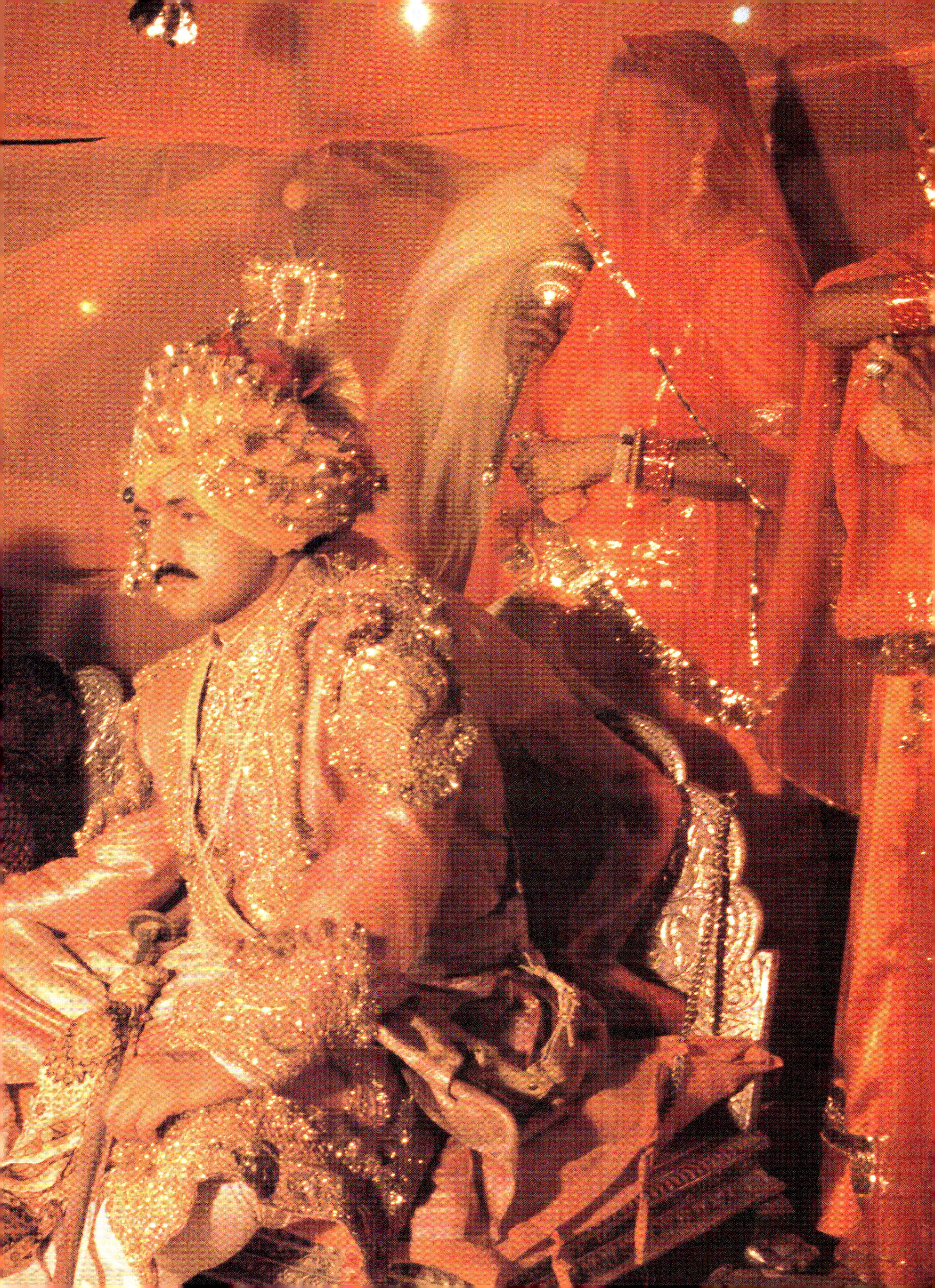

Maharaja Hemant Singh of Dholpur (left), Maharaj Kumar Brijraj Singhji of Kotah (centre), and the Maharaja of Narsinghgarh tying the SEHRA on Prince Nawed Ali Khan of Rampur before his marriage ceremony. The SEHRA covering the groom's face is adorned with gold threads and flowers made of GOTA, gold ribbon.

pages 126-127, top centre: Prince Nawed Ali Khan of Rampur looks at his bride Princess Yaseen's face in a mirror just after their NIKAH ceremony. This ritual is known as AARSI-MUSUF. Princess Yaseen is the daughter of the Nawab of Sawanur and her wedding trousseau included numerous JODAS, sets, of traditional Rampur FARSHIS. The heavy gold embroidery and workmanship on her bridal costume made it virtually impossible for her to walk. In the period preceding the wedding, costumes in red and yellow are sent from the groom's side to the bride, as these colours are symbols of fertility. The Rampur court had strict dress codes and women were required to wear elaborate silk and satin FARSHIS everyday and even at night.

from the remainder of the palace and guarded by eunuchs with drawn swords. The *mardaana*, the male quarters, contained his private apartments. Passionate about the arts, Nawab Hamid Ali Khan had a separate wing housing a music room, an art gallery for his Mughal miniatures and what is now a library for rare manuscripts. A guest section was created for visiting dignitaries. In 1923 a lift was installed for the visit of Lord and Lady Reading. Unfortunately it did not work when they arrived, the current having been switched off by someone! The Nawab, however, compensated by presenting Lady Reading with a dress of gold tissue, 'all embroidered in bullion'.

Commenting on Ramnagar, the palace which was built by Balwant Singh in Benares a mile above the city, on the opposite bank, Prevost Battersby stated that the 'curious fort-like Palace lies in flood-time like an ivory crown in the green swirl of the river . . . .' In the mid-nineteenth century the ruler Iswari Prasad Narain Singh invited musicians and poets to the palace and boasted a grand collection of contemporary paintings. His own apartments however were totally different: they were practically without any furniture or decoration, no modern touch. The Durbar Hall displayed the wealth of the arts and crafts of Benares: ivory inlay work on chairs and doors; *Kincob* silk and gold brocade on upholstery, curtains and wall-hangings; a carpet gifted by Lord Curzon and a smaller one presented by the Shah of Iran.

Behind the Purdah

Although the women of the palace were able to observe the goings-on of the outside world from behind carefully placed marble screens, their world was an enclosed one at the back of the palace: the zenana, behind high walls and guarded doors, to which all men other than the chief and the immediate male members of his family were forbidden access. Whether introduced by the Muslims, as some argued, or already an established feature of Indian culture from the earliest days, it was considered improper for women of high caste to appear in public or in mixed company. The Rajput argument was that for the defence and protection of their honour, their womenfolk should remain in purdah or behind the curtain. Here, those ladies who formed part of the ruling chief's family enjoyed a pampered life that made up for its other restrictions. They were attended by large numbers of female attendants and passed their time in a wide of range of leisure pursuits — dancing, music, playing games in their enclosed gardens, taking part in religious festivals and ceremonies, attending to their toilette and receiving a wide range of visitors, including such traders as the sellers of bangles or saris who conducted their business from behind curtains or screens. As in the *mardana*, a strict order of precedence was observed, with the power of the ruler extending to his queen, the maharani or rani. If, as was customary in royal circles, the ruler had several wives, it was the senior rani who had the most authority – but not always. Marriages were made for reasons of state and as a means of strengthening alliances, and the status of a wife within the zenana often depended on how well her husband and her father got along. And while wives were selected because of their political links, concubines were chosen purely and simply to meet the chieftain's sexual appetite. Every royal history had its instances of powerful women, more often concubines than wives, who were said to have turned the ruler's head with disastrous consequences. A notorious example was that of Maharaja Jagat Singh of Jaipur who in the 1800s, and despite already having twenty-one queens and twenty-four concubines, became so enamoured with the dancing-girl Ras Kapoor that he gave her half his kingdom before his nobles finally intervened to have her removed and imprisoned.

The more powerful the ruler the more he felt free to indulge himself. The last major figure among the princes to do so on a grand scale was the Sikh Maharaja Bhupinder Singh of Patiala, who had a voracious appetite in every sense and whose harem at the time of his death in 1938, was rumoured to exceed three hundred and fifty concubines in addition to his official wives. Among the Rajputs, however, a much more damaging vice was the excessive consumption of opium and hashish. Opium was regularly taken whenever friends met and to seal agreements but, according to James Tod, its consumption among the Rajputs reached a point where it became endemic and, in his opinion, 'robbed the Rajpoot of half his virtues'.

One of the first princely states to break the traditional mould in making alliances was Cooch Behar where, in the late nineteenth century, a young English-educated maharaja, Nripendra Narain, chose for his bride a commoner, Sunity Devee, the daughter of the Bengali social reformer Baba Keshub Sen. At first the orthodox members of the Cooch Behar family objected to Sen's radical views on rites and customs. However after a great deal of behind-the-scenes activity, the alliance was concluded. Nripendra Narain became a member of his wife's sect, the reforming Brahmo Samaj movement, and with her support, set up schools and other modern institutions in the state. This example also proved to be beneficial in that it became a guiding light to other women to step out from behind the purdah and take part in social activities.

The women of Cooch Behar's ruling family continued to be unorthodox and forward looking. Nirpendra Narain's younger son, Jitendra Narain, fell in love with Indira, the daughter of the Maharaja of Baroda, a conservative Hindu. A storybook romance followed with its share of intrigues and clandestine meetings. It culminated in a registered marriage in London, soon after which, Jitendra Narain became the Maharaja of Cooch Behar. It took five years for the Baroda family to reconcile to the marriage.

top: THE NEWLY WED COUPLE OF PRINCE NAWED ALI KHAN AND PRINCESS YASEEN. TRADITIONALLY ROYAL WEDDINGS WERE VERY LONG AND THE AFFAIRS LASTED FOR OVER TEN DAYS. DURING THE COURSE OF THE WEDDING HUNDREDS OF GUESTS HAD TO BE PROVIDED FOR AND ENTERTAINED.

pages 124-125: THE WEDDING CEREMONY OF RANVIJAY SINGH, A MEMBER OF THE RATHORE CLAN OF JODHPUR, TO PRINCESS PURNIMA KUMARI OF LUNAWADA.

A GILDED *HOWDAH* WITH INTRICATE DESIGNS AND UPHOLSTERED COMFORT – SUCH SEATS OF LUXURY WERE FOUND IN EVERY ROYAL FAMILY. THEY WERE MOUNTED ON RICHLY ADORNED ELEPHANTS ON CEREMONIAL OCCASIONS WHEN THE RULER USUALLY RODE IN REGAL SPLENDOUR RIGHT THROUGH THE CITY.

pages 130-131: TRADITIONAL *VAJRAMUSHTI* FIGHTERS ATTACK EACH OTHER IN AN AGE-OLD RITUAL DURING DUSSEHRA IN MYSORE. THE FIGHTERS WEAR TOOTHED KNUCKLE-DUSTERS ON THEIR FIST AND, IN THE OLD DAYS, WERE KNOWN TO FIGHT EACH OTHER TO DEATH. A LIVERIED REFEREE WATCHES THEM. NOWADAYS THE FIGHT COMES TO AN END THE MOMENT ONE OF THEM DRAWS BLOOD.

The third unconventional romance of Cooch Behar involved Gayatri Devi, the daughter of Maharaja Jitendra Singh and Maharani Indira, who became the third wife of Sawai Man Singh, the Maharaja of Jaipur. This marriage too was opposed by both families but grew into a great romance with Jai and his beautiful young wife becoming pacesetters of reform and iconic images of the modern maharaja and maharani. Gayatri Devi took bold initiatives in womens' education, fashion trends and entered politics. The purdah had become a memory of the past!

Of Sports and Princely Pastimes

When not attending to his chief at court or his own estates, the Rajput male spent much of his life out of doors, most of it on horseback – accompanying the ruler on military campaigns that lasted for months or even years, on winter tours of his kingdom, or hunting. As James Tod records, hunting lions, tigers, bears and wild boar was the Rajput's chief diversion. 'With the sovereign and his sons all the chiefs sally forth, each on his best steed, and all animated by the desire to surpass each other in acts of prowess and dexterity. It would appal even an English fox-hunter to see the Rajpoots driving their steeds at full speed, bounding like the antelope at every barrier with their lances balanced in the air, or leaning on the saddle bow slashing at the boar.' When he was not hunting the Rajput was practising his fighting skills. 'Everything around him speaks of arms and strife,' noted Tod. 'Riding in the ring with the lance in tournaments, defence of the sword against the lance, firing at a mark with a matchlock and throwing a dart or javelin from horseback, are favourite amusements. In these martial exercises the youthful Rajpoot is early initiated and, that the sight of blood be familiar, he is instructed, before he has strength to wield a sword, to practise with his boy's scimitar on the heads of lambs and kids. In this manner the spirit of chivalry is fed.'

Prithiviraj Chauhan's expertise with his bow and arrow won him the beautiful Sanyogta. Col. James Tod wrote of Maharaja Sheodan Singh, who was a perfect shot and well versed in music: 'Like Tell, he placed a mark on his son's head and hit it successfully. He could kill an eagle on the wing, and divide a ball on the edge of a knife.'

With the arrival of the British Raj the Rajputs and other rulers were no longer allowed to make war against their neighbours, so they channelled their martial instincts into blood sports. After hunting the Asiatic lion to the point of extinction, they came to regard the tiger as their natural and most noble prey – to the extent that the killing of tigers began a royal prerogative. All the large princely states established royal forests or game preserves where only the ruler and his guests were allowed to hunt. Hunting scenes became a favourite subject for court artists, most notably in the linked kingdoms of Bundi and Kota, which developed one of the most famous schools of Rajput painting. Some states became famous for the scale of their sport: in Jaipur, Gwalior and Rewa it was tigers; in Bharatpur duck and other wildfowl; in the desert state of Bikaner sand grouse. Ironically, because this royal exclusiveness continued into the early 1970s, it made possible the preservation of some of India's most endangered wildlife with the conversion of these former hunting forests into game reserves and what are now national animal sanctuaries. Ranthambhor, where Queen Elizabeth and Prince Philip shot tiger in the 1960s as guests of Maharaja Jai Singh II of Jaipur, is now a national park and a haven for the tiger, panther and other rare species. Similarly, the lakes and canals so carefully developed by the Maharaja of Bharatpur into the finest duck-shoot in India, and where in 1938 his guest Lord Linlithgow, the Viceroy of India and his party shot no less than 4,273 ducks in one day, is now Keoladeo Ghana Bird Sanctuary, the finest in India.

Mysore's famous *Kheddas*, elephant round-ups, were originally conducted to capture wild elephants so that they could be put in the service of the state. For three months teams of elephant hunters drove the wild elephants towards a trap, culminating in a grand finale where the rounded-up wild elephants were tied up with the help of tame elephants, only to be tamed in their turn. In Mysore, as in all larger states, hundreds of elephants were kept in specially-built stables, mainly to participate in formal processions on state occasions.

Sita – Paradigm of Rajput Womanhood

The annals of Rajput history abound with stories of the devotion, sacrifice and love of their women. Sati, giving herself up on the funeral pyre of her husband, and *jauhar*, commiting suicide rather than falling into the hands of an enemy, were resorted to by every Rajput woman when the light of her husband's life was diminished.
Sita's plea to Rama, when he contemplated becoming a hermit, was exemplified by the Rajputani character:

A woman's bliss is found, not in the smile
Of father, mother, friend, nor in herself:
Her husband is her only portion here,
Her heaven hereafter. If thou indeed
Depart this day into the forest drear,
I will precede, and smooth the thorny way.
A gay recluse
On thee attending, happy shall I feel,
Within the honey-scented grove to roam,
For thou e'en here canst nourish and protect;
And therefore other friend I cannot need.
Today most surely with thee I will go,
And thus resolved, I must not be deny'd.
Roots and wild fruit shall be my constant food;
Nor will I near thee add to thy cares,
Nor lag behind, nor forest-food refuse,
But fearless traverse every hill and dale.
Thus could I sweetly pass a thousand years;
But without thee e'en heaven would lose its charms.

Pleased to embrace thy feet, I will reside
In the rough forest as my father's house.
Void of all other wish, supremely thine,
Permit me this request – I will not grieve,
I will not burden thee – refuse me not.
But shouldst thou, Raghuvu, this prayer deny
Know, I resolve on death.

-Vide Ward, *On the History, Literature and Mythology of the Hindus*, vol. ii. p.408.

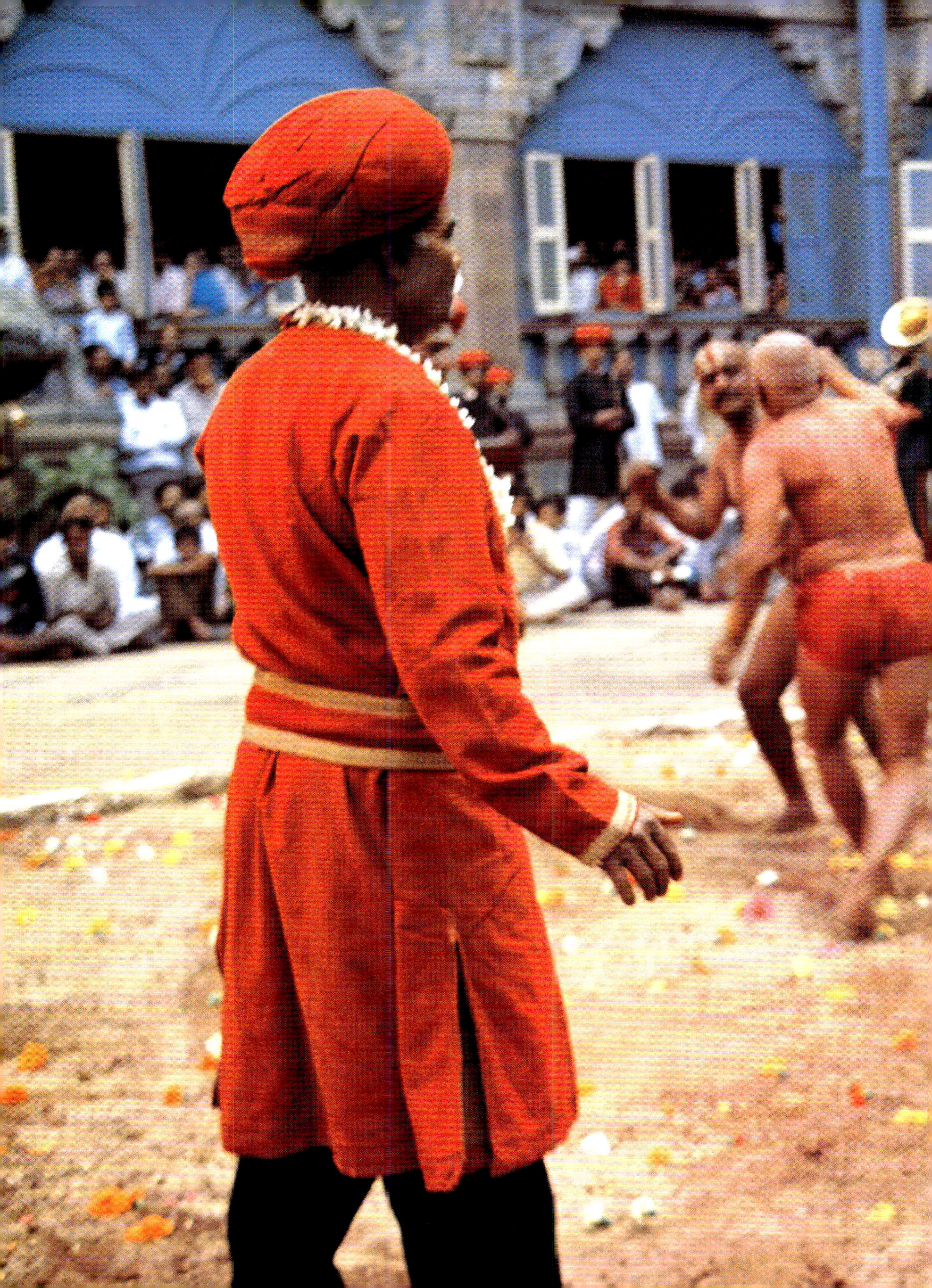

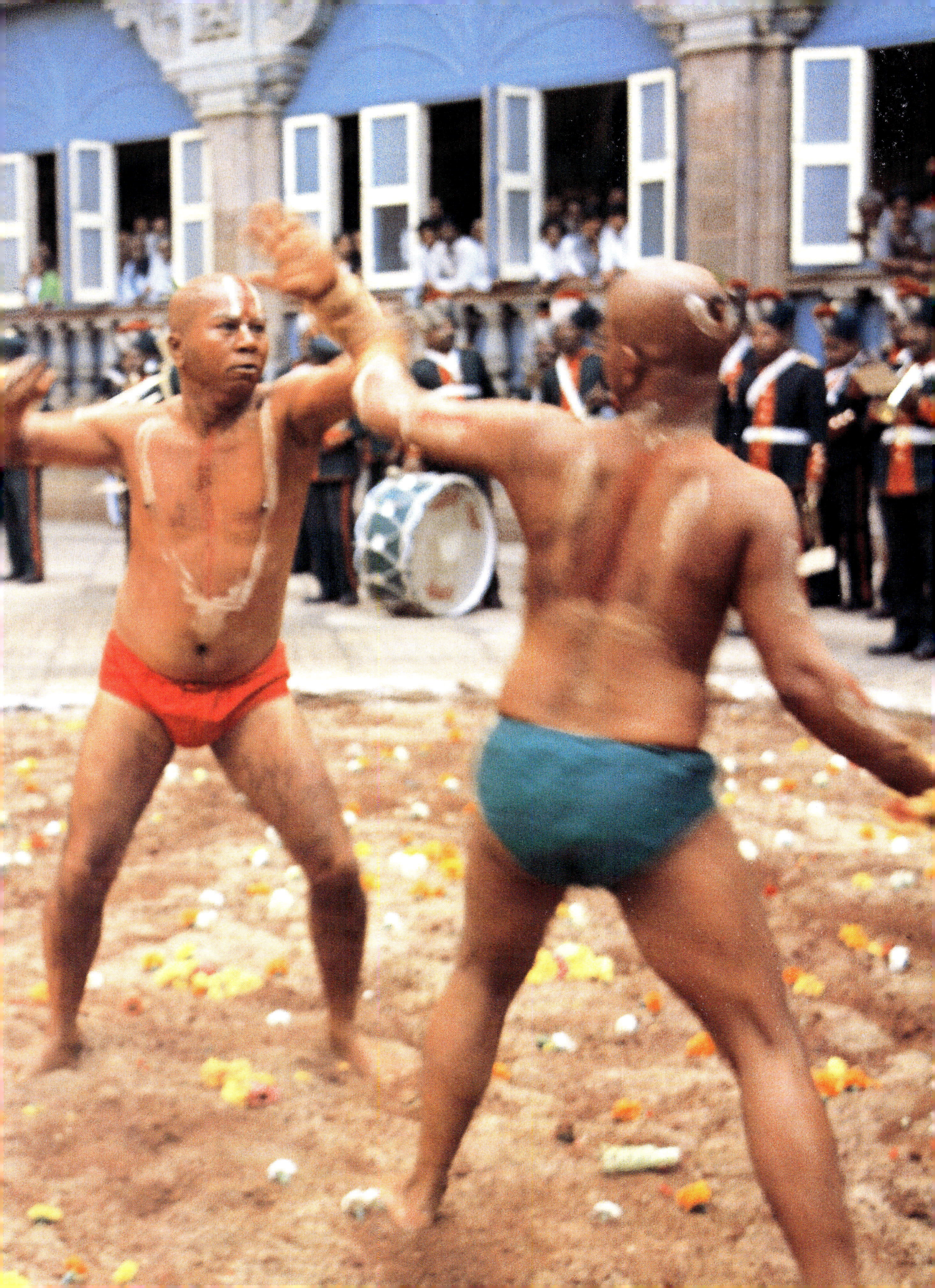

Maharaja Sayaji Rao of Baroda was a keen hunter, racehorse enthusiast and cricketer. What gave him much greater pleasure was the entertainment provided by his troupe of performing parrots who could ride bicycles and fire cannons. Polo, which seems to have originated from Persia, became a favoured princely game, specially in Rajasthan. In some princely states, it was even played by royal women, although always behind screens. Tennis was played professionally: Kapurthala and Palanpur produced a number of princely tennis champions. The Maharajas of Cooch Behar, Indore, Morvi and Lohlapur all enjoyed horse-racing and bred horses.

Riding with hounds in pursuit of jackals emerged as another princely sport. While some rulers included their hounds in their usual hunts, others organised dog races. Pig-sticking, popular in western India and Jodhpur, required hard riding and great stamina, with the danger of being charged at by the wild boar being chased. In many of the princely states of western India, hunting black buck with cheetahs and doves with caracals was extremely popular. This was considered a clean sport because the prey was either killed immediately or went free. Every state had its own shikar department manned by professional huntsmen who had followed this occupation for generations,

A COURTESAN FROM LUCKNOW WITH HER ATTENDANT. PATRONISED BY RULERS, COURTESANS WERE IMMORTALISED BY POETS. THEY MOVED THROUGH THE CITY IN CURTAINED PALANQUINS, LEAVING WHIFFS OF PERFUME BEHIND. IN RAJPUT STATES COURTESAN-DANCERS PROVIDED ENTERTAINMENT AT DURBARS WHERE THEY DANCED DRESSED IN ALL THEIR FINERY TO THE ACCOMPANIMENT OF MUSIC. IN CERTAIN STATES LIKE HYDERABAD THIS ROLE WAS ALSO PERFORMED BY *HIJRAS*, TRANSVESTITES, WHO DRESSED, DANCED AND SANG AS WOMEN. ON MANY OCCASIONS, FOR THEIR SERVICES THESE *NAUTCH* GIRLS RECEIVED MONEY, JEWELS AND EVEN *JAGIRS*, LAND, FROM THE IMPRESSED RULER.

top: MADE IN JAIPUR IN THE 19TH CENTURY, THIS NECKLACE COMPRISES EMERALDS AND DIAMONDS SET IN GOLD, IN A WESTERN DESIGN.

Fads and Foibles

Unbridled wealth, privilege and power without responsibility, as a result of the British reducing them to the status of figureheads, were all factors that allowed some of them to develop fetishes and indulge their fantasies.

- The Nawab of Junagadh staged elaborate wedding festivities for his hundreds of bejewelled pedigree dogs.
- Maharaja Jai Singh of Alwar used widows as tiger-bait, but always shot the tiger before it could take the bait. He owned a gold-plated Lanchester, and after his death, was driven through the streets of Alwar, seated upright in his Lanchester.
- The Maharaja of Bharatpur bankrupted his state by arranging mammoth duck-shoots, and buying scores of Rolls-Royces and converting them into shooting-brakes.
- Maharaja Bhupinder Singh of Patiala collected wives and concubines by the score, maintained around three and a half thousand domestic staff, spent sixty per cent of the state's income on himself, and was ultimately banned from Simla because no woman was safe from him. Such was his craving for food that he ate three chickens at a tea.
- Madhav Rao Scindia of Gwalior had his own railway; his 'second' railway ran over tracks on the dining table: a miniature silver train on which circulated cigars and wine!
- Mir Osman Ali, the tenth Nizam of Hyderabad, piled up his wealth in stacks of gold bricks, chests of diamonds and pearls and mounds of silver rupees. He was said to have been gifted with three hundred cars, and used the famous Jacob diamond as a paperweight. In spite of his wealth, he was a miser. Visitors invited to tea were offered only one biscuit each; he himself smoked the cheapest cigarettes; wore the same cap for thirty years and used the same stick for forty; rode in a run-down Buick while his cars rotted in the stables, and wore such shabby clothes that he was often mistaken for a servant.

TOP LEFT: THE MAHARAJA OF GWALIOR'S UNIQUE SILVER TRAIN RAN ON AN ELECTRIC TRACK, LAID OUT ON A BANQUET TABLE. WHILE GUESTS ATE THEIR DINNER, THE TRAIN CHUGGED AROUND CARRYING CIGARS, CHOCOLATES AND OTHER DELICACIES. TOP RIGHT: THE MAHARAJA OF JAISALMER'S GERMAN SHEPHERD GUARD DOGS LOOK OUT AT THE EVENING SUN FROM THE *JHAROKAS*, WINDOWS, OF VIJAY MANDIR PALACE. ABOVE: THE PRIDE OF THE ALWAR COLLECTION OF CARS: A 1925 CUSTOM-MADE LANCHESTER, WHICH WAS HALF CAR AND HALF ROYAL COACH. THERE WERE TWO SEATS IN FRONT AND A COACH AT THE BACK.

Kashmir and Jammu

KASHMIR

1339
Muslim invaders in the vale of Kashmir. Almost the entire population converted to Islam.

1752-1819
Kashmir – a province of Afghanistan.

JAMMU

Ruled by the Dogra Rajputs till Muslim invasions.

Early 18th century
The Dogra Rajputs in control again.

1780
Captured by Ranjit Singh but Gulab Singh, the ruler allowed to remain a semi-independent raja.

1846
Kashmir sold to Gulab Singh of Jammu by the East India Company to pay for the Second Sikh War. Thus becoming the independent ruler of Jammu and Kashmir, he seized the outlying principalities with the help of the Sikhs and Dogras.

Maharaja Hari Singh of Jammu and Kashmir being driven at a slow, leisurely pace through Palanpur in 1936 by Nawab Taley Muhammad Khan. Attendants and the police escort the car. Maharaja Hari Singh built an elegant palace amidst perfectly manicured gardens on a hill beside the Dal Lake in Srinagar. top: H. H. the Maharaja of Kashmir, G.C.S.I. Kashmir became a favourite resort of the officers of the British Raj, rich travellers of the world and wealthy Indians.

many of them drawn from the local Adivasi population. Bhupinder Singh of Patiala had a private zoo, orchestra and a private cricket team. He loved pedigree dogs and bought them in scores. Out of the seventy-two cars he owned, three dozen were Rolls-Royces.

Invoking Divine Blessings

Every ruler also had a duty to act as a patron of religion, nowhere better exemplified than at the temples of love at Khajuraho, in Bundelkhand. The site comprises two groups of temples; the oldest are covered in exquisite, and mostly erotic, stone carvings dating from the ninth to the eleventh centuries. They were the work of the Chandella Rajput rulers of Kalinjar. Today Khajuraho is a World Heritage Site.

Every royal house had its own family deity, worshipped daily in its own shrine within the palace and attended by the family priests. But there was also the state deity or patron god/goddess, and in some kingdoms the ruler described himself as no more than the *dewan* or chief minister of the kingdom, the real ruler being the state deity. In Udaipur the Maharanas have always described themselves as chief servants of the state deity, Shiva, worshipped in a form known as Eklingji, and guardians of the temple which houses it. The Kalika Mata Temple, built by Rana Hamir, was dedicated to the goddess Kali, the patron goddess of Chittor. The Kumbh Shyam Temple, built by Rana Kumbha, was dedicated to Viraha, the boar avatar of Vishnu. Within this temple compound is a small shrine dedicated to Lord Krishna, to whom Mira Bai, the celebrated sixteenth century poetess and saint of Chittorgarh, devoted her life.

Rulers also led the annual religious festivals, the most important being Holi in spring and Dussehra in autumn. Holi was a communal festival that welcomed the onset of spring and the harvesting of winter crops. It is celebrated by the throwing of crimson powder in thin plates of mica at one another or squirting it from syringes, with no distinctions made in caste or rank.

Dussehra, by contrast, was very much a warrior's festival, extending over ten days and commemorating the war waged by Rama against the demon Ravana, who had abducted his wife. It was also celebrated to herald the second harvest season. In every Hindu state this was the leading festival of the year, with *Ramleelas* being enacted every day. On the tenth day enormous effigies of Ravana, his son Meghnadh and brother

above: The marriage ceremony of Maharaja Brijraj Singh of Jaisalmer to the daughter of a Nepalese Rana. A lady washed the Maharaja's feet with water from a silver jug in keeping with the age-old Nepalese custom. The bride is dressed in a traditional Rana costume of velvet covered with heavy gold embroidery. Her veil-covered headdress is reminiscent of medieval English women.
top, left to right: The Maharani of Jodhpur, Maharaja Gaj Singhji of Jodhpur, the Maharani of Udaipur, and Maharana Mahendra Singhji of Udaipur perform a *hawan*, religious ceremony, at the fort of Chittor during the *Jauhar Samaron*.

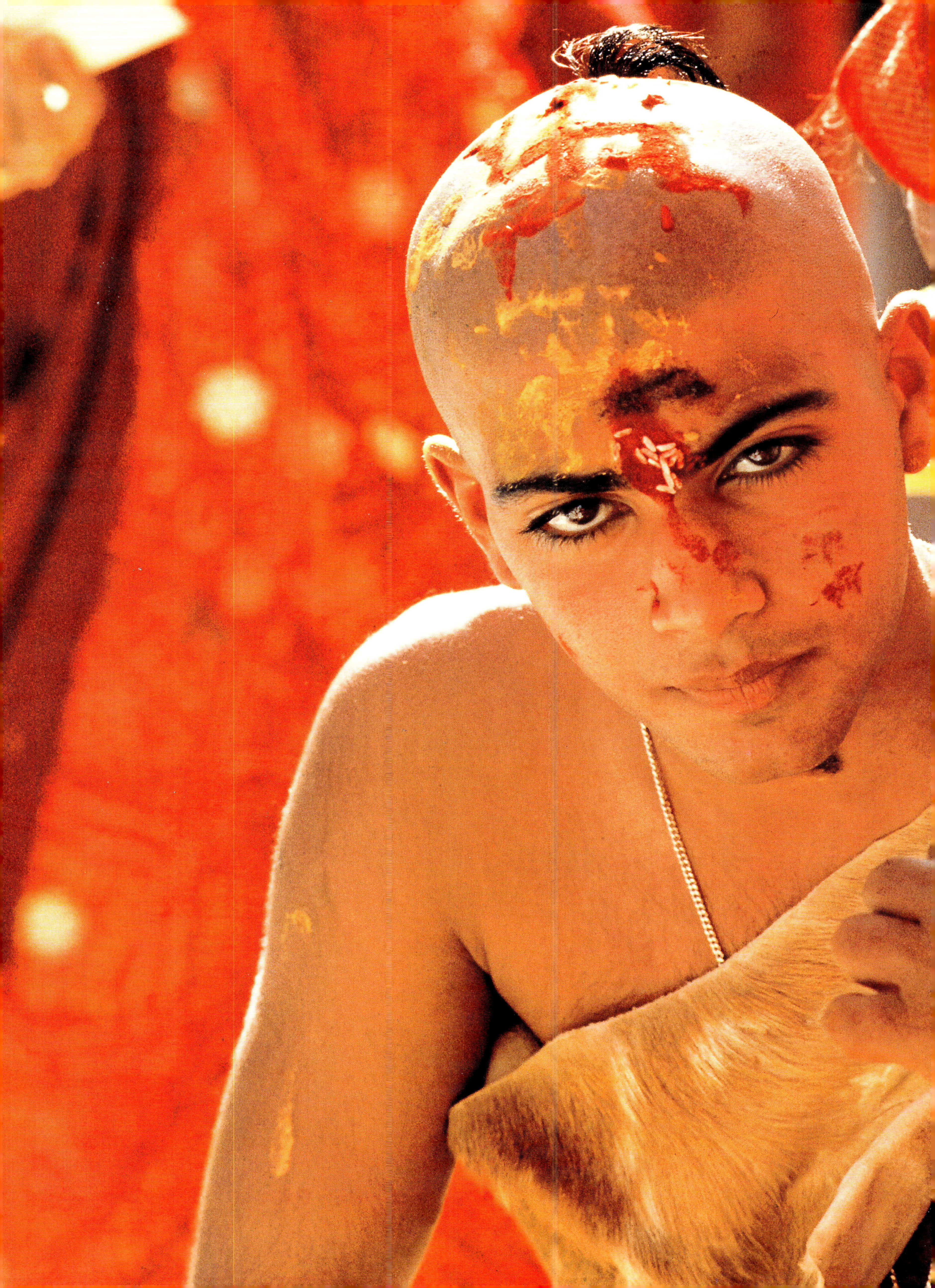

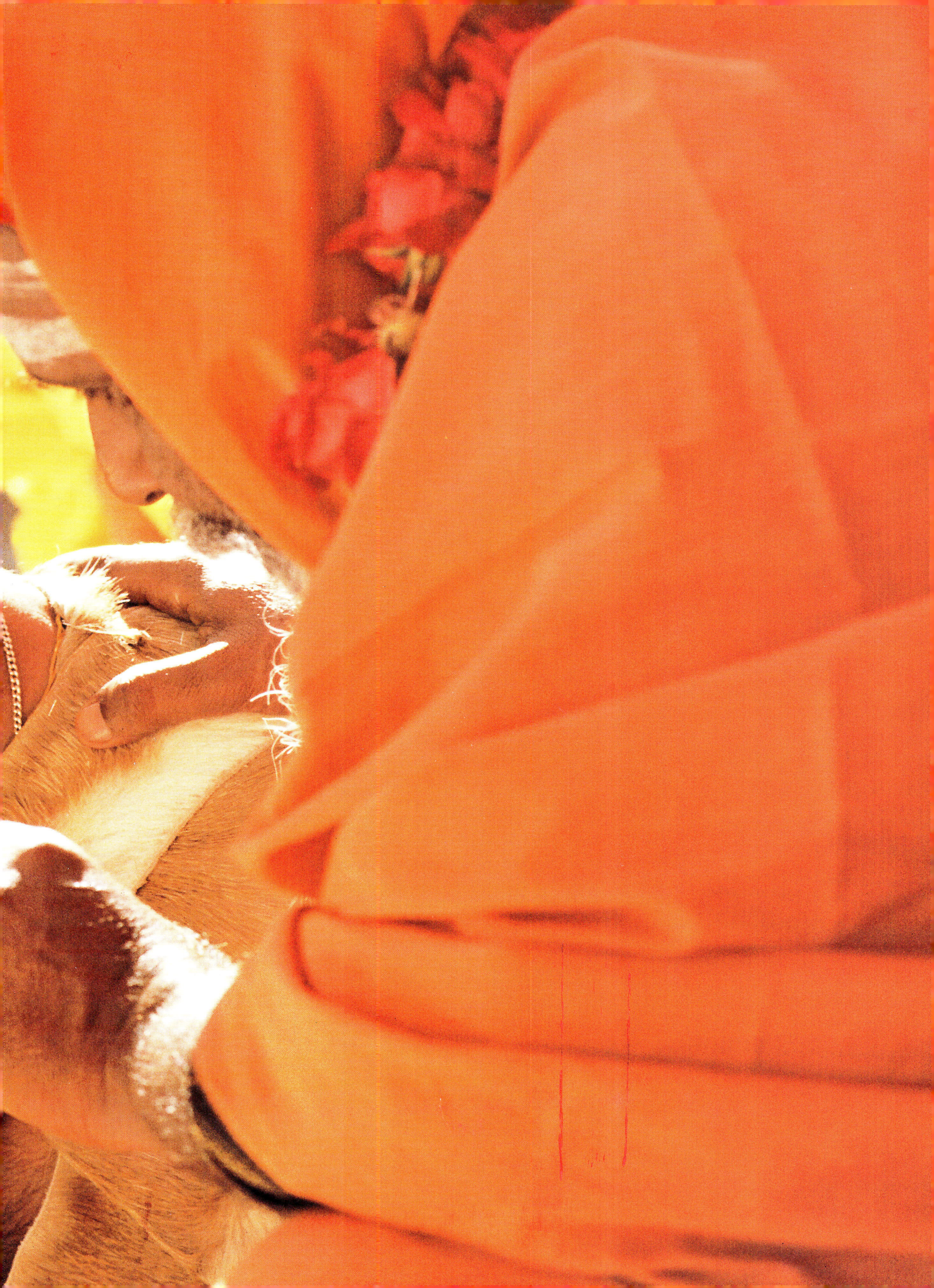

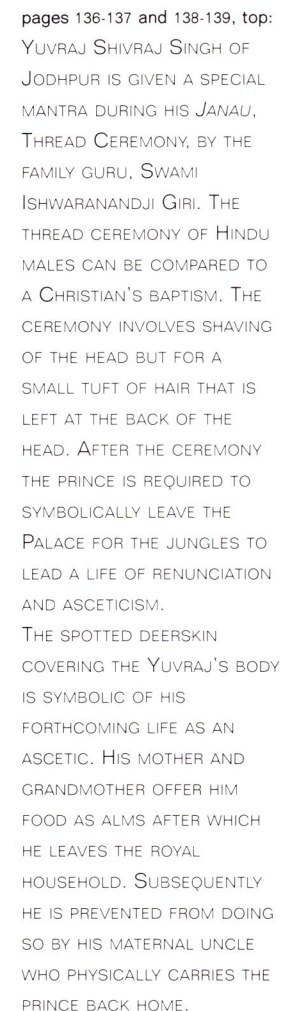

pages 136-137 and 138-139, top: Yuvraj Shivraj Singh of Jodhpur is given a special mantra during his Janau, Thread Ceremony, by the family guru, Swami Ishwaranandji Giri. The thread ceremony of Hindu males can be compared to a Christian's baptism. The ceremony involves shaving of the head but for a small tuft of hair that is left at the back of the head. After the ceremony the prince is required to symbolically leave the Palace for the jungles to lead a life of renunciation and asceticism.
The spotted deerskin covering the Yuvraj's body is symbolic of his forthcoming life as an ascetic. His mother and grandmother offer him food as alms after which he leaves the royal household. Subsequently he is prevented from doing so by his maternal uncle who physically carries the prince back home.

Kumbhakarna were burnt in a shower of fire crackers. After the ritual slaughter of a large number of buffaloes and goats, the *shastra puja* was performed, when all the instruments of war were first taken out in parade in front of the ruler, who then led his men in making offerings to them and obtaining the priest's blessings. The womenfolk would come together in the courtyards of their zenanas to dance the Ras Garba, while the men in their part of the palace would perform their own Banaoli Dantia dances with swords or sticks and small shields. The festival culminated in a grand parade from the palace through the streets of the town or city, an annual display of pomp and pageantry much celebrated in painting. Although held on a more modest scale today Dussehra is still an important event in the former princely states – and especially in Mysore. Marking the end of the monsoon and the beginning of the 'season of warfare', the Maharaja ascended Chamundi Hill bedecked in his finery and became a god for a few days. The parade of elephants today is a faint echo of the grand parades that used to take place in the past.

In Rajasthan, the essentially local spring and late summer festivals of Gangaur and Teej continue as colourful popular celebrations. Gangaur is also connected with the worship of Shiva and Parvati. Colourful processions are taken out by performing artists in their honour. Teej celebrates the onset of the monsoon and the unification of Shiva and Parvati. Women, attired in their finery, enjoy playing on swings

Dressed in a traditional white *angarakha* and the *Shindeshahi Pagdi*, headgear, Yuvraj Jyotiraditya Scindia goes through the *Bahuman* ceremony preceding the marriage ceremony of his sister, Princess Chitrangadaraje (veiled). A *zari dupatta* is draped over his left shoulder. The Princess of Gwalior's marriage to Yuvraj Vikramaditya Singh of Kashmir was one of the last lavish royal weddings of the twentieth century. Maharani Madhaviraje Scindia is seated on the right. The colour yellow is worn on the day of the *Haldi* ceremony when turmeric paste is applied to the bride's skin as a beauty treatment.

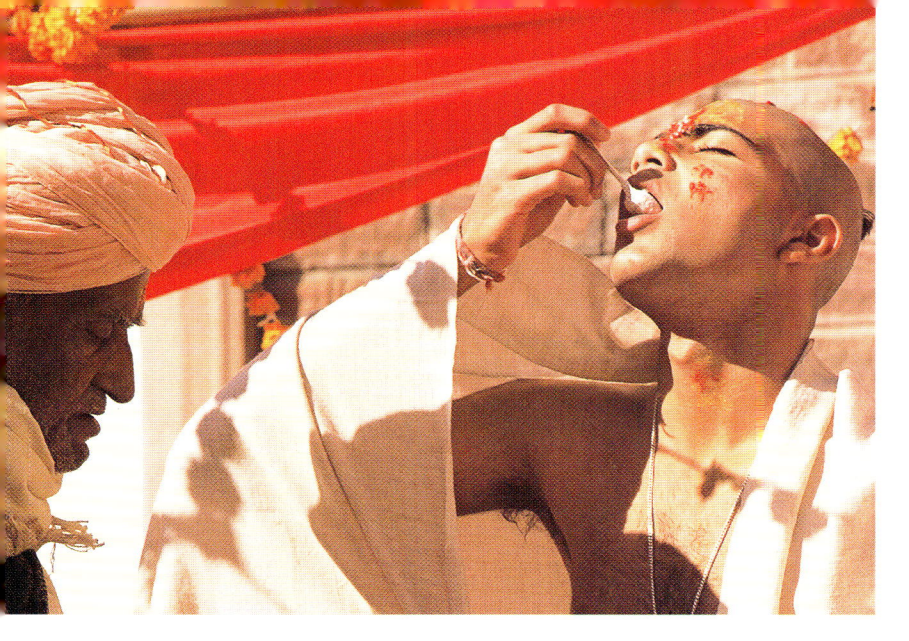

hung from trees. In Jaipur silver and gold images of Parvati are taken out in procession in sliver palanquins.

Diwali, the Festival of Lights, comes a fortnight after Dussehra. It celebrates the return of Rama to Ayodhya after defeating Ravana. Oil lamps are lit everywhere, turning the place into a fairyland. Fireworks, sweets and bonhomie complete what is perhaps the main festival celebrated in north India, and the goddess Lakshmi and lord Ganesh are worshipped.

Until recently the ancient bond between Kshatriya rulers and the Brahmin priesthood was maintained in every Hindu state, often extending beyond the hereditary *rajpurohits* to Brahmin ministers and officials who acted as the state's chief administrators. But other castes also enjoyed hereditary positions. The state heralds, bards and genealogists were always Bhats and Charans, while the local Bhils, Meers and other tribal people were huntsmen or guardians of the state treasure. A remarkable example of this hereditary occupation lies in Jaipur where one family from the local Minas has for centuries guarded the Kachhawa clan's treasures, said to be hidden deep underground beneath a fort overlooking the palace-fortress of Amber. Even the current Maharaja of Jaipur is said to be unaware of its exact location. Only once in his lifetime is the ruler of Jaipur permitted to see this treasure – and to choose one item for his personal use. In the mid-1970s Government troops supervised by officials of the Inland Revenue dug deep into the hillside in search of this treasure but failed to find it.

bottom: MEMBERS OF THE JODHPUR COURT FEED EACH OTHER LIQUID OPIUM FROM THEIR PALMS IN A RITUAL CALLED *AKHA TEEJ*. OPIUM WAS EXTENSIVELY USED ESPECIALLY AT THE TIME OF WAR. IT REMOVED FEAR AND FATIGUE FROM WARRING SOLDIERS AND THEY COULD MARCH, RIDE OR FIGHT FOR LONG DURATIONS.

Artistic
and Regal

Patronage
Splendour

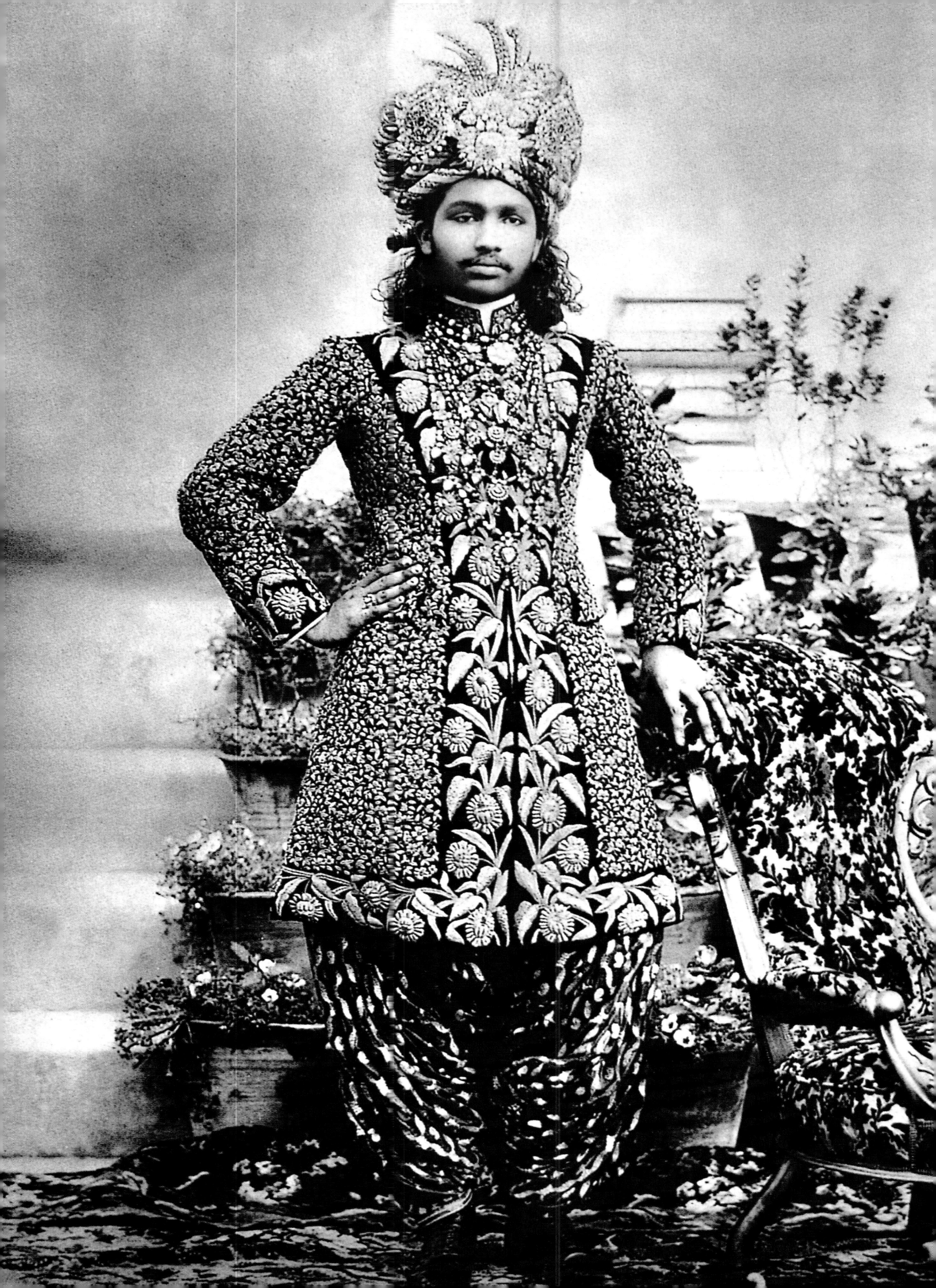

PATRONAGE OF THE arts and crafts had long been a feature of Indian kingship, and even under the Sultanates and the Mughals, the old kingdoms and principalities had continued as centres of culture, where almost every form of artistic endeavour, from weapon-making, miniature painting and music to gem-cutting, silk-weaving and stone-carving, flourished.

Promoting Arts and Crafts

With other princely states Jaipur came to excel as a centre for all the traditional crafts, largely due to the foresight of the enlightened Sawai Jai Singh II, who, modelling himself on his supposed ancestor Rama, set out deliberately to recreate the ideal state, *Ramrajya*, that was both modern and in conformity with tradition. With the help of his architect Vidyadhar, he began, in the 1720s, to build a new city on a grid pattern divided into seven sectors, reflecting the astrologically lucky number seven. His vast new city palace, with more than fifteen hundred rooms, occupied one sector, and large plots were set aside for temples and town houses of his nobles. Equal space was also set aside for traders and craftsmen, markets and bazaars. Invitations were sent out to traders, artists and skilled craftsmen such as goldsmiths, silversmiths, gem-setters, enamellers, embroiderers, bangle-makers, weavers of textiles and carpets, block printers of cloth (*chhapai*) and stonemasons, inviting them to settle in Jaipur and offering them various tax concessions. The result was an explosion of manufacturing and trading that led to the prosperity of the state and its artistic regeneration. It also set an example for other states to follow.

Today Jaipur is the largest centre for ornamental ware in the world. Enamelling objets d'art such as vases,

top: Set in platinum, this emerald and diamond *sarpech*, turban ornament, is complemented with cascading briolette drops. Yashwant Rao Holkar, Maharaja of Indore, had it made in 1936.

facing page: Nawab Sadiq Muhammad Khan of Bahawalpur spent lavishly on European-cut stones, particularly diamonds of South Africa. Although he lived a short life, his collection of bejewelled turbans was the envy of many.

pages 140-141: Set against a blue enamelled ground, this enamelled *chamar*, whisk holder, is studded with diamonds, in *kundan*-style, in gold. Probably made in 19th century northern India, its grandeur is highlighted by an elephant-head finial.

143

A VELVET AND *KARCHOBE* WORK *TOPI*, CAP, MADE FOR A CHILD PRINCE IN GWALIOR IN THE EARLY 20TH CENTURY. THE LOWER EDGE OF THIS *TOPI* IS LINED WITH MANGO MOTIFS, A PATTERN COMMON IN HINDU DESIGNS.

pages 144-145, top centre:
A JEWELLED *CHAURI*, FLYWHISK, ITS RED, GREEN AND WHITE ENAMEL WORK STUDDED WITH DIAMONDS, MAKES IT A LIKELY SPECIMEN FROM 19TH CENTURY RAJASTHAN.
centre: A RAJPUT SHIELD.
bottom: MALE LEATHER *MOJDIS*, SLIPPERS, FROM GWALIOR, DECORATED WITH SEED PEARLS (EARLY 20TH CENTURY).

facing page, right: A WRITING SET IN MUGHAL STYLE, MADE IN THE EARLY 18TH CENTURY. WHITE NEPHRITE JADE ADORNED WITH RUBIES, EMERALDS AND DIAMONDS SET IN GOLD ARE ARTISTICALLY USED. POSSESSION OF SUCH OBJECTS DENOTED RANK.

facing page, bottom:
A JEWELLED DAGGER OF EMPEROR ASHOKA'S TIME – THE BLADE AND HILT ARE MADE FROM SINGLE PIECES OF STEEL. THE HILT IS INLAID WITH EMERALDS AND RUBIES IN GOLD.

facing page, top right: A 17TH CENTURY *BAJUBAND*, ARM-PLATE, OF TWO STEEL PLATES CURVED AND ENTWINED WITH IRON PINS. A FLORAL DESIGN IN GOLD DECORATES THE SURFACE.

bowls, trinkets, boxes and plates is done in brass and silver. A detailed lacquered design covering the entire surface is called *marori;* floral and leaf motifs spread over a lacquered background are known as a *bichi* design; and *chikan* refers to generously spread out floral ornamentation on a lacquered background. Metalware of another kind is produced in Pratapgarh, near Chittorgarh. Geometric and floral interwined lines, battle and hunting scenes, and religious figures are cut out on thin gold sheets and the silhouetted pattern then transferred and fused onto glass. Known as *thewa* this process is used to make vases, jewellery and artifacts.

Stone-carving too reached its peak of excellence in Rajasthan's *havelis*, forts and palaces. Sandstone and marble have always been the preferred materials. The brilliance of the craft lies in the fine chiselling and filigree design of balconies, windows and facades.

Leather *juttis*, shoes that can be easily slipped on, are typical to Rajasthan. Hard at first, they soften with wear. They have curved tips with colourful tassels. Leather and camel hide are used to make saddles, water containers, purses and musical instruments. Wood inlaid with copper, bone and silver wire is used to make exquisite furniture, screens, caskets and doors. Smaller items like lamps, statues of deities and toys are coloured and given a lacquered finish. Enormous teak doors studded with metal spikes, brass and ivory were taken away to Agra by Akbar. The City Palace boasts doors framed by brilliant frescoes. Sawai Ram Singh introduced the craft of blue pottery, originally from Persia and China, into Rajasthan in the nineteenth century. Made of ground quartz stone with floral and geometric designs, Sanganer's vases, jugs and wall plates which were traditionally done in blue and emerald, are now being done in yellow and brown too. A paper-thin variety of blue pottery called *kagzi* is made in Alwar.

Woven cotton floor coverings called dhurries and beautiful hand-knotted carpets with Mughal designs provide a striking contrast to the *pattu*, sturdy woven woollen material. The chunky carved silver jewellery, once worn exclusively by rural women, is now fashionably ethnic. Jaipur is the largest emerald-cutting centre in the world and the state's rich deposits of precious and semi-precious stones such as garnets, rubies, lapis lazuli, amethysts, topaz and jade are cut and faceted to perfection. *Minakari,* ornamental and enamelled jewellery, and *kundan,* gold enamel work, remain high on any connoisseur's list.

Schools of painting sprang up in the princely states. The Kishangarh School acquired fame in the eighteenth century for its paintings on Krishna's life as did some of the Himalayan hill states such as Kangra. In Kota and Bundi paintings of hunting scenes achieved a level of perfection never surpassed elsewhere. In Jaipur the portraits made of rulers are the finest examples of Hindu portraiture ever made. The frescoes in the *havelis* of Shekhawati and the palaces of Bikaner, Jodhpur and Jaisalmer; the murals of Samode; the *phads*, large paintings on coarse cotton cloth, depicting the valour of Pabuji – a warrior-saint of Jodhpur; *pichwais*, devotional paintings on cloth in the traditional style – all bespeak the patronage of the Rajput rulers.

In the early nineteenth century the Gaekwad rulers of Baroda promoted arts and crafts. Three outstanding results of this royal patronage were a carpet woven in pearls and diamonds, a pair of cannons cast in silver, and another pair in gold.

In Rampur and Hyderabad culinary skills were developed to a high degree. Rampur was believed to have over three hundred cooks in its kitchen, each specialising in one particular dish. Sayyad Raza Ali gathered musicians from all over. He had a fine collection of richly carved musical instruments, many of which were very old. He also acquired a collection of fifteen thousand oriental manuscripts which included a volume of Persian poetry with annotations made in the margins by the Mughal emperors Babur and Shah Jehan. They were given pride of place in a library with a magnificent collection of miniature paintings from the sixteenth to eighteenth centuries.

Wood and ivory inlay work on wood, and the *Kincob*, silk and gold brocade of Benares, put the kingdom on a par with those excelling in arts and crafts.

Evolution of Textiles

The maharajas played a large role in the development of textiles, techniques and styles. In Deogiri in the fourteenth century, the manufacture of the fine muslin apparel worn usually as a surcoat by the nobility, was perfected to such a degree that the historian Khusrau remarked: 'A hundred yards of it can pass through the eye of a needle . . . It is so transparent and light that it looks as if one is in no dress at all but has only smeared the body with pure water'.

Kashmir's wool and silk weavers were famous for their double-interlocked, twill-tapestry technique known as *kanni* which was worked with the soft yarns of *pashmina* wool. This technique was later used in the making of the Cashmere paisley shawls that became a rage in Europe in the nineteenth century. The superfine *shahtush* shawl made from the fleece of the Tibetan

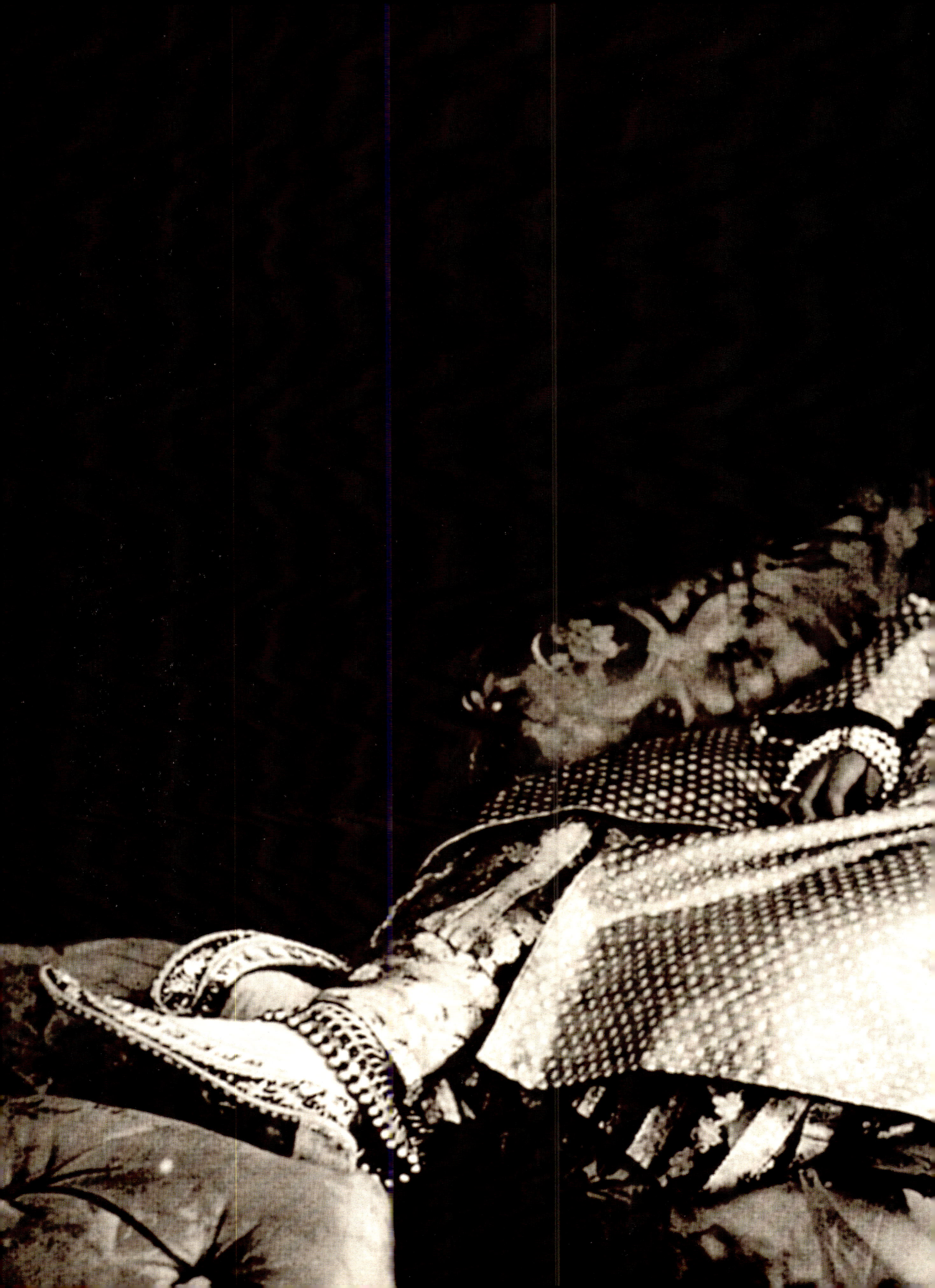

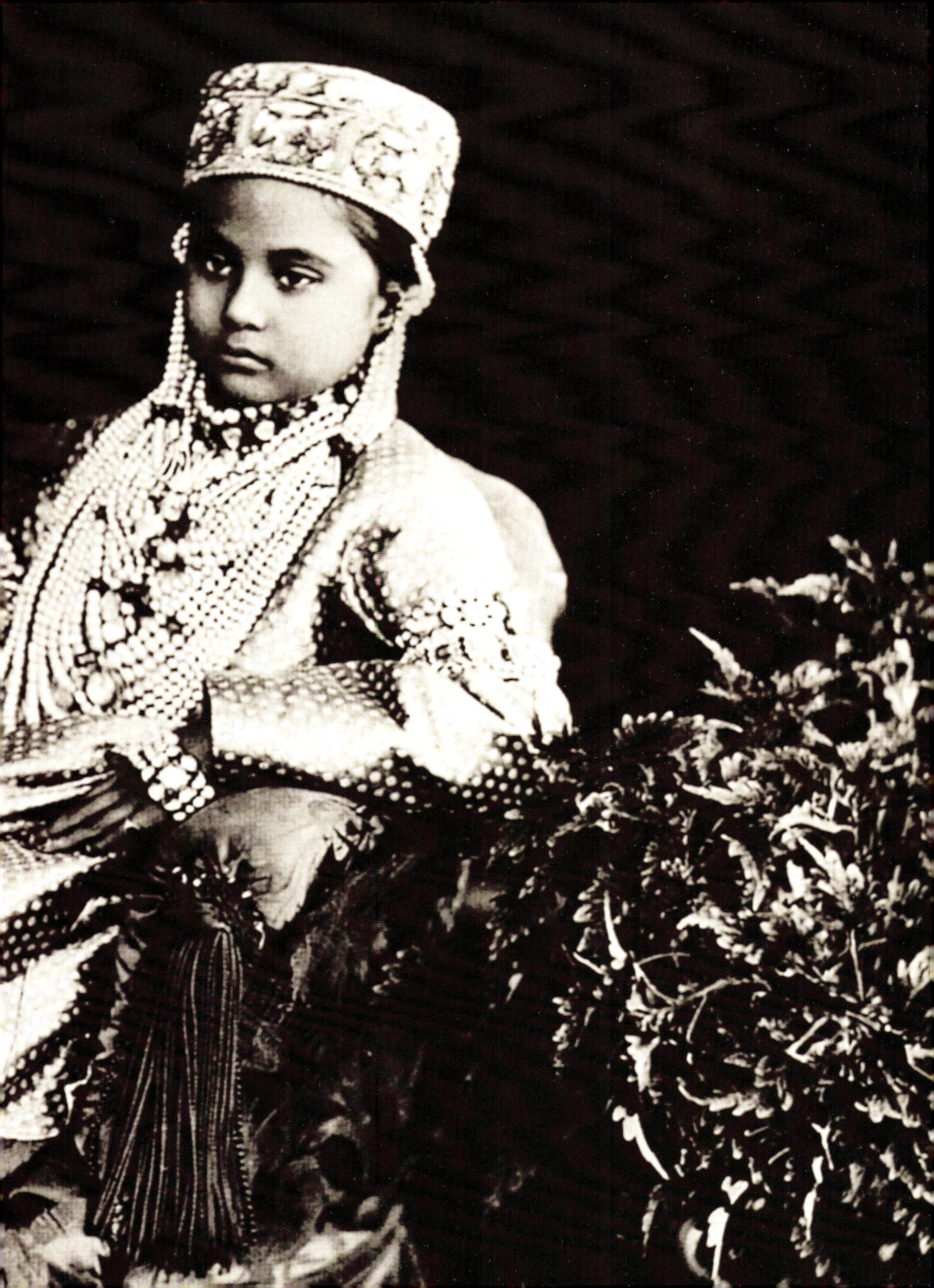

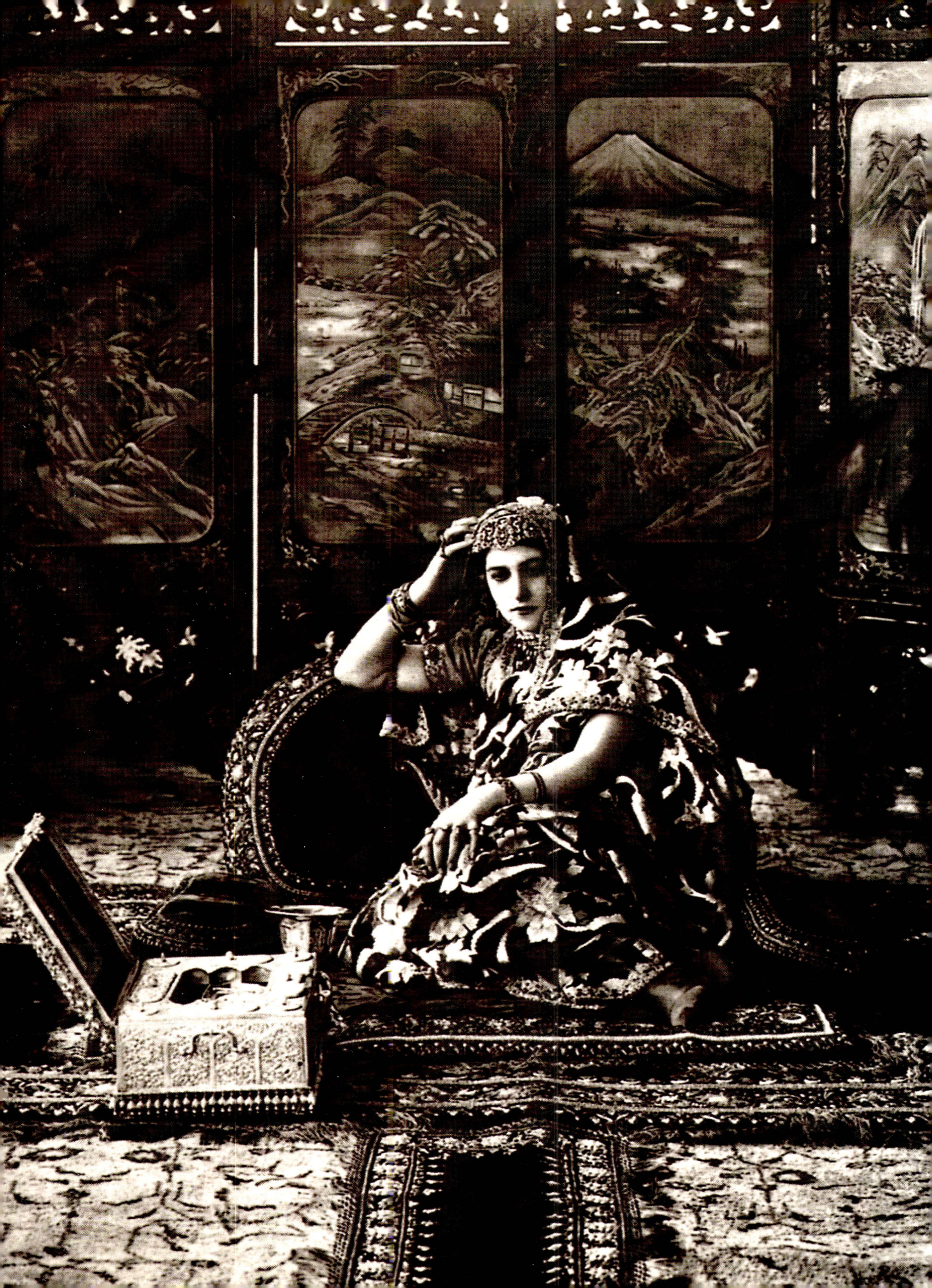

antelope, and banned today, was traditionally left plain with embroidered edges. Favoured motifs were the *hans,* swan, and the *kamal,* lotus. *Zardozi,* gold embroidery, was used to embellish royal robes, with pearls and precious stones being added for effect.

The kingdom of Benares was no less well known for its silk-weavers and sari-makers, specialising in the threading of spun gold and silver, and the production of what was known in Europe as *Kincob. Kinkhwab,* literally, small dreams, was used to describe woven gold brocade. A particularly sought after textile woven in Benares was known as Ganga-Jamuna, the gold and silver threads representing the intermingling of these two rivers.

Rajasthan's *bandhani,* tie and dye fabrics, with their eye-catching colour combinations, were renowned. The *lehariya* design, an elegant wavy pattern, was best done in Udaipur. The block-printed textiles of Sanganer and Bagru, Barmer's block prints on blue and red fabric known as *ajrak,* on which were embroidered glass pieces and motifs, and the finest cotton weaves of Kota are perennial favourites even today.

Meanwhile the styles of dress that increasingly gained popularity among the aristocracy were the *angarakha*, kurta, and *chogha* for men, and the *ghaghras* and *odhanis* for royal women. Among the heirlooms of the Rajmata of Kutch is a *ghaghra* made of seventy-seven yards of fabric heavily embroidered in gold. Colours like red and yellow came to be associated with fertility and were sent by the groom's family when a princess got married. *Ghaghras* later made way for saris, with French chiffon as the favoured fabric and hand-woven brocade borders made in Benares. Among the men headgear was important, because the manner in which the *pag,* turban, was tied denoted both the clan and the caste to which the wearer belonged. The Rajputs always wore long turbans known as *safas,* whereas the Marathas had their own distinctive boat-shaped turban.

facing page: IN THE 19TH CENTURY THE SARI OVERTOOK THE *GHAGRA* IN POPULARITY. DRESSED IN ONE, MAHARANI ANITA DELGRADA, ORIGINALLY A SPANISH DANCER, COMMONLY REFERRED TO AS THE SPANISH MAHARANI, CAUSED MUCH AGITATION WHEN SHE MARRIED MAHARAJA JAGATJIT SINGH OF KAPURTHALA.

pages 146-147: SPHERICAL, PEAR-SHAPED, BAROQUE AND OVOID — THE QUALITY OF HYDERABADI PEARLS IS UNMATCHED. WEARING A VARIETY OF PEARL NECKLACES IS SAHEBZADI NIZAM-UN-NISSA BEGUM, ELDEST AND FAVOURITE DAUGHTER OF MAHBOOB ALI PASHA.

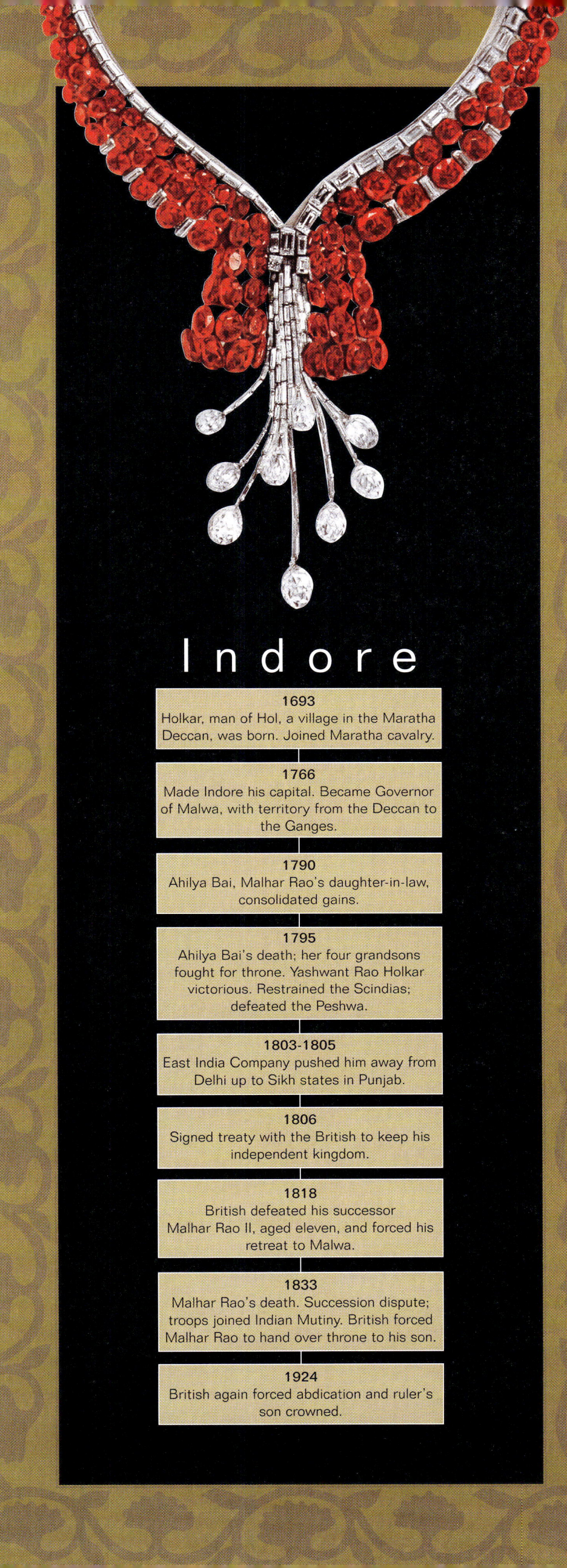

Indore

1693
Holkar, man of Hol, a village in the Maratha Deccan, was born. Joined Maratha cavalry.

1766
Made Indore his capital. Became Governor of Malwa, with territory from the Deccan to the Ganges.

1790
Ahilya Bai, Malhar Rao's daughter-in-law, consolidated gains.

1795
Ahilya Bai's death; her four grandsons fought for throne. Yashwant Rao Holkar victorious. Restrained the Scindias; defeated the Peshwa.

1803-1805
East India Company pushed him away from Delhi up to Sikh states in Punjab.

1806
Signed treaty with the British to keep his independent kingdom.

1818
British defeated his successor Malhar Rao II, aged eleven, and forced his retreat to Malwa.

1833
Malhar Rao's death. Succession dispute; troops joined Indian Mutiny. British forced Malhar Rao to hand over throne to his son.

1924
British again forced abdication and ruler's son crowned.

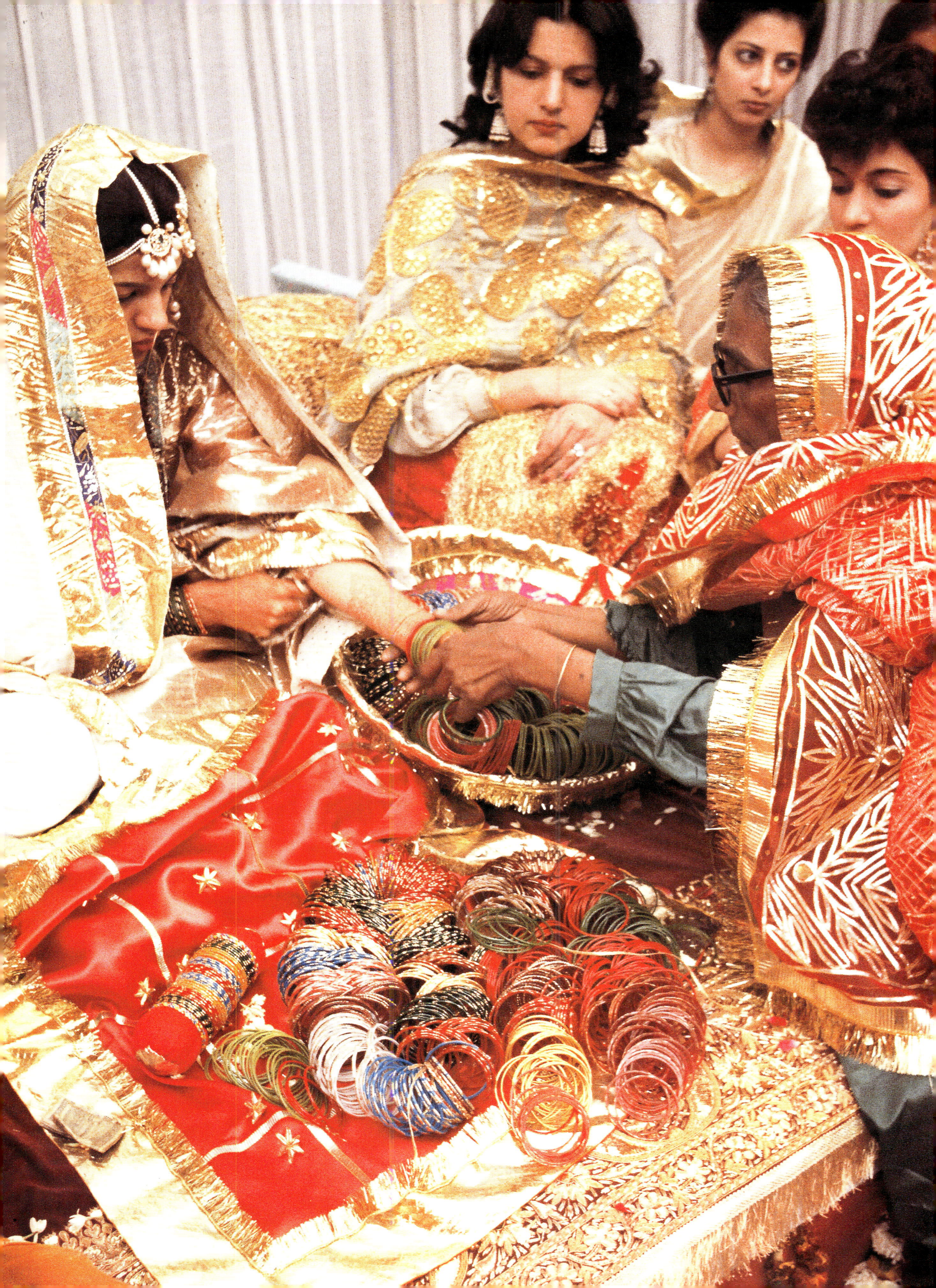

MAGNIFICENT JEWELLERY COLLECTIONS

By the standards of the Mughal emperors and the Sultanates of the Deccan none of the maharajas were hugely wealthy except the Nizams of Hyderabad and Berar, who acquired enormous riches over the centuries and spent very little on modernising their states. When Nizam Osman Ali Pasha became ruler of Hyderabad in 1911, he became the richest man in the world, much of his wealth comprising gold and silver bullion, gems and pearls. When an American heiress wore her priceless black pearl necklace at dinner in Hyderabad in the 1930s, the Nizam showed her not only boxes of pearls of greater size and quality than hers but scores of jewels, each worth a king's ransom. From his father he had inherited the 162-carat Jacob diamond, which he used as a paperweight. Another uncut diamond was the size of a lime. He had himself bought ten square emeralds, each the size of a flat egg, at the time of the 1911 Delhi Durbar. When his collection of pearls was washed and spread out on the roof of one of his palaces to dry, the entire roof was carpeted with pearls. Despite this wealth the Nizam lived and dressed like a pauper and when his estate was assessed by his heirs in 1967, tens of millions of bank notes were found rotting in his cellars. Even so, there remain seventy million dollars in gold coins and bullion and half as much in jewellery and precious objects — a delicate matter that continues to be the subject of negotiations between the Nizam's heirs and the Government of India.

Gold being the metal of royalty, and silver the metal of nobility, most royal jewels were set in gold. In royal circles the male of the species wore the best and the most — and none more than the heads of the clan. The classic royal jewel was the *sarpech*, turban ornament, made up of a plume-like *jigha* of precious jewels pinned to the front of the turban, usually with

facing page: A FAMILY *CHOODIWALI*, BANGLE-SELLER, WITH PRINCESS YASEEN ALI KHAN OF RAMPUR DURING HER *MOOH DIKHAHI* CEREMONY. THIS CEREMONY, LIKE MANY OTHERS, IS PERFORMED BOTH IN HINDU AND MUSLIM WEDDINGS IN INDIA. DUE TO LACK OF PATRONAGE THE TRADITIONAL ROLES OF SUCH PEOPLE AS THIS FAMILY BANGLE-SELLER ARE ALMOST FINISHED.

page 149: CREATED BY MAUBOUSSIN FOR YASHWANT RAO HOLKAR IN 1937, THIS NECKLACE OF BAGUETTE DIAMONDS AND FACETED RUBIES, IS SET IN PLATINUM. THE NINE DIAMOND DROPS AT THE END MAKE IT A PIECE DE RESISTANCE.

The Koh-I-Nur Diamond

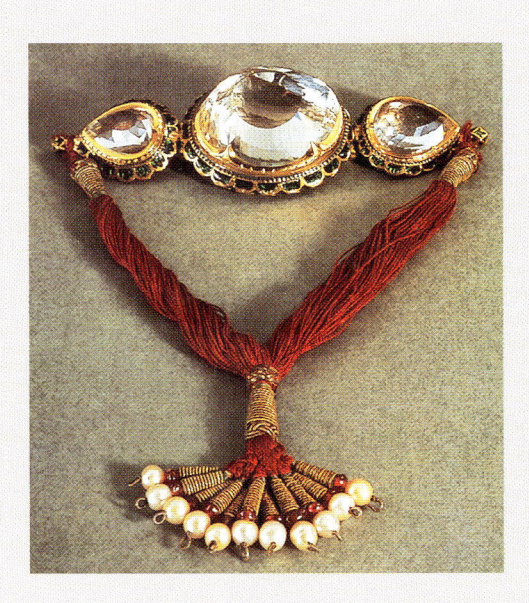

The most talked about diamond in the world, the Koh-i-Nur, Mountain of Light, was actually seen only in the sixteenth century, during the Mughal emperor Shah Jehan's reign. Said to have been owned by the first Mughal emperor Babur, and then by his son Humayun, the diamond was supposedly from the Golconda mines. Weighing 186 carats, its fluctuating destiny certainly matched the chequered fortunes of the rulers of India. Nadir Shah took it away forcibly in 1739 and after his death, it became the property of his general, Ahmad Shah Abdali. The latter succeeded in unifying Afghanistan and the diamond remained in their possession for almost fifty years. In 1812 the throne of Shah Shuja, in whose care the diamond was then, was usurped. Ranjit Singh, to whom Shah Shuja appealed for help, offered to do so in exchange for the Koh-i-Nur. Agreeing and then resisting from doing so, Shah Shuja finally had to hand it over to Ranjit Singh's treasury. Wearing it and having it reset several times, it was last with Ranjit Singh in an enamelled *bazuband*, arm-band, placed between two smaller diamonds. When the British conquered Punjab in 1849, the young son of Ranjit Singh was obliged to present it to the East India Company, who briefly lost it. It was then presented to Queen Victoria as a gift.

The Koh-i-Nur was displayed amidst much fanfare at the Great Exhibition of 1851. Its lack of brilliance, which some attributed to its smooth cut, caused Prince Albert to order it to be re-cut by the Dutch company, Coster. After five weeks it was returned in its new form: a shallow oval, 105.60 metric carats in weight — much smaller than its original size. One wonders, as many surmised then, whether it simply refused to 'shine' for its captors! In 1937 the Koh-i-Nur was fitted in the Maltese Cross at the front of the crown made for Elizabeth, George VI's consort. It remains in the crown of Queen Elizabeth, the Queen Mother, today.

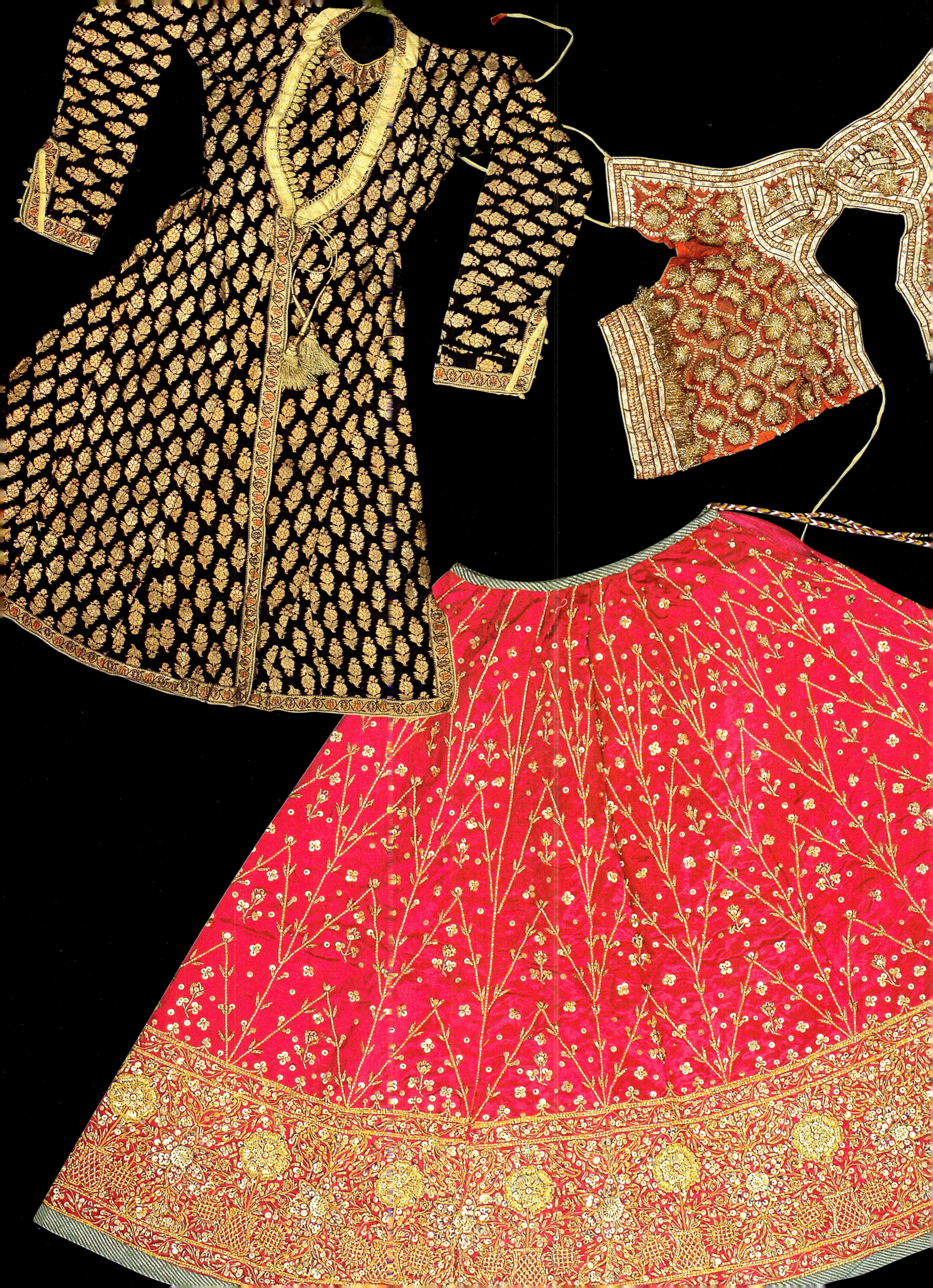

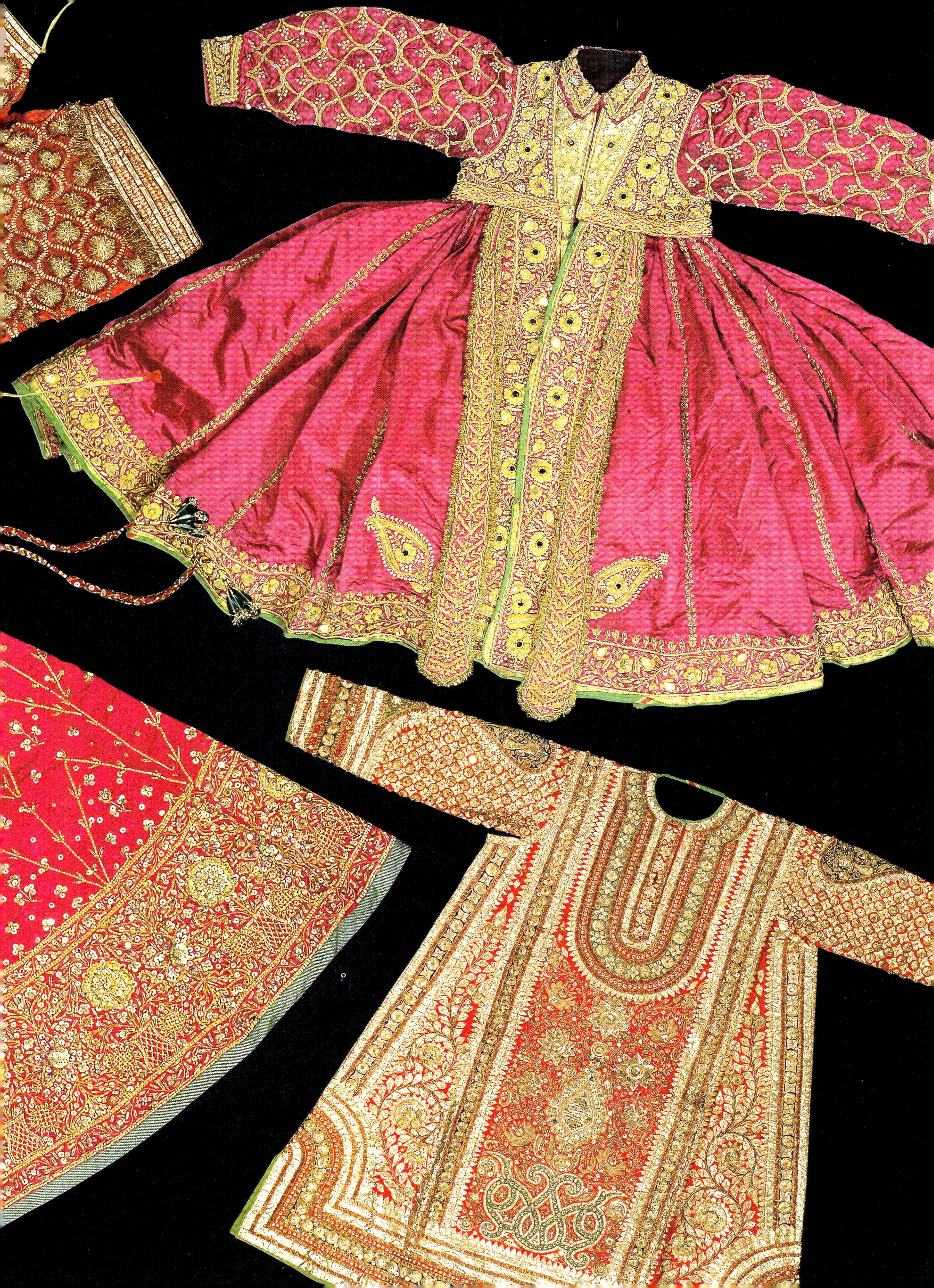

one large gem at the centre, and hanging beneath it the base or *sarpati*, usually made in three sections with one large central stone, each surrounded by lesser gems, the two pieces being linked to the turban by swags of pearls. Many such *sarpechs* and jewelled armbands were of ancient origin, but they were not as grand as the necklaces of many maharajas in the nineteenth century, most of which were acquired in Europe by jewellers, reset and then sold to the maharajas in the Victorian years.

The second richest prince in India, Maharaja Khande Rao Gaekwad of Baroda, paid $ 400,000 in 1867 for the 128.5-carat Star of the South diamond. It was given a triumphal parade when it arrived in Baroda and added to a collection of diamonds that already contained the 76.5-carat English Dresden, the 70-carat Akbar Shah (said to have been one of a pair of tear-drop diamonds that had formerly been the eyes of the Mughals' famous peacock throne looted by the Persians), the Empress Eugenie (once owned by the Russian Empress Catherine the Great's favourite general, Potemkin) and the yellow Moon of Baroda. The French traveller Louis Rousselet was allowed a glimpse of these jewels when he visited Baroda in the late 1860s and later wrote of 'streams of diamonds, diadems, necklaces, rings, bracelets, costumes and mantles embroidered with pearls and precious stones of marvellous richness . . . .'

Khande Rao of Baroda was followed by his brother Mulhar Rao. A distant relative was next chosen to be the new Gaekwad, a boy of twelve named Sayaji Rao. After years of careful tutoring and guardianship by British administrators, he turned out to be a model ruler. He shared a fondness for pearls with his queen,

top: A *MANGA MALAI* NECKLACE FROM TAMIL NADU. THIS 19TH CENTURY GOLD NECKLACE IS INLAID WITH MANGO-SHAPED BURMESE CABUCHON RUBIES. THE 'MANGOES' ARE ENJOINED WITH FLAT CHAINS THAT PASS THROUGH LOOPS BEHIND EACH PIECE.
right: A SPECIAL BUCKLE OF RUBIES, EMERALDS AND DIAMONDS MADE FOR MAHARAJA GANGA SINGH OF BIKANER BY BOUCHERON.
pages 152-153: TRADITIONAL MALE AND FEMALE COSTUMES OF INDIAN ROYALTY. THE COSTUMES SHOWN HERE INCLUDE
bottom right: A *KURTA* FROM AMRITSAR, PUNJAB. top right: A *PESHWAZ* FROM CHAMBA, centre: A *GHAGRA* FROM KOTA, top centre: A *CHOLI* FROM JAIPUR, top left: AN *ANGARAKHA*.

facing page, extreme right: A BELT OF EMERALDS, SET WITH DIAMONDS AND PEARLS IN GOLD AND A FABRIC BACKING, MADE FOR MAHARAJA SHER SINGH OF PUNJAB, C. 1840.
facing page, right bottom: MAHARAJA YADAVENDRA SINGH AND MAHARAJ KUMARI SURINDER KAUR OF PATIALA DRESSED IN GROWN-UP ATTIRE.
facing page, top: MAHARAJA YADAVENDRA SINGH OF PATIALA WAS ONE OF THE MOST HANDSOMELY DRESSED MAHARAJAS. WITH STRINGS OF PEARLS ON HIS SILKEN TURBAN, MASSIVE BUT BEAUTIFUL NECKLACES OF DIAMONDS AND EMERALDS, DIAMOND BRACELETS, A DIAMOND COLLAR SET IN PLATINUM, DIAMOND BUTTONS AND A GEM-COVERED SWORD IN A JEWELLED SCABBARD, THE TALL AND HANDSOME MAHARAJA LOOKED STUNNING TO SAY THE LEAST.

Patiala

Late 18th century
The Sikhs, who had been militarised by the tenth guru, Guru Gobind Singh, organised themselves into twelve *misls*, groups, and pushed the Mughals out of Punjab. Baba Ala Singh led one of the *misls* and in 1752, established his kingdom at Patiala.

1808
Ranjit Singh combined the *misls* into one state and made a treaty with the British, fixing the Sutlej river as the boundary between them.

1830
Ranjit Singh died. The British entered Punjab.

1848
Only those Sikh states which fell on the 'British' side remained independent. Patiala was the largest.

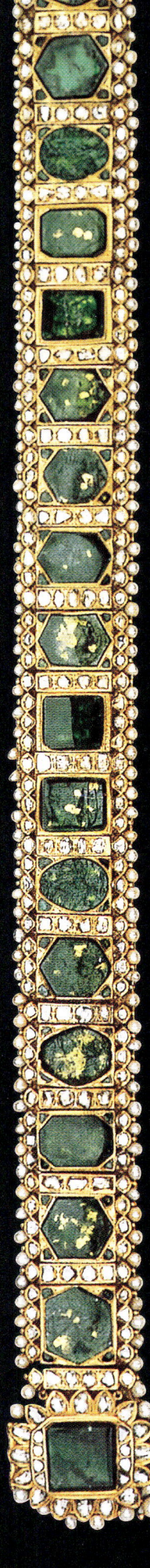

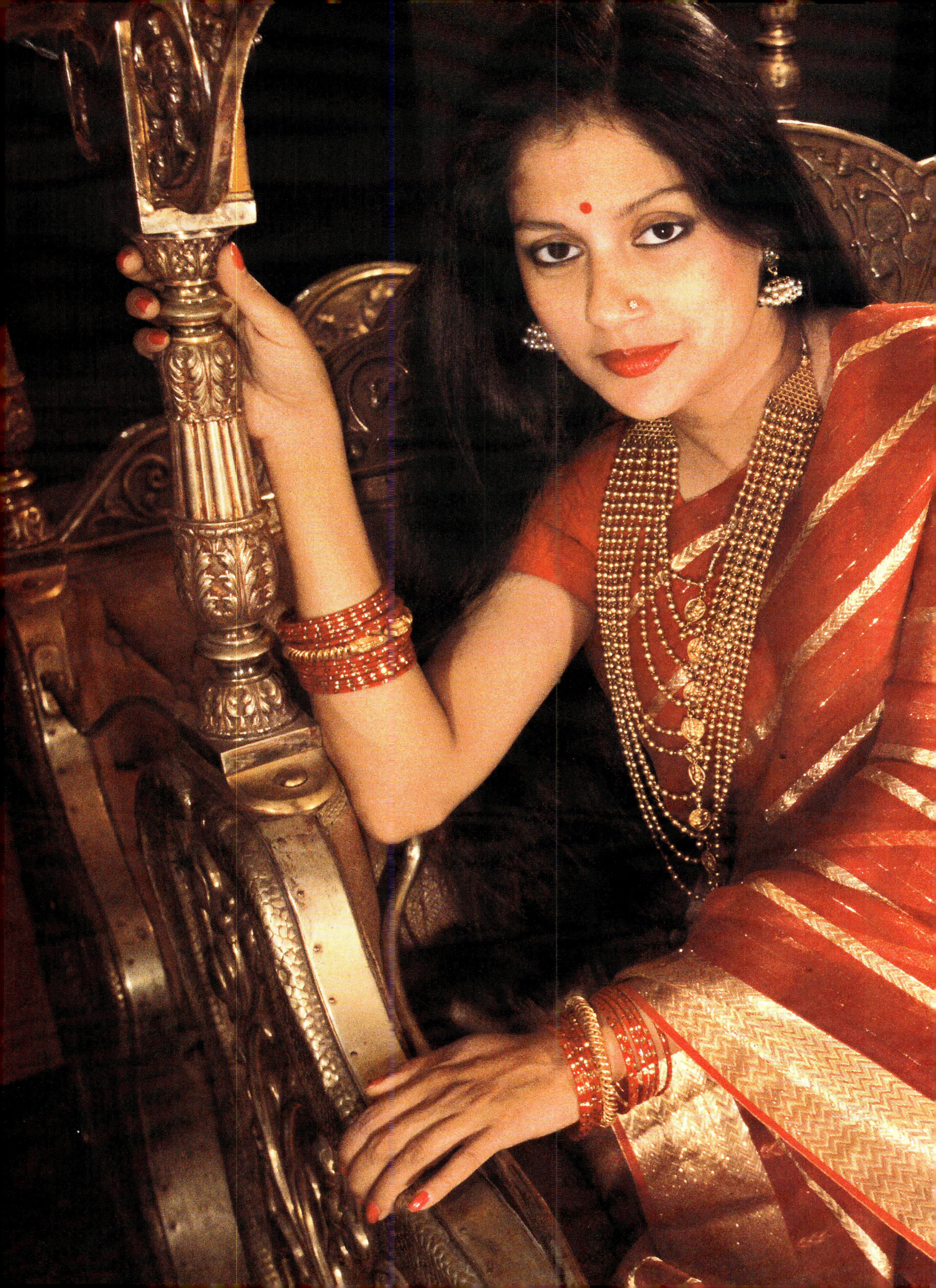

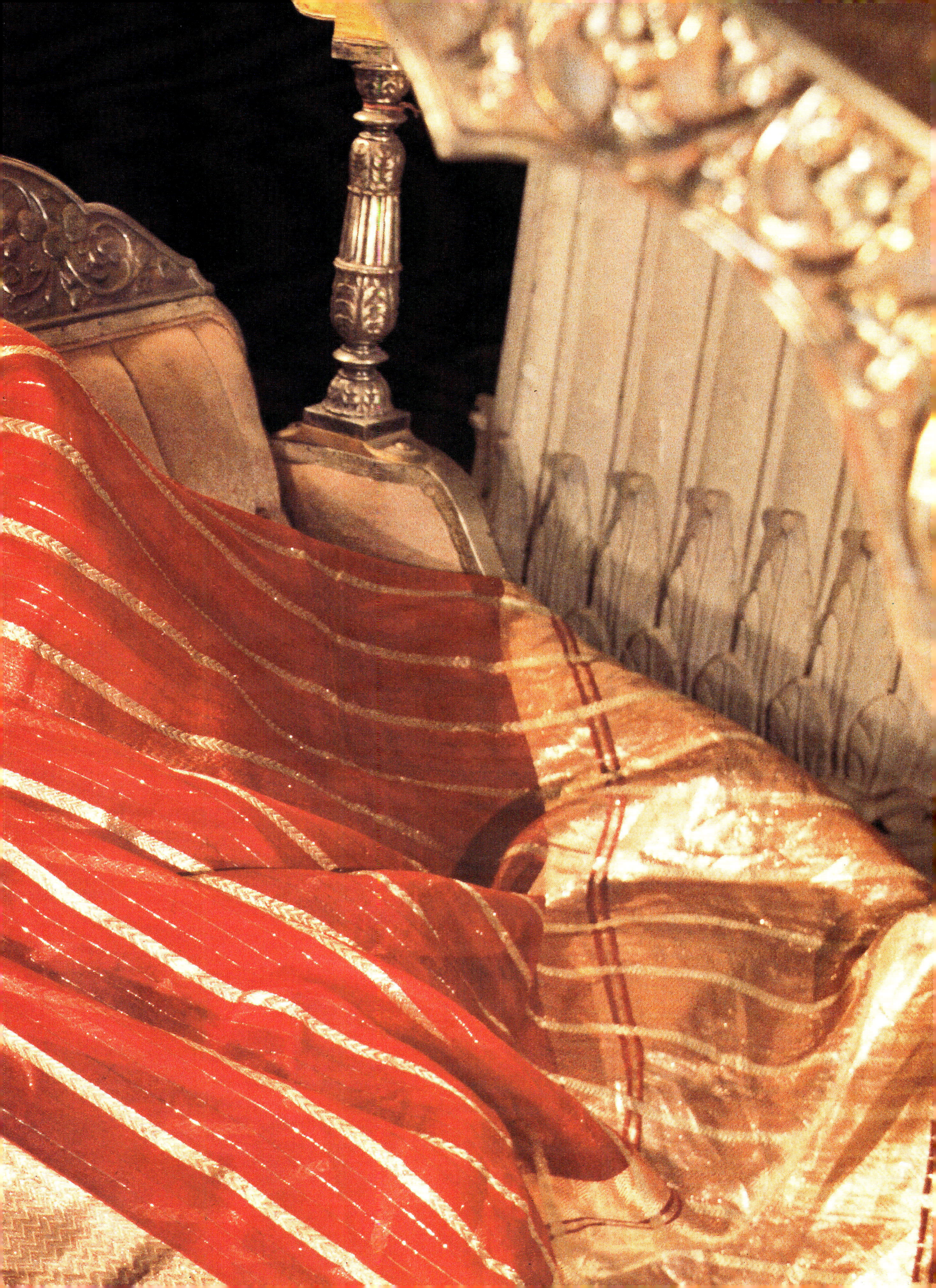

below: A STUNNING PENDANT OF DIAMONDS IN A FLOWER-HEAD DESIGN AND A LARGE FOILED TABLE-CUT DIAMOND IN THE CENTRE. SITTING ATOP ARE TWO BIRDS IN DIAMONDS, WITH RUBY BEAKS. THE REVERSE (see facing page, bottom) IS IN GOLD WITH FINELY ENAMELLED FLOWER AND BIRD MOTIFS. THIS PIECE IS FROM THE NIZAM OF HYDERABAD'S COLLECTION.

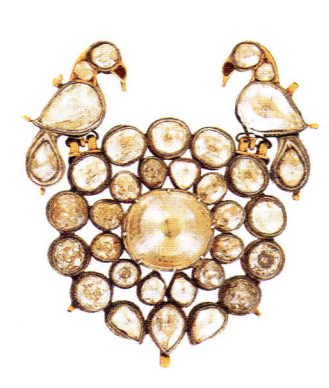

top: SHAH JEHAN BEGUM, THE GREAT GRANDMOTHER OF THE CURRENT BEGUM OF BHOPAL, WAS A POWERFUL MID-19TH CENTURY MUSLIM RULER. APART FROM THE TRADITIONAL BHOPALI KURTA AND CHURIDAR, SHE DONS A SATIN ROBE SHOWING THE STAR OF INDIA, BESTOWED ON HER BY QUEEN VICTORIA. THE TRADITION OF WOMEN RULERS OF BHOPAL STARTED WAY BACK IN THE MID-19TH CENTURY WITH KUDSIA BEGUM WHO WAS THE REGENT, RULING UNTIL HER DAUGHTER SIKANDER BEGUM CAME OF AGE. SIKANDER BEGUM MARRIED ONE OF HER COUSINS WHO ALSO DIED YOUNG. SHE TOO ONLY HAD ONE DAUGHTER, SHAH JEHAN, AND SO BECAME THE REGENT. AFTER HER DEATH IN 1868, SHAH JEHAN TOOK OVER BUT UNFORTUNATELY SHE ALSO LOST HER HUSBAND EARLY AND HAD ONLY ONE DAUGHTER, NAWAB SULTAN JEHAN BEGUM.

Maharani Chimnabai, whose favourite jewellery was a seven-stringed necklace of pearls, each the size of marbles. Maharaja Sayaji Rao lived a somewhat simple life, even borrowing money from the British. On his death, however, a search of his palace revealed wealth valued at sixty-two million rupees. It included 'silver coins that could be counted by millions, magnificient pearls and diamonds by the tens of thousands, rubies, emeralds, and other gems by thousands, and wrought and melted gold by maunds [an Indian weight measure of approximately eighty pounds]'. All his sons had died before him, so his grandson, Pratap Sinha, succeeded him. He was deprived of his titles and privy purse by the Government of India in 1951.

Almost as wealthy as the Gaekwads of Baroda were the Scindias of Gwalior and the Holkars of Indore. All three families had acquired much of their fortunes from their conquests of Rajput states. Tukoji Rao II of Indore inherited almost half a million pounds worth of jewellery and doubled it over the next fifteen years. He bought two beautiful pear-shaped Golconda diamonds from Chaumet, the French jeweller, one of 46.95 carats and the other of 46.70 carats.

Bhupinder Singh of Patiala inherited the De Beers diamond, an enormous light yellow diamond from South Africa. Its weight is today calculated at 234.5 metric carats, making it one of the largest polished diamonds in the world. A penchant for platinum led him to Cartier to make a forehead ornament like the traditional *chand mang-tika* for his senior maharani, Bhaktavar Kaur. Fringes of pearls surrounded four concentric crescent moons set with diamonds around a miniature portrait of the maharaja. At a Viceregal Ball in Delhi in 1924, Bhupinder Singh made his appearance in 'a brocaded coat entirely concealed by diamonds'.

The rulers of Cooch Behar, Kapurthala, Gwalior, Patiala, Hyderabad, Kashmir, Indore, Mysore and Rampur all loved Western-designed jewellery. Ganga Singh of Bikaner ordered a belt buckle from Boucheron set with many diamonds, rubies and emeralds, and with a central brilliant of 3.60 carats.

Jagatjit Singh of Kapurthala ordered a *sarpech*, turban ornament, from Cartier for his golden jubilee. A pagoda-like tiara, it was set in emeralds, diamonds and pearls, many from Jagatjit Singh's collection itself: fifteen large and uncommon emeralds, a brilliant hexagonal emerald of 177.40 carats placed at the centre, topped by a smaller hexagon, a half-moon, and an inverted pear-shaped emerald.

Indian maharajas gifted magnificent jewels to the British Crown and its representatives in India as proof of their allegiance to them. Robert Clive left Indian with 'a million for himself, two diamond drops worth twelve thousand for the Queen, a scimitar, dagger and other matters covered with brilliants for the King'.

Much of the artistry that flourished under princely patronage allowed the ruler to display his wealth and that of his tribe and his kingdom in his person and in his surroundings. On state occasions and religious festivals he and his retainers dressed in the finest clothes and wore the most ostentatious jewellery that their *toshakanas* or treasuries contained. The more powerful the ruler, the larger his *toshakana*, much of it filled with booty gathered in wars against his neighbours and often amassed over centuries. As might be expected in a warrior people, much of the *toshakana* was taken up with arms and armour, often of the finest quality — everything from scimitars with bejewelled blades to complete sets of elephant armour. Due to their years as generals of the Mughals, Jaipur and Jodhpur excelled in their collections of war booty, whereas weakened states such as Udaipur lost much of their former wealth to the newer and stronger Maratha states of Baroda, Indore and Gwalior. However, not all this accumulated jewellery or finery was the ruler's personal property. It was mostly family or tribal wealth held in trust, with the current head of the family or tribe merely acting as its guardian. Only in later years under British rule, when taxation added greatly to the ruler's revenues, did the maharajas acquire and build up their own personal collections of private jewellery and other precious objects.

pages 158-159, top centre: A RARE 19TH CENTURY IMAGE OF THREE AVADHI NOBLEWOMEN (WITHOUT PURDAH) HOLIDAYING IN RANIKHET. WEARING TRADITIONAL JEWELLERY, THEY ARE CLAD IN THE FASHION OF THEIR TIME — IN *FARSHI PYJAMAS* AND EMBROIDERED *DUPATTAS*.

top right: RAJMATA SAHIB MOHINDER KAUR OF PATIALA.
pages 156-157: PRINCESS YASHODHARARAJE SCINDIA OF GWALIOR SEATED IN HER FATHER'S SILVER HOWDAH. THE PRINCESS IS CURRENTLY A MEMBER OF THE LEGISLATIVE ASSEMBLY IN MADHYA PRADESH. SHE IS A PROFICIENT RIDER AND IS VERY CLOSELY INVOLVED WITH PROMOTION OF EQUINE SPORT IN INDIA. AT ONE TIME HER LATE FATHER, MAHARAJA JIWAJIRAO SCINDIA, WAS THE LEADING RACEHORSE OWNER OF THE COUNTRY AND HIS STABLES PRODUCED NUMEROUS CHAMPIONS.

Acknowledgements

I would like to thank the following people, without whose kindness, generosity and trust this book would not have been possible. First and foremost I owe an immense debt of gratitude to the late Maharaja Madhavrao Scindia of Gwalior. In 1983 he helped open the doors of princely India for me by introducing me to most of the royal families appearing in this book. At that time I had been commissioned to shoot the pictures for Charles Allen's best-selling *Lives of the Indian Princes*, my very first photographic assignment. Thanks to His Late Highness I gained a privileged access which enabled me to witness and photograph the otherwise hidden world of the Maharajas. My sincere thanks to Maharaja Ranjitsinh Gaekwad of Baroda for readily contributing the Foreword to this book, and to my old friend Charles Allen for agreeing to write the text.

Among the many princely families who opened their doors to me, I must list my debt in alphabetical order: The late Yuvrani Mahendra Kumari of Alwar; Their Highnesses, the late Rajmata Shanta Devi Gaekwad of Baroda, Maharani Shubhangini Raje Gaekwad of Baroda, Yuvraj Samarjit Singh Gaekwad of Baroda; the late Maharaja Brijendra Singhji of Bharatpur, Maharaja Vishwendra Singhji of Bharatpur; the late Maharaja Dr Karni Singhji of Bikaner, Rajmata Sushila Kumariji of Bikaner; Princess Bhawani Kumari of Burdwan; Maharani Vasundhara Raje of Dholpur; Maharajkumar Shatrujit Deo of Dharangdhara; the late Maharawal Lakshman Singhji of Dungarpur; the late Rajmata Vijaya Raje Scindia of Gwalior, Rajmata Madhavi Raje Scindia of Gwalior, Princess Yashodhara Raje Scindia of Gwalior, Maharaja Jyotiraditya Scindia of Gwalior; Rajmata Gayatri Devi of Jaipur, Maharaja Brigadier Sawai Bhawani Singhji, MVC, of Jaipur, Maharani Padmini Devi of Jaipur, Princess Diya Kumari of Jaipur; Rajmata Mukut Rajya Laxmi of Jaisalmer, Maharawal Brijraj Singhji of Jaisalmer; Maharaja Dr Karan Singh of Jammu and Kashmir, Maharani Yasho Rajya Lakshmi of Jammu and Kashmir, Yuvraj Vikramaditya Singh of Jammu and Kashmir, Yuvrani Chitrangada Raje of Jammu and Kashmir, Maharaj Ajatashatru Singh of Jammu and Kashmir; Rajmata Krishna Kumariji of Jodhpur, Maharaja Gaj Singhji of Jodhpur, Maharani Hemlata Raje of Jodhpur, Yuvraj Shivraj Singh of Jodhpur; Maharaja Krishna Chandra Pal of Karauli; the late Maharao Bhim Singhji of Kotah, Maharao Brijraj Singhji of Kotah, Maharani Uttara Devi of Kotah, Bhanwar Ijyaraj Singhji of Kotah, Bhanwarani Kalpana Devi of Kotah; Maharaja Srikantdatta Wodeyar of Mysore, Maharani Pramoda Devi Wodeyar of Mysore; Maharaja Madhukar Shah of Orchha; Maharaja Amrinder Singh of Patiala; the late Rajmata Anant Kunverba of Porbandar; the late Nawab Zulfiquar Ali Khan of Rampur, Begum Noor Bano of Rampur, Nawabzada Naved Ali Khan of Rampur, Nawabzadi Yaseen Ali Khan of Rampur, Princess Saman Ali Khan of Rampur; the late Maharaja Martand Singhji of Rewa; Raja Hari Sen of Suket; the late Nawab Masoom Ali Khan of Tonk; Maharaja Kirit Dev Burman of Tripura; Maharana Mahendra Singhji of Udaipur and M.K. Arvind Singhji of Udaipur.

In England, the late Tony Colwell, Gita Mehta, Abner Stein, Mrs Uma Phalke, Dr Indrajit Phalke, Mark Shand and Don McCullin. In India, my mother-in-law Smt Kamla Devi Jadhav, my wife Manjula Patankar, my sister Shreelekha Singh, my brother-in-law the late Kunwar Rajendra Singh Dundlod, Alpana Khare, Manjulika Dubey Raghu Rai, Naveen Patnaik, Ritu Kumar, Martand Singh, Radhika Singh, Harpreet Singh, Kesri Singh Mandawa, Randhir and Manjula Singh Mandawa, Yadvendra and Arpana Singh Samode, Rani Devika Devi, Reena Ribjit Singh, Maharaj Saubhag Singhji, the late Maharaj Saroop Singhji, R.K. Ranvijay Singh, K.K. Singh, Captain Shamsher Khan, Thakur Raju Singh, Thakur Sundar Singh, Mahendra Singh Nagar, Nahar Singhji, R.K. Mehra, Ravi Pasricha, Harry, Lakshman and Statfotos. In New York, Max Vadukul. Finally, I would like to thank all the princely families of India who allowed me access into their private space and also extended their most generous and gracious hospitality. To them my deepest gratitude. For me the journey has been an extremely rich and rewarding one and I hope I have not inadvertently caused hurt or offence to anyone along the way. If I have failed to mention any person to whom thanks are due I humbly apologise for the oversight.

ADITYA PATANKAR

PICTURE CREDITS

THE PUBLISHERS WOULD LIKE TO EXPRESS THEIR APPRECIATION TO THE PHOTOGRAPHERS, MUSEUMS AND ARCHIVES FOR KINDLY PERMITTING THE REPRODUCTION OF THEIR WORKS AND FOR THEIR SUPPORT. EVERY EFFORT HAS BEEN MADE TO OBTAIN AND FULFIL THE COPYRIGHT FOR ALL THE IMAGES DEPICTED IN THE BOOK. HOWEVER, SHOULD THERE BE ANY FURTHER CLAIMS, THE INDIVIDUALS CONCERNED MAY KINDLY APPROACH THE PUBLISHER.

(A-ABOVE, B-BOTTOM, T-TOP, C-CENTRE, L-LEFT, R-RIGHT, E-EXTREME)

© ADITYA PATANKAR: FRONT COVER; 6-7; 8-9; 10-11; 12TR; 13TR; 14-15; 18T; 18A; 22; 23; 24; 28-29; 33; 36TL; 36-37; 37TR; 40-41; 44; 45; 46; 47; 50-51; 52TL; 52TR; 53TL; 53TR; 54; 55; 56R; 57TB; 60-61(ALL); 62-63; 64TL; 64B; 64-65; 65TR; 65B; 70-71; 74B; 79; 82-8; 90B; 91TL; 91B; 96-97; 98B; 99TR; 102-103; 104TL; 104-105; 105TR; 110T; 110-111TC; 111T; 111B; 112-113; 114TR; 118-119; 121; 124-125; 126TL; 126-127TC; 127TR; 130-131; 133TL; 133TR; 135T; 135A; 136-137; 138-139 (ALL); 144TL; 144BL; 146-147; 150; 152-153 (ALL); 155B; 156-157; 159TR.

© ASHMOLEAN MUSEUM, UNIVERSITY OF OXFORD: 85.

© AKG LONDON LTD.: 32.

© BHARATH RAMAMRUTHAN: 34B; 35TR; 35BR; 39BR; 48EL; 48L; 56BL; 61; 65T; 65B; 68; 69; 84B; 89B; 99TR; 123T; 132T; 143 (COURTESY: ARCHIVES MAUBOUSSIN, MAHARAJAS' JEWELS); 144-145BC; 152T; 154T; 158BL; 159TR; 159BR.

© BBC HULTON LIBRARY: 38; 80B; 115T.

© BRITISH LIBRARY: 16; 17; 57TR; 68-69; 75; 78; 84T; 123B.

© DINODIA: 96-97; 110B.

© ILLUSTRATED LONDON NEWS PICTURE LIBRARY: 80T.

© MAGNUM PHOTOS LONDON: 95B; 133B.

© MAHARANA MEWAR HISTORICAL PUBLICATIONS TRUST: 66T; 67; 79R.

© NATIONAL MUSEUM, NEW DELHI: 12-13; 20-21; 34C; 34-35TC; 43R; 73; 94B; 95T; 144C; 145TR.

© PRIVATE COLLECTIONS: 1; 2-3; 4-5; 12TL; 13TL; 19; 25; 26-27; 30; 31TL; 31B; 34TL; 39TL; 42T; 42TL; 42-43; 49; 56T; 57TL; 58B; 59; 60; 66B; 72; 74TL; 74TR; 81; 86; 88; 89T; 90T; 91TR; 98T; 99TR; 100-101; 106-107; 108; 109; 114L; 114BR; 115A; 116TL; 116-117; 117TR; 117B; 120T; 120B; 122; 128; 132B; 134TR; 134B; 142; 148; 149; 152B; 155T; 158TL; 158-159TC; BACK COVER.

© ROYAL COLLECTION: 76-77; 151T; 151B; 155ER.

© ROYAL COMMONWEALTH SOCIETY: 92-93; 94T.

© SALLY AND RICHARD GREENHILL: 111; 116B.

© SAWAI JAI SINGH BENEVOLENT TRUST: 58T; 64.

© VICTORIA & ALBERT MUSEUM: 39TR; 140-141; 145BR.

BRITISH INDIA AND THE INDIAN STATES

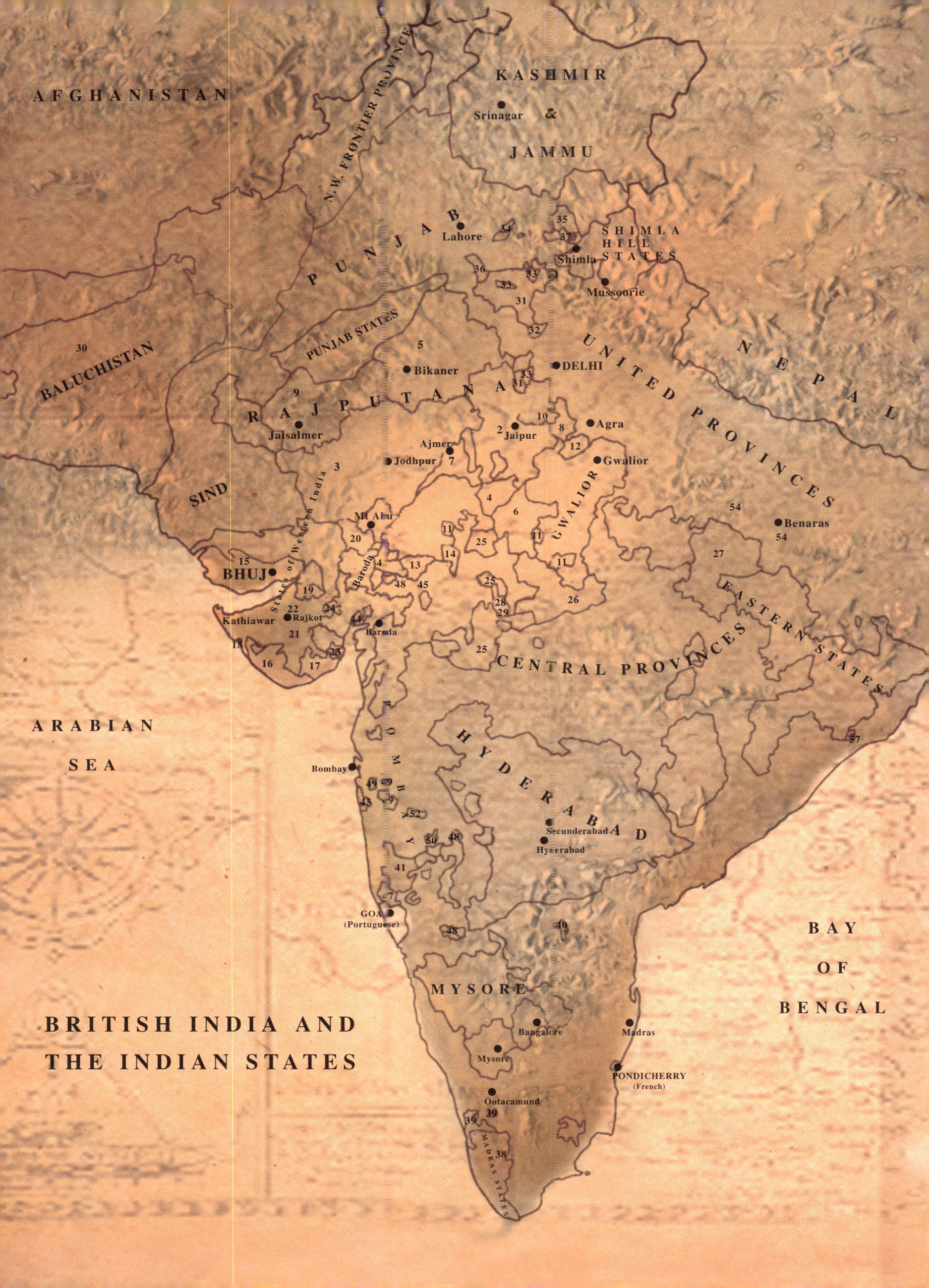